Dreams

ETERNAL THEMES IN ART
FROM GIOTTO TO KUSAMA

Dreams

Markus Eisen

PRESTEL
MUNICH · LONDON · NEW YORK

CONTENTS

Eternal Themes in Art

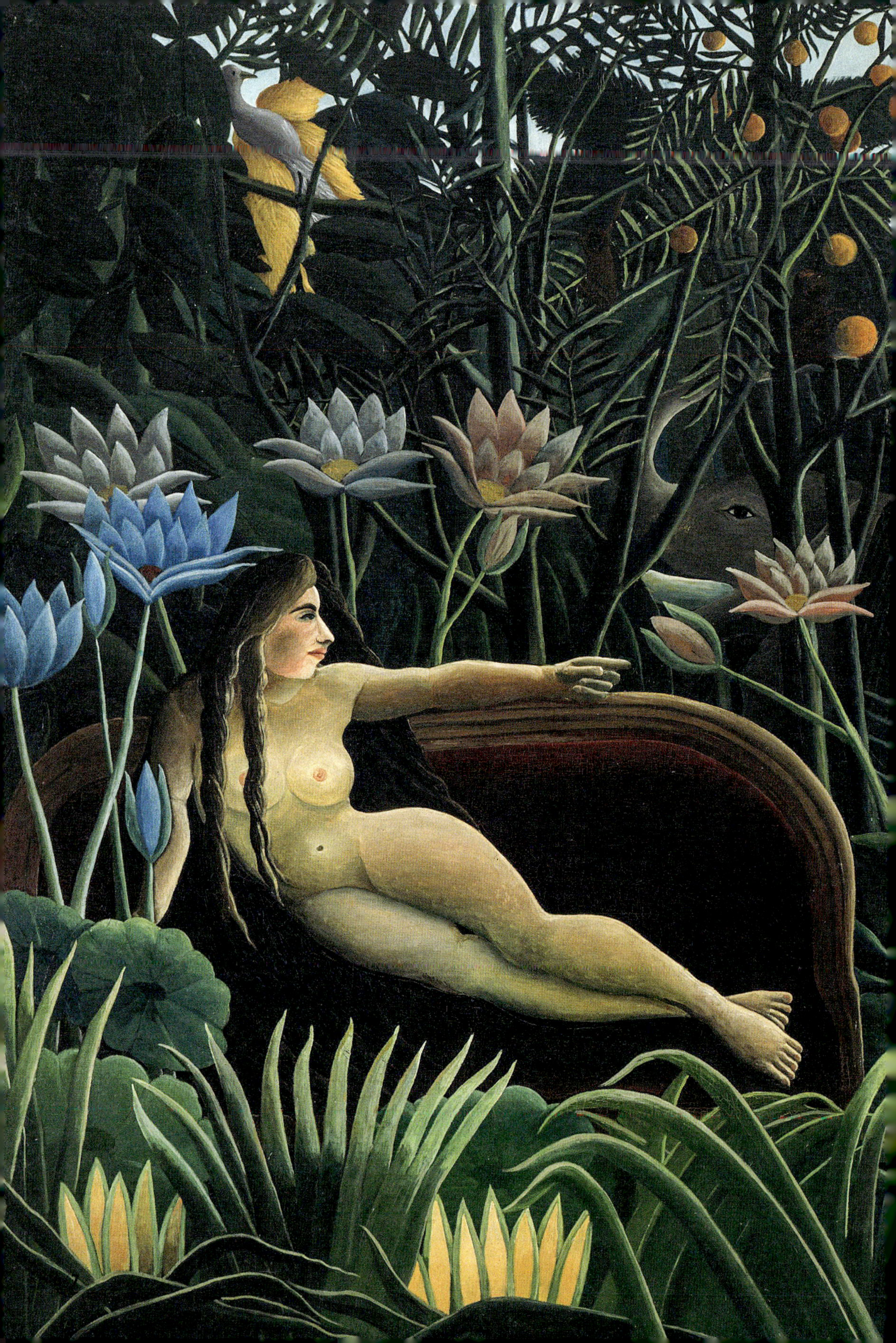

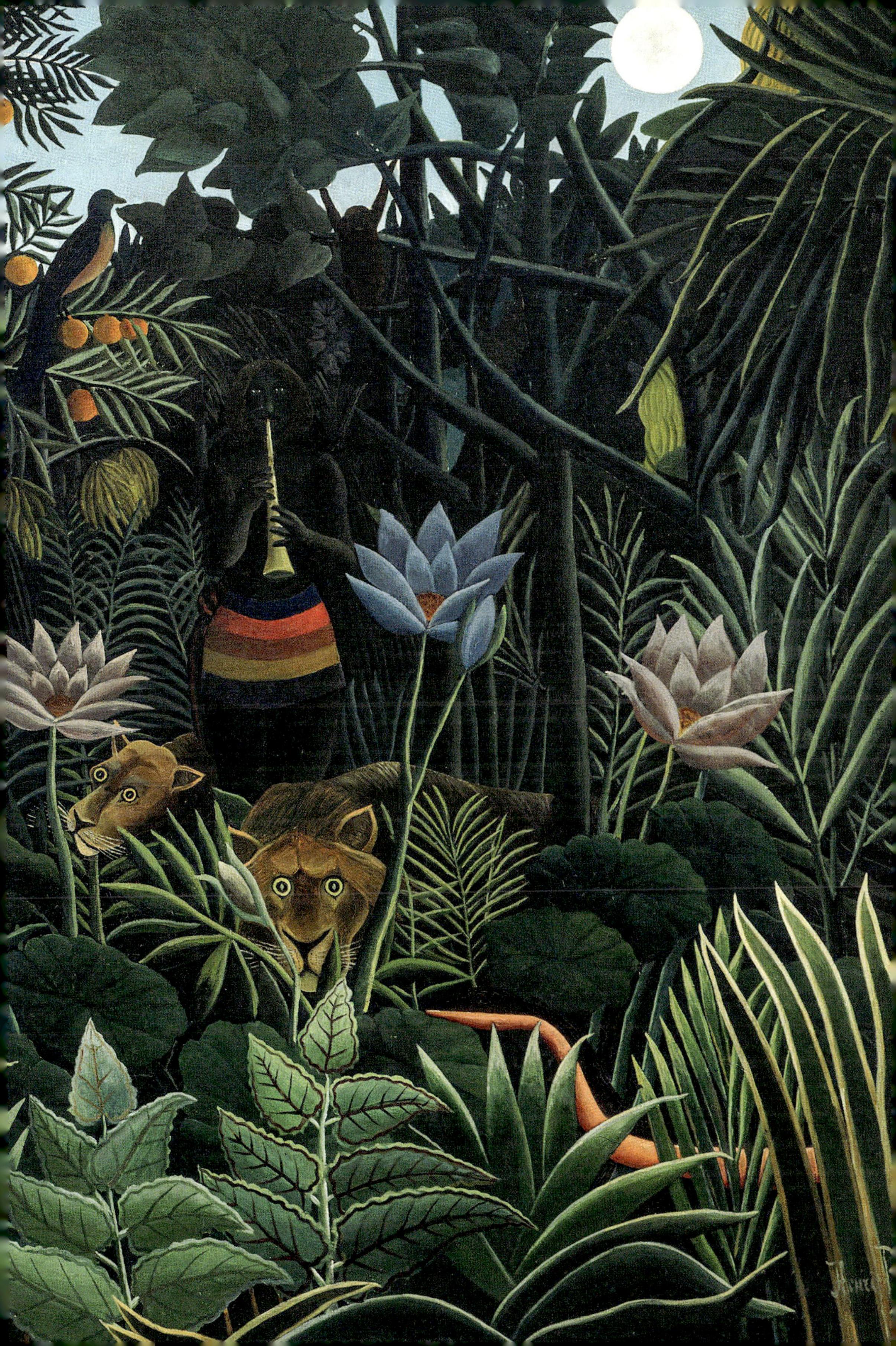

INTRODUCTION

Dreams are inescapable. They arrive unbidden, seemingly asserting themselves night after night for each and every one of us, even if, upon waking, we often find ourselves unable to recall them. The most fantastical scenarios, the most extraordinary chains of events, often take on a life of their own. Set against the immediate, tangible reality of what is seen and experienced in dreams, the imaginative play and fantasies of the waking mind appear almost drab, weak, even superficial. Dreams have a compelling presence, an overwhelming intensity and are full of tangled situations and baffling phenomena. They elude rational understanding and resist scientific analysis; as soon as our investigations move beyond purely medical and physiological observation and attempt to grasp the actual content of dreams, we quickly encounter insurmountable obstacles. The dream as such remains subjective, confined to each individual, in some ways resembling religious or artistic experience. In this sense, the world of dreams forms a realm set apart from the world of the ordinary, only partially subject to the laws and norms of everyday reality, unfolding instead in a seemingly untameable, uninhibited space.

Across all periods and cultures, people have grappled with dreams, which in turn have played a significant role throughout history. Dreams permeate religious texts, literature and fine art, shaping superstitious beliefs from the earliest times up to the present day. What has changed over the centuries, however, are the opinions on the nature and origin of dreams. In the distant past, dreams were often understood as visions sent from outside ourselves, received by the dreamer from a real, if variously imagined, source. In more recent times, dreams were perceived as emerging from the depths of our own minds, with dream imagery interpreted as a manifestation of our deepest desires. Some dreams have even been seen as a gateway to other, supernatural or divine worlds; while in others, the emphasis shifts inwards, with dreams understood as offering access to the unconscious and to our innermost secrets. Both share the conviction that at least some dreams carry genuine significance and can supply us with vital insights into our own lives – provided we are able to interpret them. This holds true for both the dream readers of antiquity and the psychoanalysts of modernity.

It is hardly surprising that artists have repeatedly engaged with the strangely unfamiliar yet at the same time uncannily familiar world of dreams, incorporating them into their works, whether because a patron wished to have a significant dream experience preserved, or because a dream itself provided the artist with a creative impetus. In the visual arts, thousands of works take up dreams in strikingly diverse ways. Among them are pieces by some of the most outstanding artists from disparate epochs, many of which have had a lasting influence and retain enduring aesthetic significance. It goes without saying that dream art can never escape the cultural, religious and social circumstances of the historical environment in which it was created. Such works reflect the most diverse conceptions of dreams: at times these are directly visible and legible in the way an image is composed; at other times, specific facets of dream experience become accessible through the circumstances of an image's production and reception. The present selection thus offers both a journey through the history of art and an exploration of the history of dreams.

We begin with two examples from the remote past, both involving the direct intervention of a divine being in human life. According to legend, a god struck a bargain with Thutmose IV in a dream: if he were to free the Sphinx from its sandy grave, the prince would become Pharaoh. Shortly after the year 1400 BC, he had a stele erected to commemorate this event; it still stands, three and a half millennia later, at the very place where the dream occurred – between the front legs of the Sphinx itself (p. 15). This monument to an event that once held world-historical importance is followed by an image that records the experience of a single individual while at the same time reflecting the religious practices of the day. A Greek votive relief from the fourth century BC depicts a man being healed by the god Amphiaraus, which occurred in a dream (p. 17). The person who had been cured commissioned the work himself and had it set up in the temple grounds in gratitude. In both instances, part of the work's aura derives from the circumstance that it was ordered by an individual who, by their own account, encountered a god while in a dream state. The two objects, then, are immediately bound up with an awe-inspiring and deeply moving religious experience.

... And they say that life is a dream: not so;
not dream alone. Dream is a fragment of life.
A tangled fragment in which face
and being clasp and intertwine [...]

RAINER MARIA RILKE, '... AND THEY SAY THAT LIFE IS A DREAM' (1906)

The works that follow engage with sacred texts and depict celebrated religious scenes once familiar to all, some marking turning points in their respective sacred narratives. Dozens of dream episodes appear in the Old and New Testaments, five of them in the Christmas story alone (p. 43), while dreams also play a role in Buddhism (p. 19). In Jewish, Christian and Islamic households, every child knows stories such as that of Jacob's Ladder, on which angels ascended and descended between heaven and earth (p. 23), or Joseph's interpretations of dreams in Egypt (p. 35). There are nevertheless many lesser-known dreams, particularly those associated with the legends of saints, including the dreams of Pope Innocent III (p. 24) and Pope Sergius I (p. 29), or the dream of Emperor Constantine the Great (p. 31). In the Middle Ages and the early modern period, such images of dreams emphasized the power and agency of God and were repeatedly commissioned from the leading artists of their time, including Giotto, Fra Angelico, Rogier van der Weyden, Piero della Francesca, Raphael and Rembrandt (pp. 21, 24, 29, 31, 35 and 43).

Around 1500, with the flourishing of the Renaissance in Europe, we encounter works that offer a fundamentally different approach to the world of dreams. Subjective experiences, personal interpretations of dream images and even dreams personally experienced by the artist now shift into the foreground, as seen in Dürer's apocalyptic vision (p. 37), but also Michelangelo's famous dream drawing (p. 39) and, strikingly, at roughly the same moment, Tang Yin's depiction of Wang Dongyuan's dream (p. 33). With this shift, the range of themes gradually expands, as a wide variety of dream subjects now furnish material for artists, including desires and longings of an amorous nature (pp. 45 and 47), at times intensified into the explicitly sexual, as in Japanese shunga imagery (p. 57), or giving rise to terrifying and abyssal nightmare visions.

Two such depictions of nightmares, created just before 1800 by Henry Fuseli (p. 48) and Francisco de Goya (p. 53), mark the transition from the early modern period to Romanticism, or even Modernism. With his aquatint *The Sleep of Reason Produces Monsters*, Goya created one of the most striking and widely discussed images of this epochal shift, giving form both to the dangers of Reason abandoned and to the menace of Reason elevated to unchallenged authority. With Romanticism, the historical past itself – albeit transfigured now by the imagination – enters the world of dream images. Like virtually no other artist, Caspar David Friedrich succeeded in visualizing a nostalgic, dreamlike yearning for what has been irrevocably lost – a past beyond recovery (p. 59) – while Thomas Cole presents a grand vision of idealized architecture, drawing on historical models (p. 62).

From the mid-nineteenth century onwards, an increasing number of works take up the grotesque and often absurd imagery of dreams – a powerful current whose influence reaches well into the twentieth century. A key figure in this regard is Odilon Redon, whose enigmatic dream apparitions (p. 67) were frequently and explicitly cited by later generations of artists. His shadowy drawings and prints of floating, disembodied eyes and heads testify to humanity's hidden depths and to unconscious realms, as they may be revealed in dream's elusive visions. An extended sequence of works by a range of artists is devoted to experimentation with such bizarre and hallucinatory forms and motifs, culminating in the great masters of Surrealism, among them Giorgio de Chirico (p. 81), Max Ernst (p. 85), Joan Miró (p. 89), René Magritte (p. 91) and Salvador Dalí (p. 103). Although their approaches differ widely, these works are united by their engagement with the irrational, creative dimension of dreams and their effort to give form to the unconscious – a path that gained considerable momentum through the concurrent establishment of psychoanalysis under Sigmund Freud.

There are also striking individual works that articulate highly personal relationships to dreams, not aligned with any particular artistic tendency but compelling in their own right, including images by Ferdinand Hodler (pp. 70/71), Edvard Munch (p. 73), Henri Rousseau (p. 77), Franz Marc (p. 79), Paul Klee (p. 83), Wassily Kandinsky (p. 87), Pablo Picasso (p. 93), Henri Matisse (p. 95), Marc Chagall (p. 97), Frida Kahlo (p. 99) and Max Beckmann (p. 101). After 1945 and the Second World War, works increasingly emerge that use dream motifs to critically engage with aspects of contemporary life or recent history – whether related to a specific nation (pp. 104/105), patriarchal systems in general (p. 109) or to colonialism (p. 115), commodity capitalism (p. 117) or false promises of freedom (p. 119). An entirely new level of radicalism is evident in works that transform the viewer into an active participant, drawing them directly into the world of dreams (p. 120), even allowing them to become the dreamers themselves (p. 113). A genuinely exceptional role is played by so-called 'Dreamtime', a central element of a living religious practice that continues to the present day, and one powerfully visualized by Australia's Indigenous artists (p. 111).

Taken as a whole, this focused selection of key, exemplary artworks offers a distinctive and compelling view of the many facets of dreaming as they unfold across the centuries and into the present. These works open a path into a world of dreams found nowhere else.

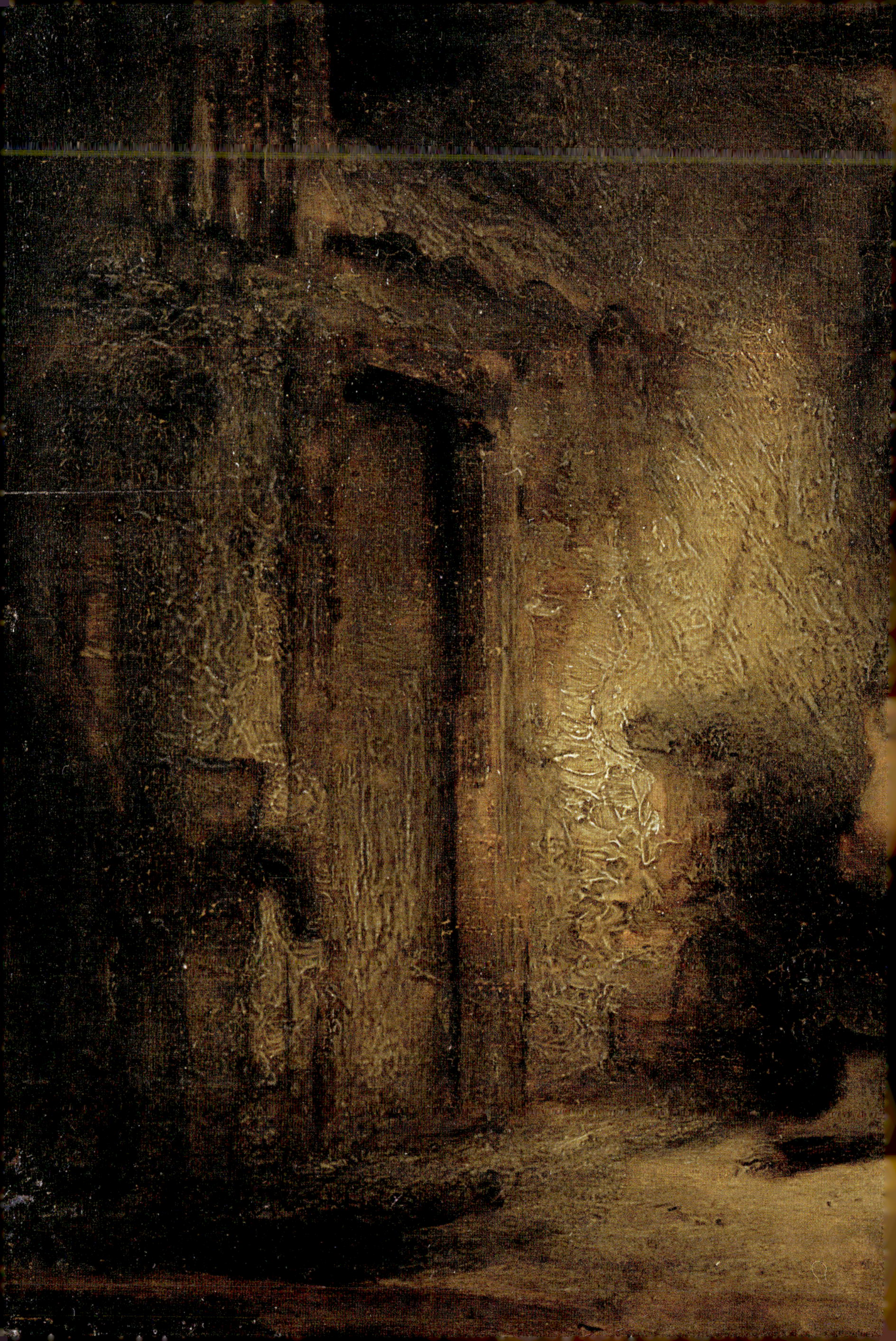

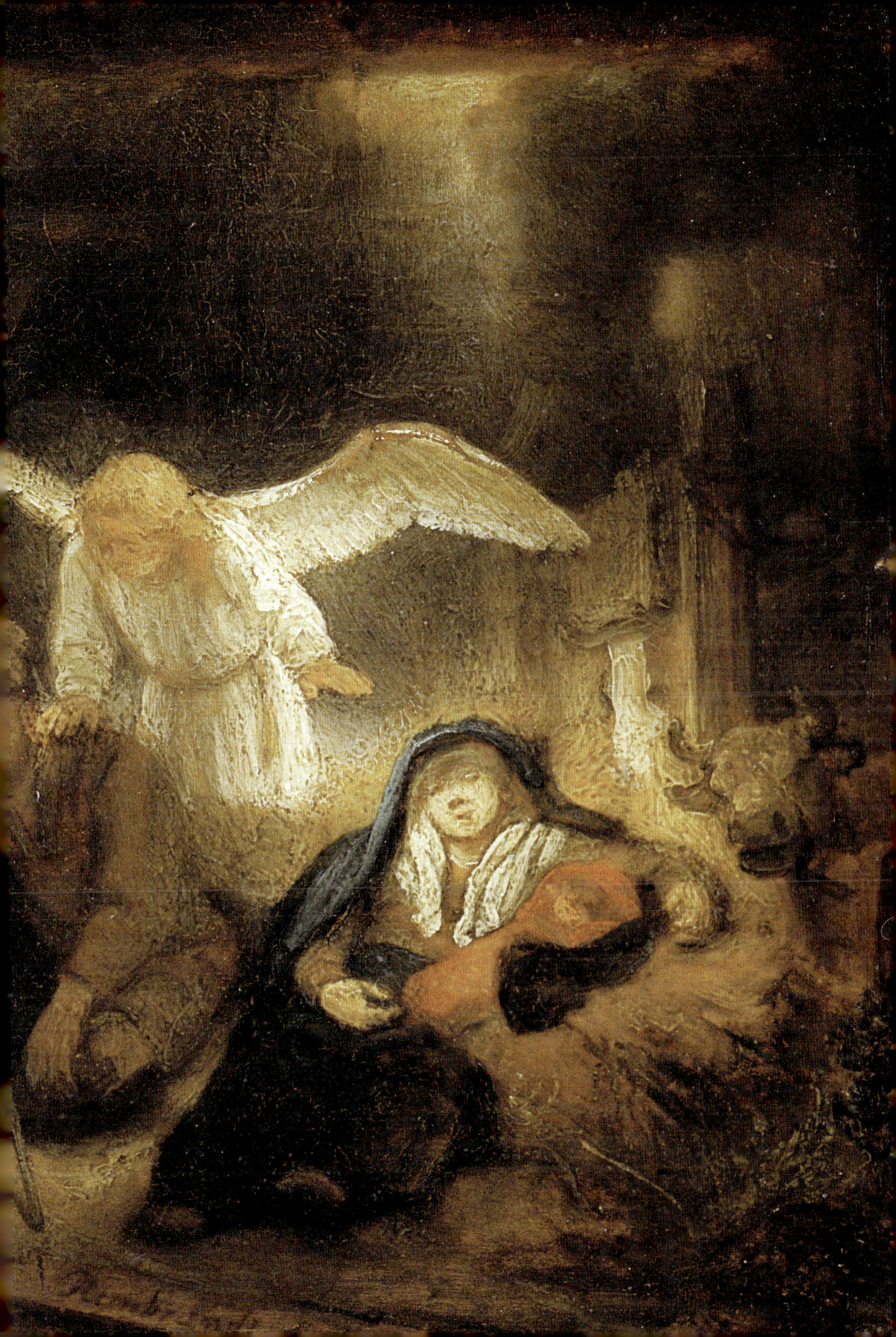

ANONYMOUS NEW KINGDOM CARVER

early 14th century BC

One of those days it came to pass that the King's Son Thutmose came,
coursing at the time of mid-day, and he rested in the shadow of this Great God.
Sleep seized him at the hour when the sun was in its zenith,
and he found the Majesty of this Revered God speaking with his own mouth,
as a father speaks with his son, saying: 'Behold thou me, my son, Thutmose. [...]
The land shall be thine, in its length and in its breadth,
that which the eye of the All-Lord shines upon.'

FROM THE INSCRIPTION ON THE *DREAM STELE OF THUTMOSE IV* (c. 1397 BC)

The celebrated stone monument known as the *Dream Stele of Thutmose IV* still stands at its original site, between the front paws of the Great Sphinx of Giza, close to the great pyramids. It recounts a fantastical story: at noon, Thutmose, the Pharaoh's young son, who often hunted in the area with a small retinue, fell asleep in the shadow of the Sphinx. In a dream, the god Hor-em-akhet-Khepri-Ra-Atum, a local form of the god Horus, appeared to him in the guise of the Sphinx, offering him a pact: if Thutmose were to have the sand removed that had accumulated around the Sphinx over the centuries, fully uncovering the powerful divine figure once more, he would one day rule over all Egypt. Upon becoming Pharaoh, Thutmose carried out the divinely ordained task and had the stele erected to commemorate the encounter, which he believed had permanently altered the course of his life, along with the history of Egypt.

Around 1400 BC, when Thutmose ascended the throne, Egypt was at the height of its power. Little is known about his reign, which probably lasted around a decade, from about 1397 to 1388 BC, but there are reasons to believe that Thutmose had not been the intended successor and therefore found it necessary to establish his legitimacy. It must, of course, have helped to strengthen his authority that a god had appeared to him in a dream and explicitly promised him sovereignty, an event of extraordinary significance in Egyptian culture. Moreover, the Sphinx was a monument of exceptional importance whose restoration represented a considerable achievement and an indicator of good governance.

The stele – measuring 3.6 metres in height (almost twelve feet), weighing approximately fifteen metric tons, and fashioned from rose granite – is a striking monument in its own right. Its fine, low-relief imagery and the positioning of the inscription correspond entirely to the formal conventions of Egyptian art, whose hieroglyphs remained unchanged for millennia, making them immediately recognizable. Appearing twice beneath the winged sun disk is Thutmose himself, who makes sacrificial offerings to the Sphinx. Below the scenes is the main inscription, all arranged in strict symmetry. Even today, the singular positioning of the stele remains awe-inspiring, set beneath the Sphinx and alongside the pyramids – monuments that were already more than a thousand years old when the god appeared to the young prince in a dream.

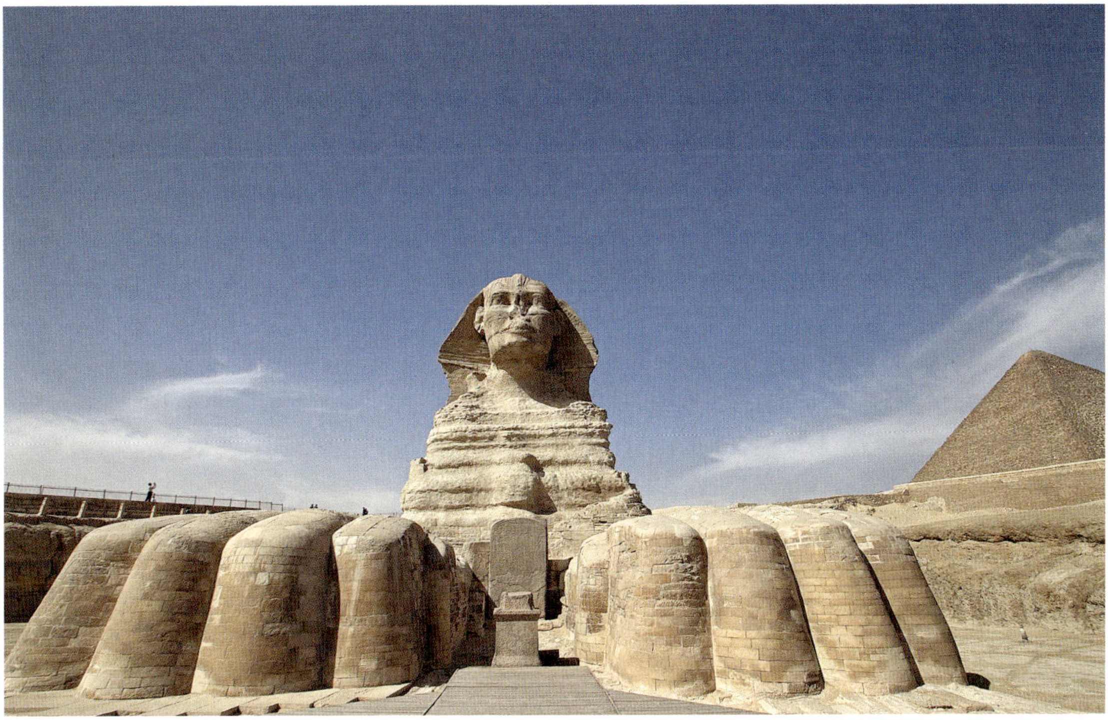

Dream Stele of Thutmose IV, c. 1397 BC, rose granite,
361 × 218 × 70 cm (142 ⅛ × 85 ⅞ × 27 ½ in.), Giza Plateau, Egypt

ANONYMOUS ATTIC SCULPTOR

first half of the 4th century BC

One who has come to consult Amphiaraus is wont first to purify himself. The mode of purification is to sacrifice to the god [...]. And when all these things have been first done, they sacrifice a ram, and, spreading the skin under them, go to sleep and await enlightenment in a dream.

PAUSANIAS, *DESCRIPTION OF GREECE* (AD 155–180)

Amphiaraus, a figure from Greek mythology, was a military commander from Argos endowed by Zeus with prophetic and healing powers. He plays a central role in a number of legends, including the story of the Argonauts, as well as Aeschylus's tragedy *Seven Against Thebes*. Amphiaraus is said to have been swallowed up at Oropos by a cleft in the earth created by Zeus and then to have been received into the ranks of the gods of the underworld. In the late fifth century BC, a sanctuary was erected among rolling hills in the vicinity of this place, its centre marked by a spring. The Amphiareion, or Sanctuary of Amphiaraus, soon became one of the most important and frequented dream oracles, as well as a powerful place of healing.

This celebrated votive relief illustrates a miraculous event in three stages. Entering the room from the right is a young man in prayer, identified by the inscription as Archinos. Immediately to his left, we see Archinos again, this time sleeping on a couch; a snake – a manifestation of the deity – bites his right shoulder, thereby healing him. On the left-hand side of the image, Amphiaraus appears in the foreground, now in human form as a physician treating the afflicted shoulder. This sequence corresponds precisely to known written sources: once the patient had shown himself worthy through purification, sacrifice and prayer, he was admitted to an enclosed, sacred space. Here, he lay on a couch covered in blankets or animal skins and surrendered to *enkoimesis*, or 'temple sleep', hoping to encounter the god personally in a dream and thus receive the desired healing. For a suffering individual, this would have been an overpowering and existentially decisive moment.

In the case of Archinos, this ritual evidently proved successful. His votive relief exemplifies the formal mastery of Greek art during the first half of the fourth century BC. The relaxed, confident pose of the god is rendered with great virtuosity, while the slightly unsteady stance of Archinos, his wounded arm dangling limply and supported by his left hand, is conveyed with impressive naturalness. Garments drape convincingly around the figures, the folds obeying natural laws. In the background, a votive tablet stands on a column; along the upper edge of the relief, two eyes stare out at the viewer, intended to ward off future illnesses from the grateful donor. This relief offers a fascinating glimpse into the mythology and ritual of the ancient world. Only towards the end of the fourth century AD was the sanctuary of Amphiaraus closed by edict of the Christian emperor Theodosius I.

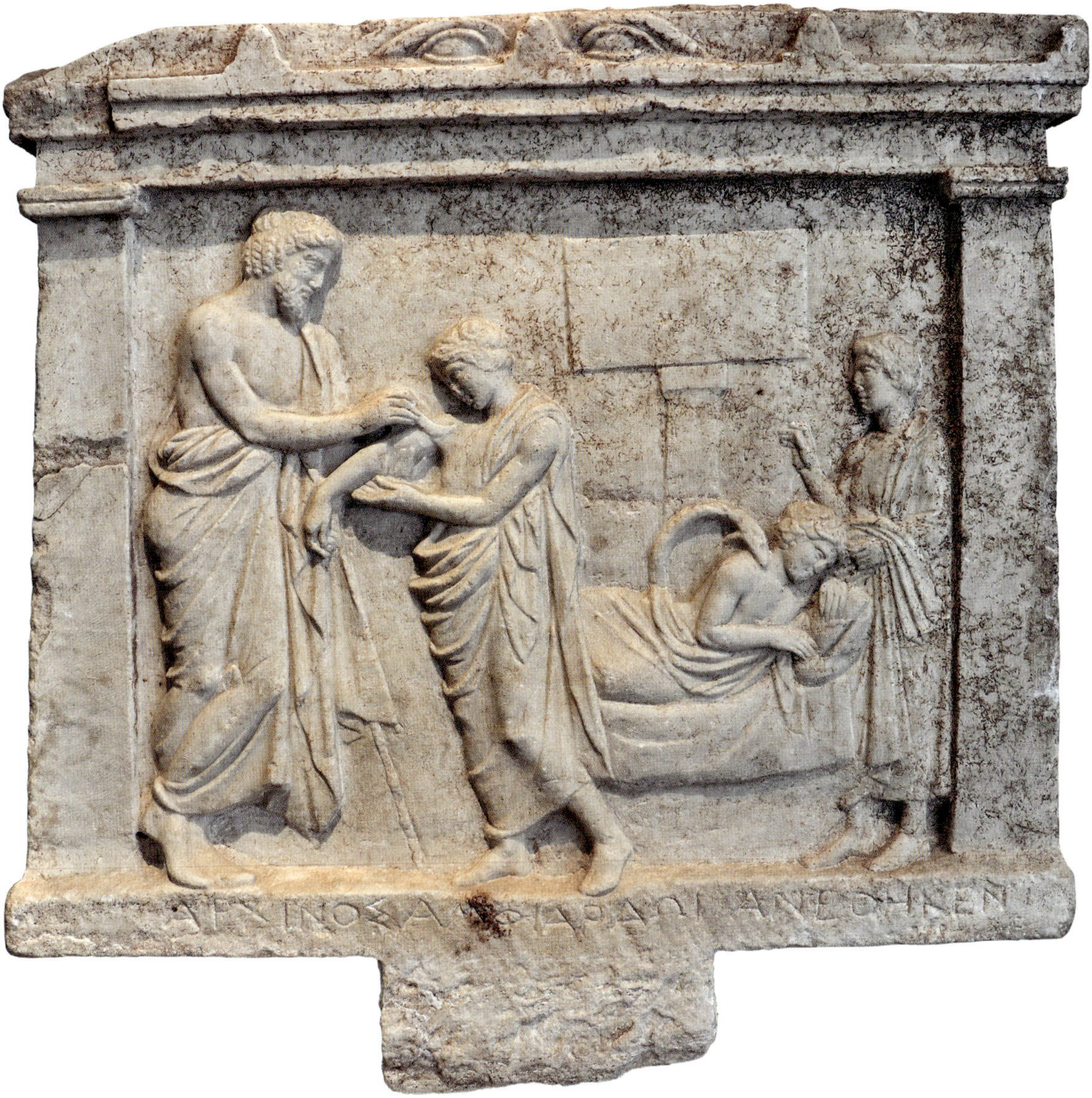

Votive Relief from the Sanctuary of Amphiaraus at Oropos, first half of the fourth century BC, pentelic marble, 49 × 54 cm (19 ¼ × 21 ¼ in.), National Archaeological Museum, Athens

ANONYMOUS SHUNGA STONE CARVER

late 2nd century BC

Queen Maya was sleeping on her pleasant bed
and saw the following in her dream:
A snowy-silver colored elephant with six tusks,
Beautiful feet, exquisite trunk, and a pretty red head,
Moving in a fine gait with joints as stable as a diamond—
That perfect elephant entered her womb.

LALITAVISTARA SŪTRA, CH. 6, SECTIONS 3 AND 4 (3RD CENTURY AD)

According to legend, Maha Maya – the childless consort of King Śuddhodana, ruler of the small aristocratic Shakya Republic in northern India – fell asleep in her husband's palace on the night of a full moon and had an unusual dream. Four ethereal spirit beings transported her to the mythic lake Anotatta in the Himalayas. After bathing, she was dressed in splendid garments, enveloped in delightful fragrance and sprinkled with blossoms. Finally, a small white elephant appeared to her, holding a lotus blossom on its tusk; the creature circled her three times before penetrating her belly from the right side. Upon awakening, she was joyful and serene, and after questioning priests well-versed in the interpretation of dreams, the momentous meaning of her vision became clear: while dreaming, she had conceived a child of great significance. Ten months later, according to tradition, in the year 563 BC, she gave birth to Siddhartha Gautama, who would come to be known as the Buddha, the founder of Buddhism.

A small circular relief from the village of Bharhut in Madhya Pradesh, central India, illustrates the dream of Queen Maya. It formed part of the stupa there, a Buddhist monument commemorating the Buddha and his teachings, which devotees are meant to ritually circumambulate in a clockwise direction. Mounted on the pillars of the railing (*vedika*), which is fashioned from dark red sandstone and surrounds the stupa, are reliefs, probably created shortly before 100 BC, which are among the oldest surviving Buddhist sculptures.

Maya, adorned with precious chains and armbands, and with her hair elaborately dressed, has fallen asleep on a divan, with one arm supporting her head and the other lying loosely at her side. She is surrounded by three ladies-in-waiting, with a jug of water at her head and an incense burner at her feet. Above her appears the dream vision: the white elephant, which touches her with its front leg. The relief does little to suggest visual depth; the individual objects and figures emerge directly from the smooth background, which itself remains undefined. This endows the central motif with powerful expressive immediacy. The surviving pillars, gateways and entablatures of this ancient structure, now more than two millennia old, were excavated in 1873, and are preserved today in the Indian Museum in Kolkata.

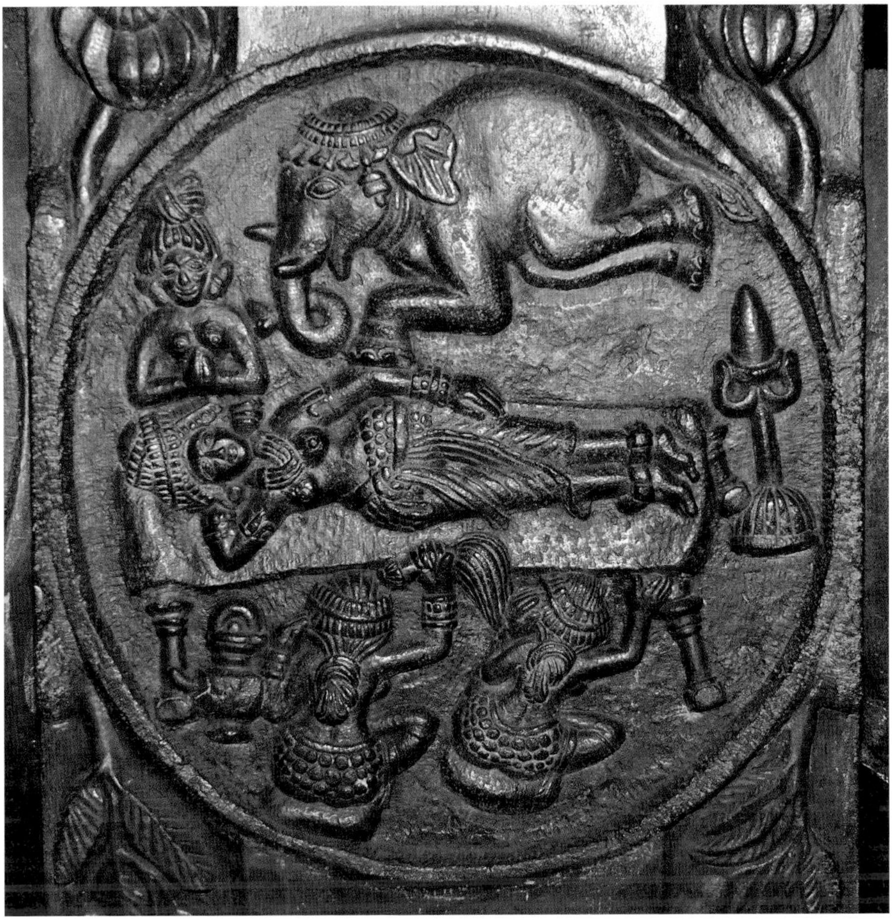

The Dream of Maya, from the stone railing (*vedika*) of the Bharhut Stupa, c. 125–100 BC, red sandstone, 38 × 38 cm (15 × 15 in.), Indian Museum, Kolkata

GIOTTO DI BONDONE
c. 1267–1337

In painting Cimabue thought that he
Should hold the field, now Giotto has the cry,
So that the other's fame is growing dim.

DANTE ALIGHIERI, *THE DIVINE COMEDY,*
PURGATORIO, CANTO 11, VERSES 94–96 (BEFORE 1321)

Throughout the history of art, few works have been universally accorded such overarching significance as Giotto's series of frescoes in the Cappella degli Scrovegni – sometimes called the Arena Chapel because of its proximity to the ancient Roman amphitheatre of Padua. These frescoes are regarded as the artist's principal achievement. In thirty-nine scenes illustrating the lives of the Virgin Mary and Christ, Giotto presents both perspectival space and human emotion with a naturalness that surpassed anything previously seen; these images, in their rendering of the visible world, paved the way for the emergence of the Italian Renaissance. Giotto's contemporaries – among them Dante Alighieri and Boccaccio – recognized his epochal achievement, and his fame has remained undiminished.

The distinctive qualities of Giotto's art become readily apparent in his celebrated fresco of *Joachim's Dream*. It is the fifth of six images that relate episodes from the lives of Sts Anne and Joachim, the parents of the Virgin Mary. This story is not mentioned in the canonical books of the New Testament; it is instead drawn from the so-called Protoevangelium of James, which was not included in the Bible. Shortly before 1300, the narrative was widely disseminated through the *Legenda aurea*, or *Golden Legend*, compiled by the Dominican friar Jacobus de Voragine. Having failed to produce a child with his wife Anne, the wealthy and pious Joachim is turned away from the temple. He then journeys into the wilderness, fasting and doing penance. On the fortieth night, an angel appears to him, announcing the birth of his child.

A diffuse light illuminates Giotto's scene. Seated on the lower right before a shepherd's hut is Joachim, fast asleep and wrapped in a cloak. On the upper left, an angel bursts downwards into the scene, piercing the deep blue of the sky, while a pair of shepherds, accompanied by white and black sheep, observe the scene from the lower left. Contemporary viewers must have been struck by the plasticity of the dreaming figure of Joachim, who rests his head on one knee, and by the naturalness with which his pose, the folds of his mantle and the shadows are rendered – all unprecedented at that time. Startled astonishment is reflected with great subtlety in the faces of the shepherds, signs of inner human emotion that had never before been depicted so convincingly in medieval art. Both landscape and figures are endowed with convincing depth, creating the illusion of space on a flat surface and presenting the viewer with a real event, as though enacted on a theatre stage. This new mode of representation marks a turning point in the history of art and has had a profound impact on creative developments all the way up to modernism.

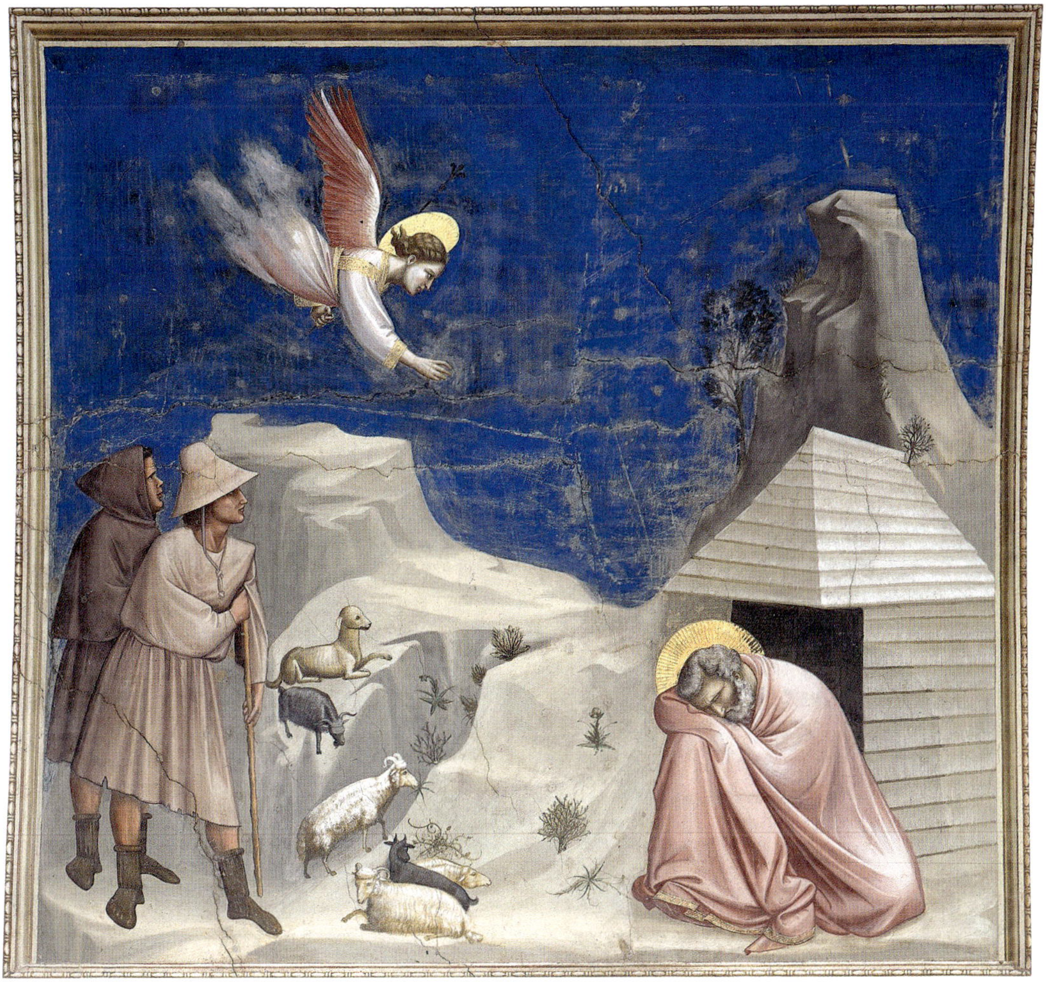

Joachim's Dream, 1303–1305, fresco, 200 × 185 cm (78 ¾ × 72 ⅞ in.),
Cappella degli Scrovegni (Scrovegni Chapel or Arena Chapel), Padua

ANONYMOUS SEPHARDIC ILLUMINATOR

early 14th century

When he reached a certain place,
he stopped for the night because the sun had set.
Taking one of the stones there,
he put it under his head and lay down to sleep.
He had a dream in which he saw a stairway resting on the earth,
with its top reaching to heaven,
and the angels of God were ascending and descending on it.

GENESIS 28:11–12

During the Seder, the ritual feast held on the eve of the Jewish holiday of Passover, it is traditional for the youngest child at the table to ask, 'Why is this night different from all other nights?' This question introduces the recital of the story of Exodus, the escape of the Israelites from Egypt, which is commemorated on Passover, or Pesach. The text from which the story of the deliverance of the Jewish people is sung, read and recited, each year at the Seder table, is called the Haggadah.

One of the best-known copies of this book is *The Golden Haggadah*, created in the Principality of Catalonia around 1320, probably in Barcelona. The volume is named for the patterned background of gold leaf in its fifty-six miniatures. These images illustrate the books of Genesis (*Bereshit*) and Exodus (*Shemot*). Each composition displays the fine line and noble elegance typical of High Gothic illuminated manuscripts. Stylistic characteristics suggest Italian and French models, while the pages of text are written in Sephardic square script. The work is among the most magnificent illustrated volumes to survive from the Middle Ages and testifies to the prominence of Jewish culture in medieval Spain and the peninsula's rich, multicultural life.

In one of the miniatures, the Hebrew patriarch Jacob is shown asleep during his flight from his brother Esau, set against a sparse landscape of only a few plants. Standing directly behind him is the famous ladder, which traverses the image diagonally against the gold ground, ascending into the heavens and reaching the divine realm at the upper edge, defined by undulating blue waves. An angel peers down from this heavenly sphere through a window-like opening, observing three of his celestial comrades ascending and descending the ladder. With great subtlety, the angels' gestures and poses convey their attentive care for the dreaming Jacob. Surrounding the image is a frame consisting of red and blue bands, the latter decorated with delicate arabesques. The elaborate production and high artistic quality of *The Golden Haggadah* suggest the exceptional importance of such books within Jewish life, as well as the considerable wealth of its patrons.

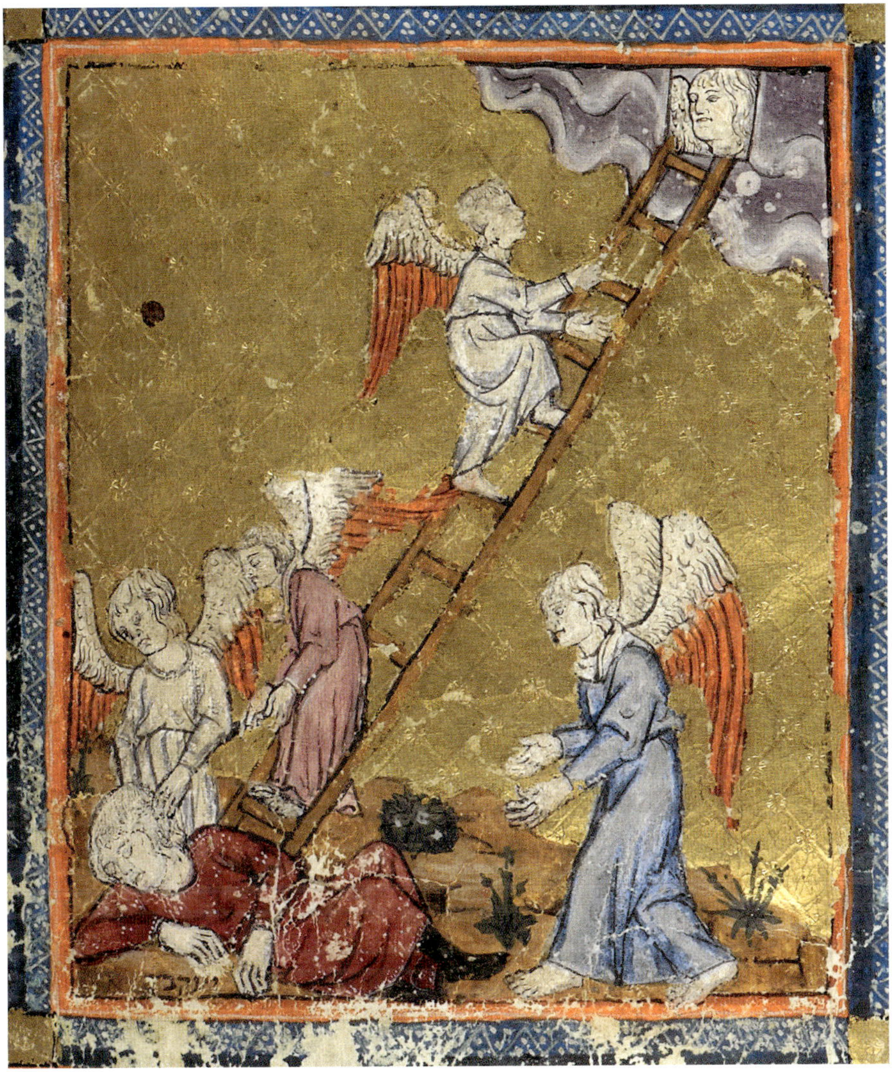

Jacob's Dream, from *The Golden Haggadah*, c. 1320, ink, tempera and gold leaf on vellum, c. 8 × 7 cm (c. 3 ⅛ × 2¾ in.), The British Library, London

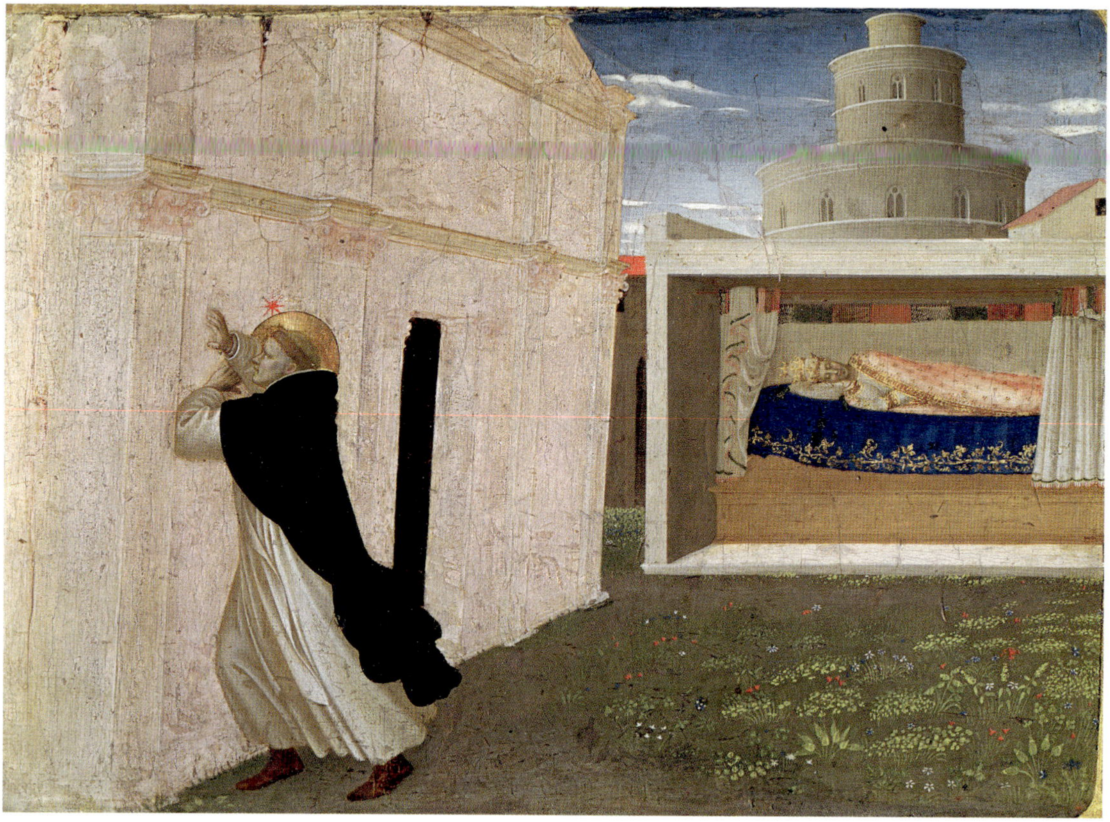

The Dream of Innocent III, 1425/1450 (second quarter of the fifteenth century), tempera on panel, 20.9 × 28 cm (8 ¼ × 11 in.), Musée du Louvre, Paris

FRA ANGELICO
c. 1395–1455

And then it happed on a night that the pope saw
in a vision that the church of Lateran was suddenly menaced
for to fall and overthrow, and as he beheld it,
all afeard, he saw on that side St Dominic running against it,
and sustained and bare it up, and kept it from falling.
And then awoke the pope, and understood the vision,
and received joyously the petition of the man of God [...]

JACOBUS DE VORAGINE, *THE GOLDEN LEGEND* (c. 1264)

Innocent III is regarded as one of the most important, yet also one of the most combative popes of the Middle Ages. An implacable opponent of any heretical deviation from the Faith, his tenure was marked by the campaign against the Cathars in southern France, whom he sought to suppress through the Albigensian Crusade, in which Dominic de Guzmán (later St Dominic) participated as an itinerant preacher. Dominic believed that the credibility of the Church was being compromised above all by growing secularization, and in 1215, he established his first community in Toulouse, with a strong emphasis on poverty, study and preaching. The pope initially rejected his request the following year to approve his new order, but changed his mind when – according to legend – he experienced a dream vision of the Lateran Basilica at the point of collapse, and then witnessed Dominic supporting it and setting it upright once again. He interpreted this vision as a divine message that Dominic was destined to rescue and restore the entire Church from its state of decay and peril.

On the far left of the predella of his celebrated *Coronation of the Virgin*, the painter and Dominican friar Fra Angelico, one of the leading figures of the early Renaissance in Florence, has depicted this dream scene with compelling simplicity. The pope sleeps in a room cut open to view, the papal tiara still on his head, clad in precious garments and on a bed covered with a blue textile woven with gold. Rising in the distance above him is Castel Sant'Angelo. The dream vision unfolds in the foreground: St Dominic, who is crowned with a halo, struggles to support the outer wall of the church as it leans perilously towards him.

In this painting, Fra Angelico demonstrates his virtuosic command of the latest artistic developments. Both the dream and the dreamer occupy the same pictorial space, and central perspective is used in an almost exemplary fashion. Dominic is placed in the foreground, while Innocent is set in the background in a way consistent with the laws of real spatial relations, but contrary to medieval convention, in which figural size indicates relative importance. With its Corinthian capitals and continuous cornice, the church façade reflects the most current architectural tastes of the time. The equally attentive yet unpretentious rendering of the meadow, with its flowering plants, lends the image a gentle and welcoming quality. The entire picture is suffused with the inner tranquillity and tender simplicity that is so characteristic of the works of Fra Angelico, known already during his lifetime as 'Il Beato' (The Blessed) – an official title granted to him by the Church in 1982 when he was beatified by Pope John Paul II.

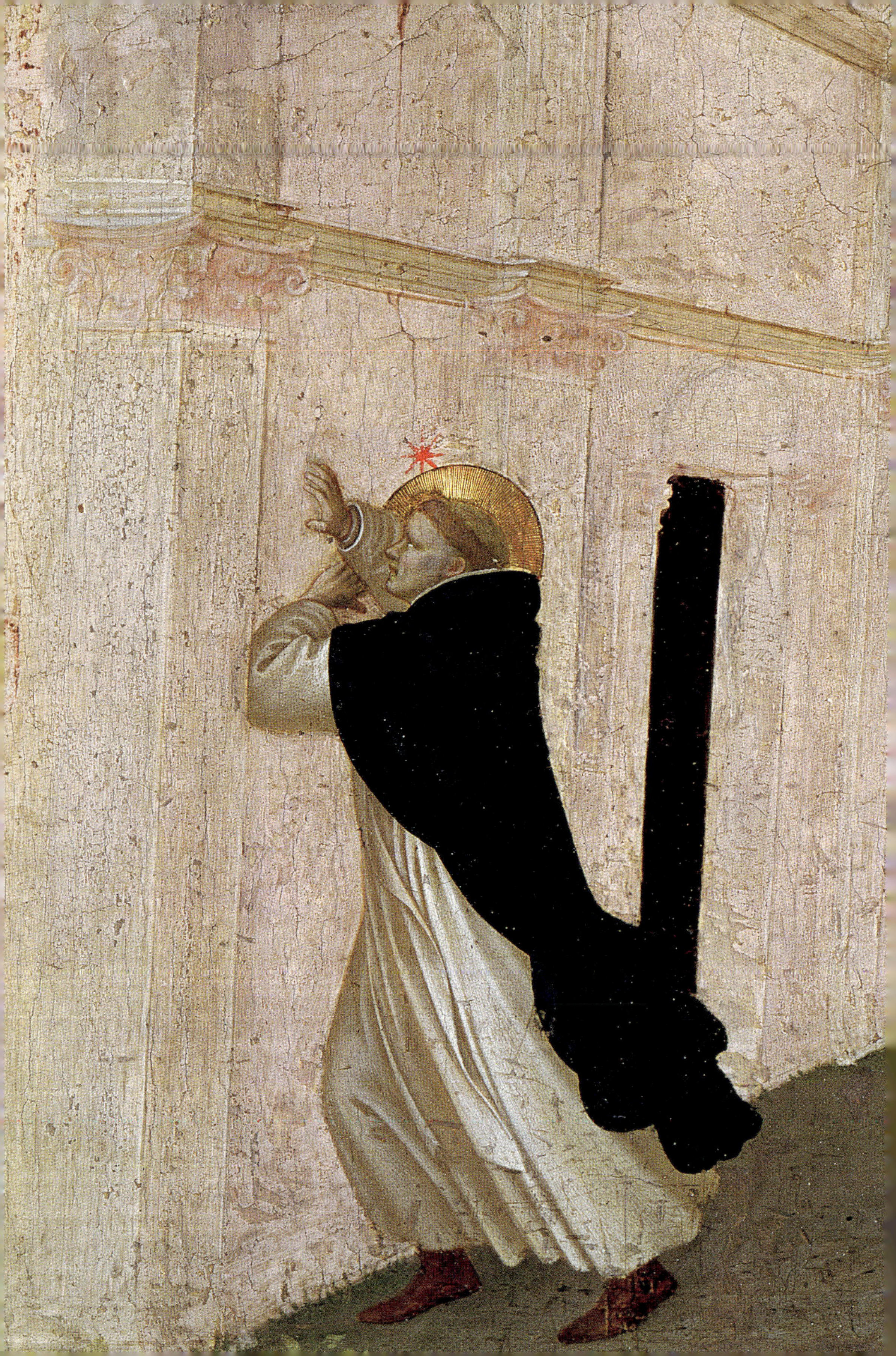

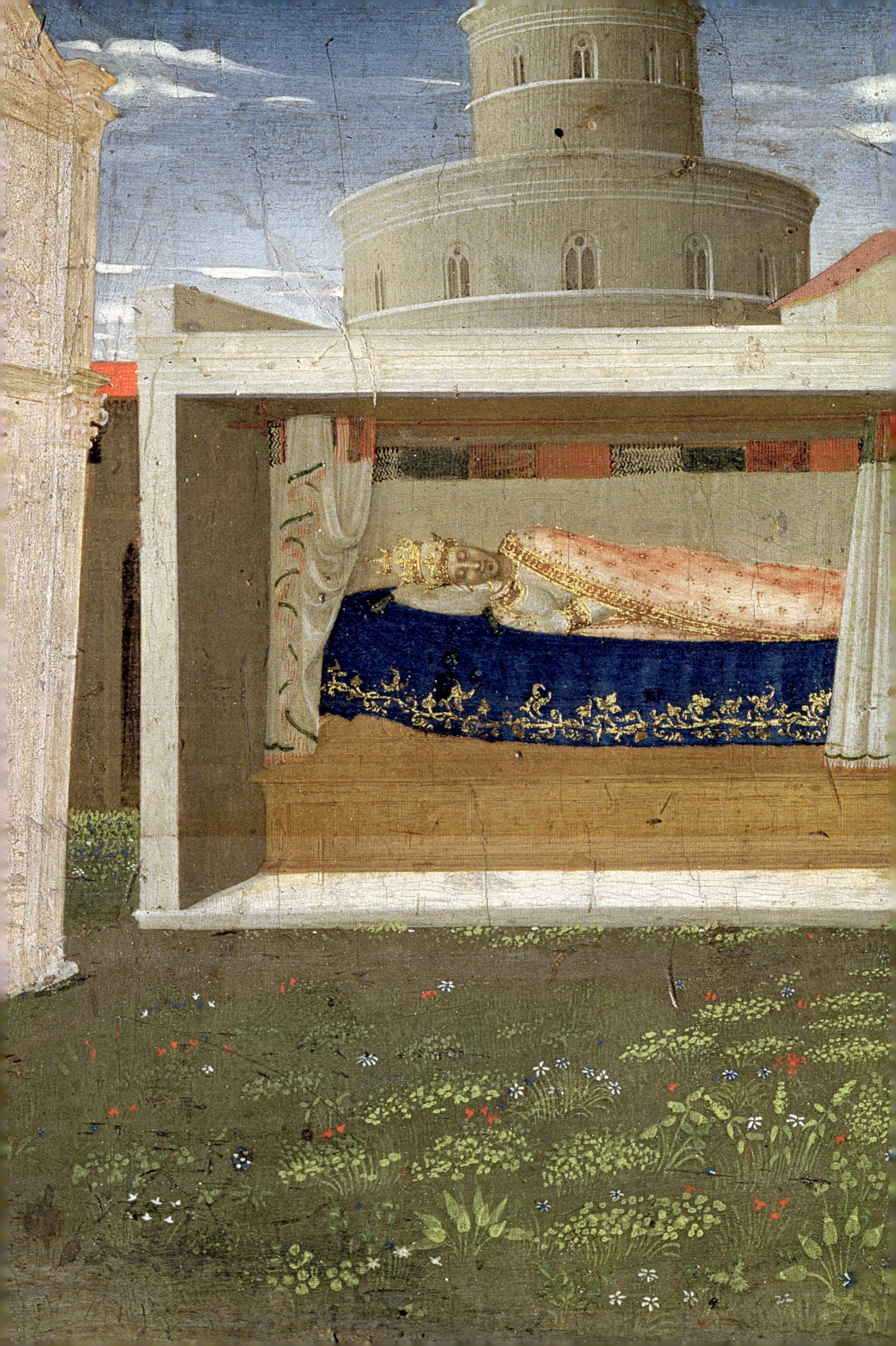

ROGIER VAN DER WEYDEN

1399/1400–1464; and workshop

The blessed Sergius [...], exhausted from night vigils and prayer,
and allowing his weakened body but little rest,
fell asleep in the early morning hours. [...] And behold!
An angel of the Lord, radiant with celestial light, stood before him in a vision:
'Hear me, brother', he said, 'and attend to what the Lord reveals to you through me.
Believe my words and do what is commanded of you with even greater zeal!'

CANON NICHOLAS OF LIÈGE, *THE LIFE OF LAMBERT, BISHOP OF MAASTRICHT* (c. 1145)

Hubert of Liège – who in some Germanic regions is counted among the Fourteen Holy Helpers and is generally regarded as the patron saint of hunters and archers – was the Bishop of Maastricht from 706 and Bishop of Liège from 716. He was venerated as a saint soon after his death in 727. A celebrated event, often illustrated by painters, is his legendary conversion, which took place when a stag bearing a cross between its antlers appeared to him during a hunt. In *The Dream of Pope Sergius*, Rogier van der Weyden – one of the leading masters of early Netherlandish painting – depicts a lesser-known scene from Hubert's life. An angel appeared to Sergius I in a dream and informed him of the martyrdom of Lambert, the Bishop of Maastricht. The angel handed him Lambert's episcopal crozier and instructed him to elevate the deceased prelate's student Hubert – then in Rome, where he could be found at St Peter's Basilica – as Lambert's successor. Upon waking, the pope found the pastoral staff lying beside him. He took it up and immediately made his way to the church, where he did in fact find Hubert immersed in prayer.

This painting was most likely executed together with *The Exhumation of Saint Hubert*, preserved today in the National Gallery in London, for the Chapel of St Hubert in the Church of St Gudula in Brussels. The scene opens onto the pope's bedchamber, where he has fallen asleep, not on his bed, but instead at a prie-dieu, still wearing his vestments, in front of an open book. An angel approaches from the left and hands him the bishop's staff, along with – in a departure from the textual sources – a mitre. On the right side of the picture, further stages of this narrative unfold in an urban setting in Rome. Accompanied by two cardinals, the pope leaves his palace, passes two petitioners and then follows a group of monks through a wooden door. The path before him runs along the Tiber, past the Ponte and the Castel Sant'Angelo, and continues all the way to the steps of Old St Peter's. Here, the pope appears for a third time, holding the crozier and mitre; the pilgrim who kneels before him is presumably Hubert. Rising in the background are the buildings and hills of Rome, although no specific locations can be identified.

Certain passages in the image – among them the cardinals emerging from the Papal Palace, the questioning glance of the first as he turns back and the subtle hesitation of the second – demonstrate the highest mastery of early Netherlandish painting, whose renown extended as far as Italy. Other elements, such as the trees in the foreground, point instead to the less confident hand of an assistant.

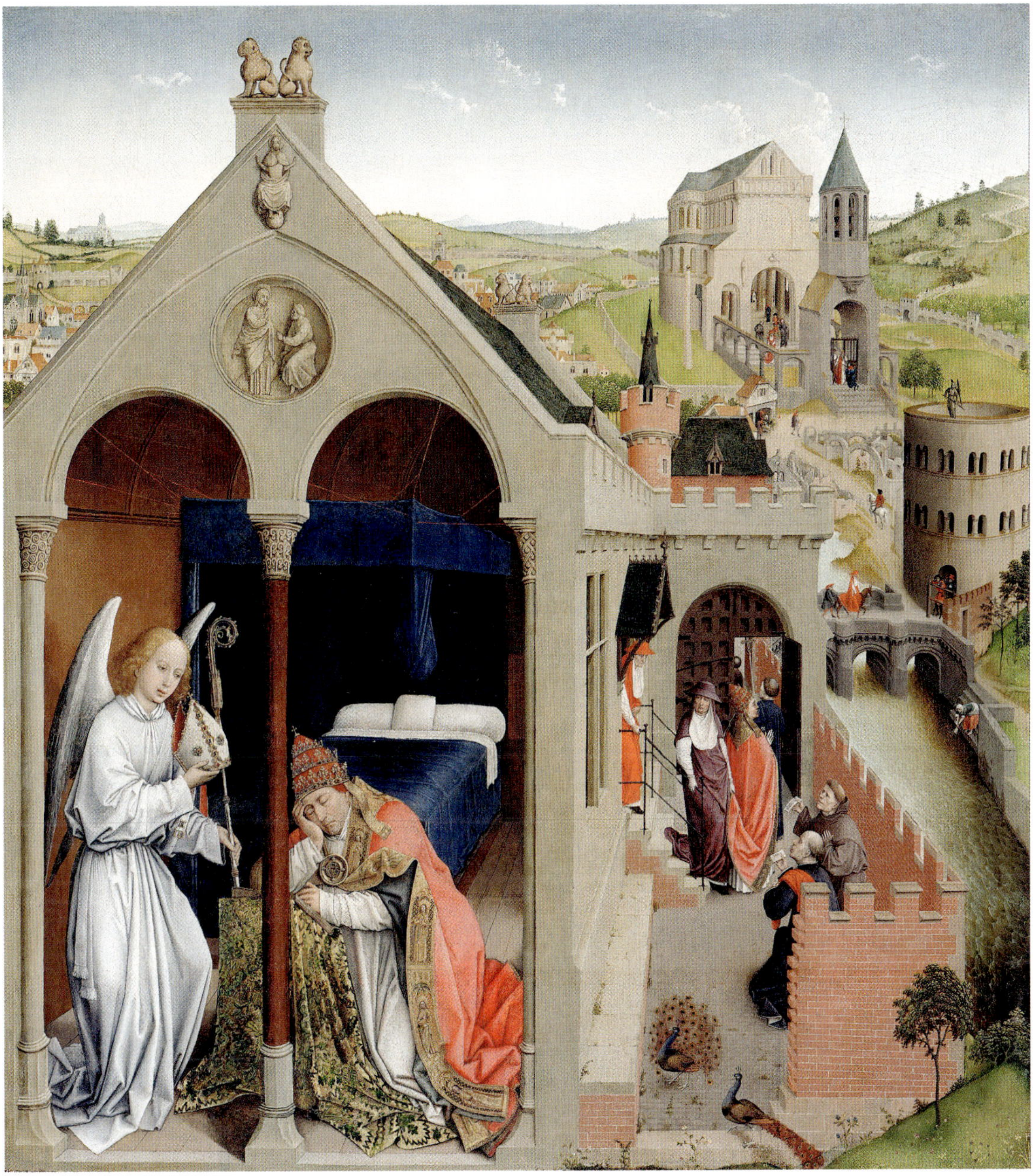

The Dream of Pope Sergius, late 1430s, oil on panel,
90.2 × 81.3 cm (35 ½ × 32 in.), J. Paul Getty Museum, Los Angeles

PIERO DELLA FRANCESCA
c. 1415–1492

Maxentius had the larger forces [...].
Fighting took place in which Maxentius's troops held the advantage
until Constantine [...], his courage renewed,
and 'ready for either success or death', moved all of his forces nearer to the
city of Rome and based himself in the region of the Milvian bridge. [...]
Constantine was advised in a dream to mark the heavenly sign of
God on the shields of the soldiers and then engage in battle.

LACTANTIUS, *ON THE DEATHS OF THE PERSECUTORS* (c. 315)

When the Bacci family of Arezzo commissioned a cycle of paintings narrating the story of the True Cross for the main choir chapel of their Tuscan city's austere Gothic Franciscan church, Christendom as a whole stood under increasing threat. In 1453, Ottoman forces had conquered Constantinople, bringing about the collapse of the Byzantine Empire. In 1456, the Ottomans laid siege to Belgrade and were repelled only after a hard-fought struggle. Given the circumstances, the story of Christ's Cross took on special significance as an emblem of victory. According to the celebrated legend of Constantine's dream, in 312, shortly before a decisive battle against his imperial rival Maxentius, the emperor was visited in his sleep by an angel, who showed him the Cross and said, 'In hoc signo vinces' (In this sign thou shalt conquer).

Piero della Francesca's fresco shows the nocturnal scene in Constantine's camp. The canvas flaps of his tent have been folded back, revealing the emperor, who sleeps peacefully, watched over by three attendants. An angel flies downwards into the scene from the upper left, a tiny golden cross held in its outstretched hand. This image is remarkable in several respects and has influenced generations of artists. To be sure, Piero has mastered the art of perspective, one of the great achievements of the early Renaissance; entirely new, however, is his virtuosic handling of light. Quite independently of the linear framework of mathematical perspective, light models the figures in three dimensions and structures physical depth. The sculptural roundness of the tent is palpable, along with the mass of the bodies, which seem to occupy real space. Yet Piero's art goes even further: light and shadow give rise to a mystical atmosphere, suggesting that we are witnessing a divine event that is to alter the course of the world, thereby transforming the dream into a transcendent vision.

Despite the dramatic events depicted by Piero, everything is suffused with a tranquil yet grave solemnity. As is typical of this artist, the composition is structured by strong horizontals and verticals, giving it a firm geometric order. On this painted stage, nothing distracts from the central moment of the vision of the Holy Cross in the emperor's dream. These qualities make Piero's fresco one of the most memorable and influential works of a century remarkably rich in masterpieces.

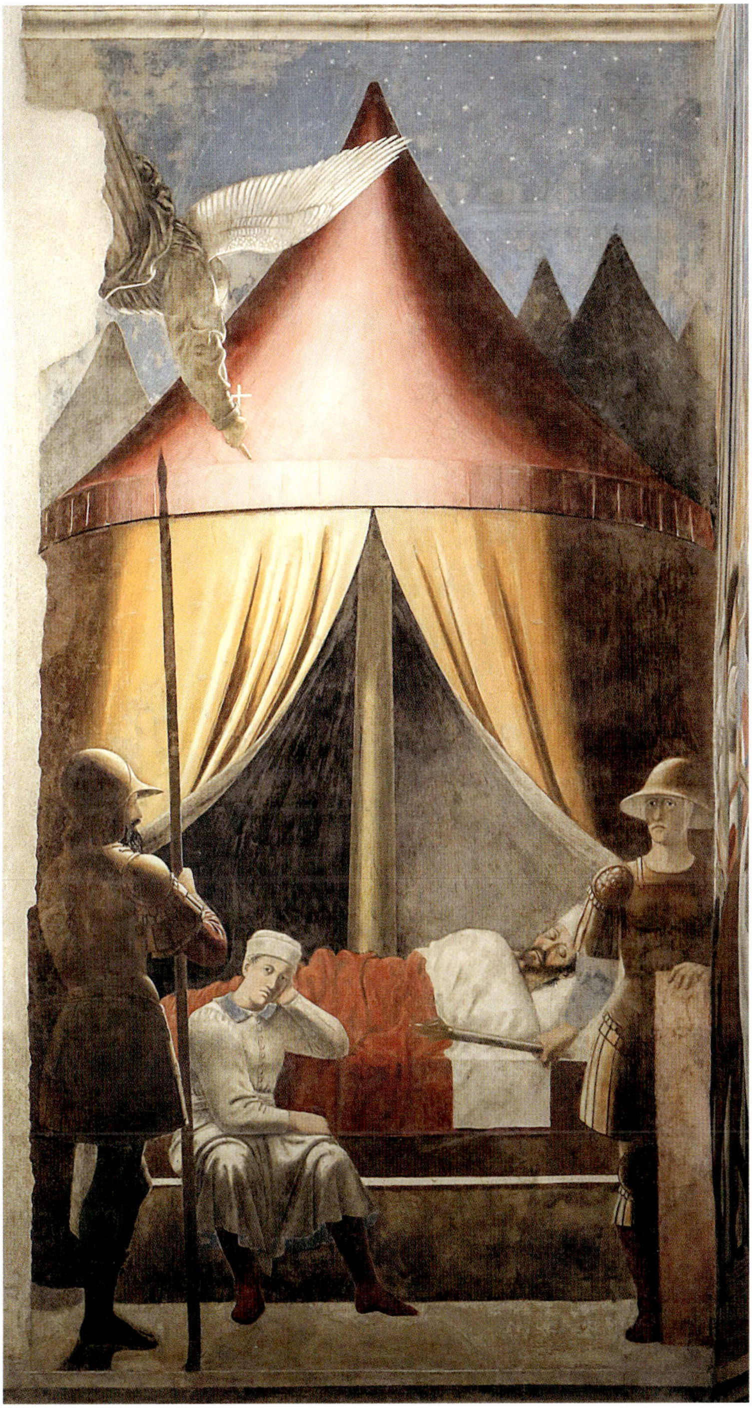

The Dream of Constantine, 1452/c. 1457/1459–1466 at the latest, fresco, 329 × 190 cm (129 ½ × 74 ¾ in.), Basilica di San Francesco, Arezzo

TANG YIN
1470–1524

Above there is heaven, below there is Suzhou and Hangzhou.

CHINESE PROVERB

In his youth, Tang Yin was a brilliant student. Within the strict system regulating appointments to government posts, he achieved one of the best results in his native province of Jiangsu, attracting the attention of influential figures, among them the eminent painter Shen Zhou. In 1499, during the Ming dynasty, Tang travelled to Beijing, the capital of China, and took part in the centralized imperial examinations together with his wealthy friend Xu Jing; had he passed, he would have enjoyed a distinguished career in the civil service. Even before the exam, however, the two were accused of bribing the official in charge and imprisoned by the authorities. Tang, who was unable to prove his innocence, was compelled to return in disgrace to his hometown of Suzhou. In this hub of non-courtly literature and art, he earned a living by selling his paintings and quickly acquired a reputation as an outstanding and inventive painter, calligrapher and poet. In the highly creative and sophisticated atmosphere of the thriving coastal city, with its growing appreciation for tranquil, inspiring and elaborately designed gardens, Tang led an extravagant life in the circle of his learned friends, becoming a popular figure in local folklore, a personality whose adventures are still told today and even adapted for the screen.

The Thatched Hut of Dreaming of an Immortal is a section of a handscroll created by Tang for a contemporary, Wang Dongyuan. The scene shows his patron asleep and dreaming within a simple hut, surrounded by his garden – a familiar Chinese symbol for retreat from the hectic, bustling world in favour of introspection, contemplation and spiritual pursuits. This accords fully with the Taoist outlook cultivated by Wang, who once saw an 'immortal' – a divine, idealized figure in Taoism – approaching him in a prophetic dream, after which he decided to name his garden 'Dreams of an Immortal'. The dream figure hovers above the delicate, virtuosically rendered mountain range, set against a misty sky in the distance. The painting imagines nature as a place of spiritual immersion, along with Wang's own desire to approach 'immortality' through meditation and a life in harmony with the 'Tao' (way).

In the mid-sixteenth century, Tang was already numbered among the 'Four Masters of the Ming Dynasty', a well-established, canonical grouping that remains valid to this day.

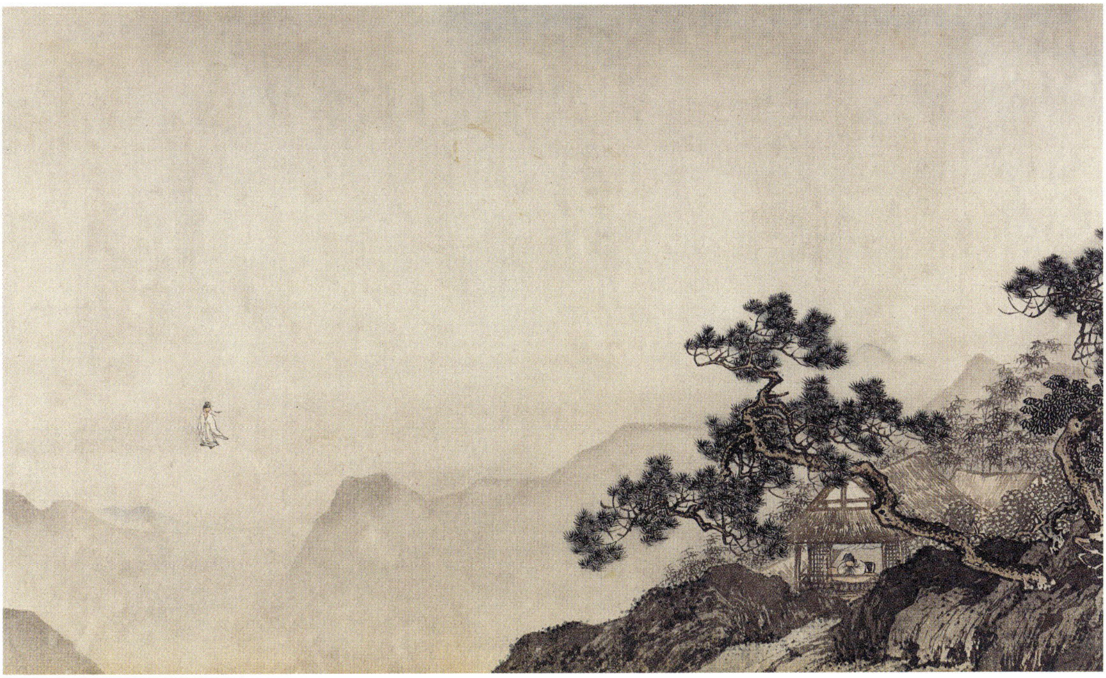

The Thatched Hut of Dreaming of an Immortal (detail), early 16th century, ink and colour on paper, 28.3 × 103 cm (11 ⅛ × 40 ½ in.), National Museum of Asian Art, Freer Gallery of Art Collection, Smithsonian Institution, Washington, DC

RAPHAEL
1483–1520; and workshop

Then Joseph said to Pharaoh,
'The dreams of Pharaoh are one and the same.
God has revealed to Pharaoh what he is about to do.
The seven good cows are seven years,
and the seven good heads of grain are seven years;
it is one and the same dream. The seven lean, ugly cows
that came up afterward are seven years,
and so are the seven worthless heads of grain scorched by the east wind:
They are seven years of famine. It is just as I said to Pharaoh:
God has shown Pharaoh what he is about to do.'

GENESIS 41: 25–28

With Raphael, the art of the Italian High Renaissance reached its splendid culmination. Upon his arrival in Rome in 1508, the precocious artist was inundated with important commissions, among them the painted decorations of the papal reception rooms in the Apostolic Palace, the so-called *Stanze di Raffaello*, which include the world-famous *School of Athens*. Raphael probably began work in 1516 in the large Loggia of Leo X, a long foyer just a few steps away from the *Stanze*. The iconographic program is vast: in the thirteen vaults, a series of fifty-two frescoes illustrate biblical narratives – an ensemble that soon came to be known as 'Raphael's Bible'. It remains unclear to what extent Raphael – who supervised the overall project – was involved in the actual execution. He likely conceived the compositions, delegating their execution to artists from his large workshop. The admirable harmony and idealized beauty of his work, however, are evident throughout the Loggia as a whole.

Displayed in the central, or seventh, vault, and given special artistic emphasis, is the story of Joseph, the great dream interpreter of the Old Testament – most distinguished for his interpretation of the dreams of the Egyptian Pharaoh. The ruler's dreams of seven fat cows being devoured by seven lean ones, and of seven plump ears of grain being swallowed up by seven withered ones, is interpreted by Joseph as a prophetic vision: seven years of abundance will be followed by seven years of famine. His interpretation convinces Pharaoh and his ministers, and Joseph, now regarded as a capable and wise advisor, is appointed governor of all Egypt.

In the fresco, Joseph stands before Pharaoh, arm outstretched and index finger raised, interpreting the sovereign's dreams, which are symbolized by a pair of gold-rimmed discs hovering above the ruler. The brooding Pharaoh, seated before him with an adviser standing behind, is lost in thought. Grouped along the right edge of the image are several men, who gesticulate vehemently, while arguing heatedly. The sovereign's composure, Joseph's commanding, self-confident demeanour and the nervous excitement of the bystanders: everything is perceptible with great immediacy in the hands and bearing of the figures.

Part of the ceremonial route for distinguished visitors, the Loggia remains closed to the public. However, Raphael's images have been widely disseminated in the form of engravings since shortly after their creation.

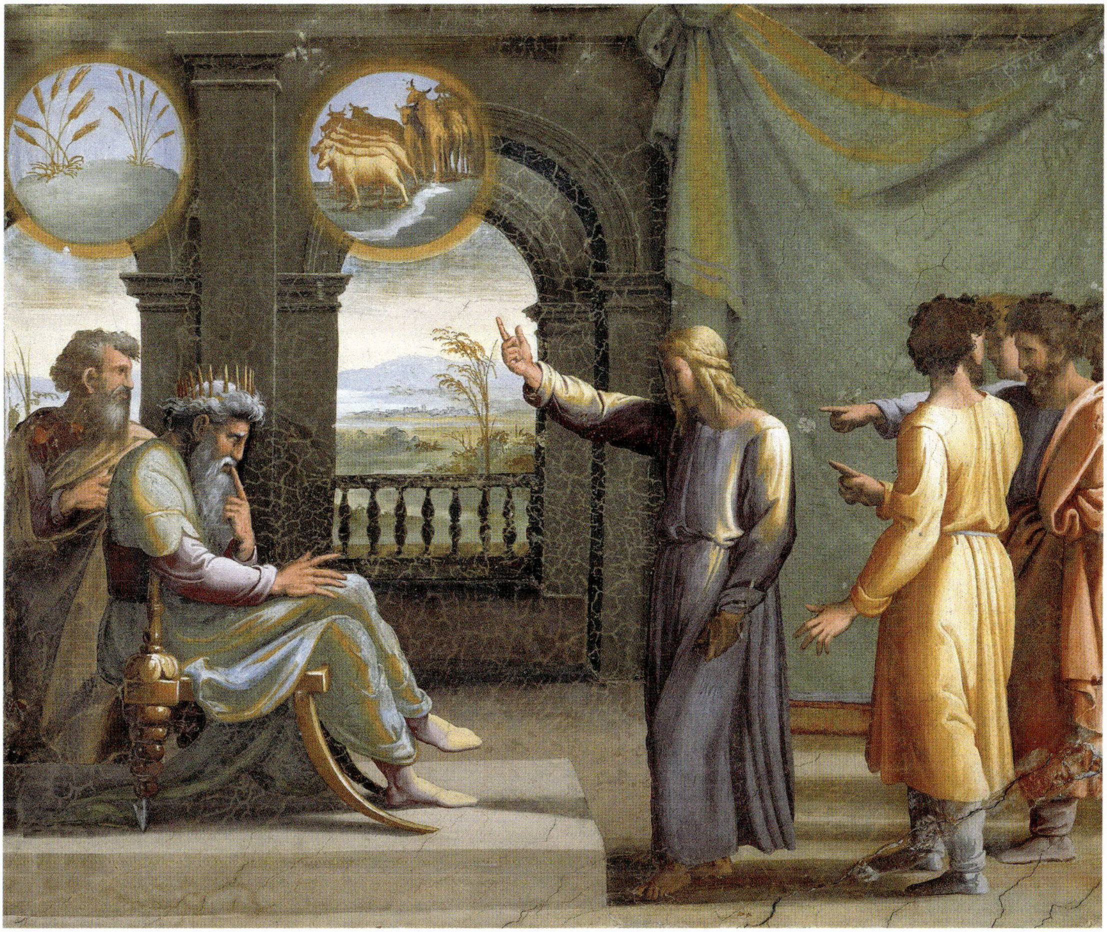

Joseph Interprets Pharaoh's Dreams, 1518/19, fresco,
c. 110 × 130 cm (c. 43¼ × 51⅛ in.), Loggia di Raffaello, Apostolic Palace, Vatican City

ALBRECHT DÜRER
1471–1528

In a dream, in a vision of the night, when deep sleep falls on people, as they slumber in their beds, he may speak in their ears and terrify them with warnings […]

JOB 33:15–16

In 1525, during 'the night between Wednesday and Thursday after Whitsunday I saw this appearance in my sleep – how many great waters fell from heaven. The first struck the earth about 4 miles away from me with terrific force and tremendous noise, and it broke up and drowned the whole land. I was so sore afraid that I awoke from it', and 'when I awoke my whole body trembled and for a long while I could not recover myself.' This account was recorded by Albrecht Dürer on the lower half of this page. Above it, in watercolour, he executed a rapid sketch of the nightmare vision that had given him such a jolt, rendering it 'just as I saw it'. The landscape is indicated only cursorily; trees and the silhouette of a town in the middle ground provide a sense of scale for the apocalyptic event occurring in the firmament above. Thirteen immense columns of water fall heavily to earth, apparently all 'with an equal slowness', the nearest having already begun its destruction, spreading explosively like an enormous wave across the landscape. A distressing vision of the end of the world.

Dürer's *Dream Vision* has no precedent in the history of art, for it neither describes nor visualizes a theologically or mythologically established narrative, but instead presents the purely subjective experience of an individual artist. Like Dürer's work as a whole, it represents a new artistic understanding of self and an unprecedented creative self-confidence on the threshold of the modern age. Here the human individual and his inner life stand at the centre. In this sense, Dürer's watercolour becomes a symbolic embodiment of the Renaissance itself.

Repeatedly, this image has been interpreted in light of the circumstances and historical events that coincided with its creation. During his lifetime, apocalyptic visions were part of Dürer's intellectual world – not uncommon in the sixteenth century. In 1499, a much-noted text by a certain Johannes Stöffler of Tübingen predicted a deluge for February 1524, a prophecy that triggered a panic that spread across Europe. His revelation was discussed in more than 130 subsequent texts, and even Emperor Charles V himself became preoccupied with the matter. Only three weeks before Dürer experienced this dream, the Peasant's War reached its tragic climax in the Battle of Frankenhausen, and just a few days earlier, a host of Franconian peasants had been defeated near Würzburg. Dürer was undoubtedly well aware of these events, and they must have affected him deeply. His watercolour provides a glimpse of a society in the grips of apocalyptic anxiety in the age of the Reformation.

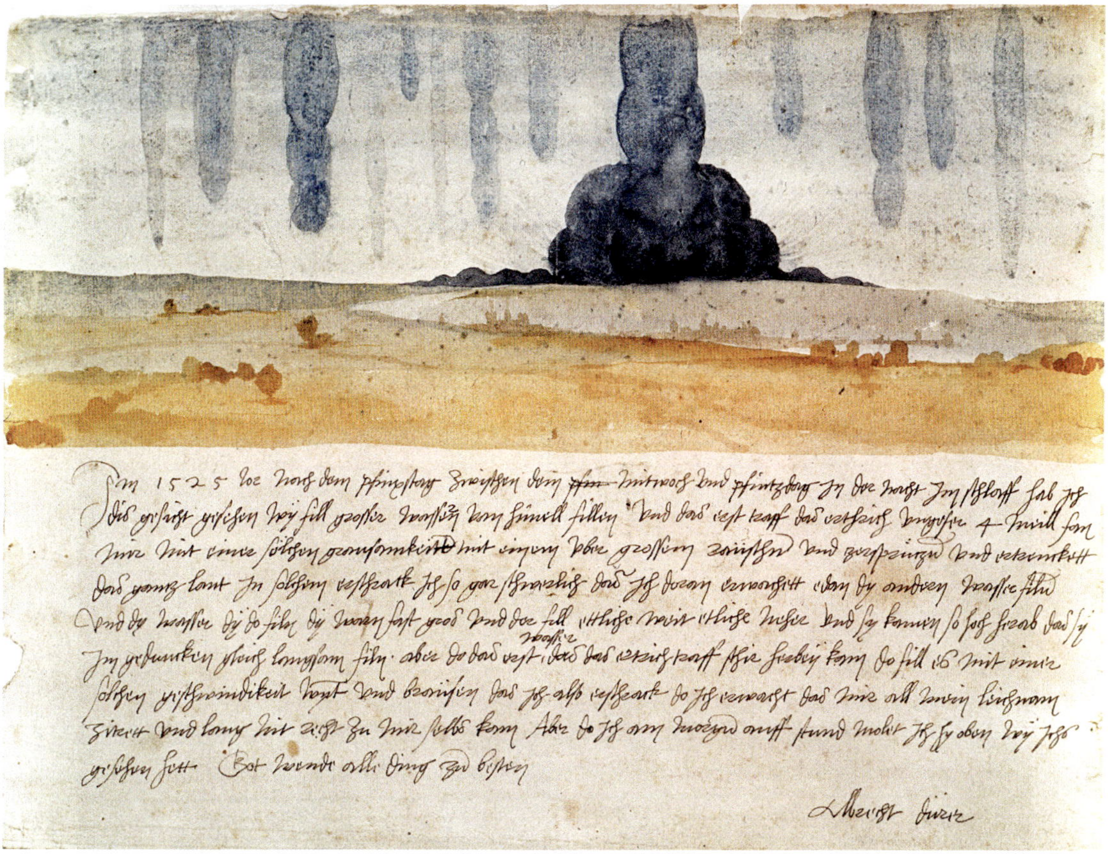

Dream Vision, 1525, watercolour and ink on paper,
30 × 42.5 cm (11 ¾ × 16 ¾ in.), Kunsthistorisches Museum, Vienna

MICHELANGELO BUONARROTI

1475–1564

O night, O sweet though sombre span of time!—
All things find rest upon their journey's end—
Whoso hath praised thee, well doth apprehend;
And whoso honours thee, hath wisdom's prime.
Our cares thou canst to quietude sublime;
For dews and darkness are of peace the friend:
Often by thee in dreams upborne, I wend
From earth to heaven, where yet I hope to climb.

MICHELANGELO, SONNET 102,
TRANSLATED BY JOHN ADDINGTON SYMONDS

Michelangelo's celebrated *Il Sogno* (*The Dream*) is among the most outstanding drawings of the Renaissance, and indeed one of the most remarkable graphic works in the history of art. Around 1533, shortly before commencing work on his fresco *The Last Judgment* in the Vatican's Sistine Chapel, he produced a series of drawings which he distributed to his closest friends, the present sheet among them. In all likelihood, its recipient was Tommaso dei Cavalieri, a pupil with whom Michelangelo retained a deep personal connection throughout his life. These compositions, given as gifts, were never intended as mere studies or preparatory pieces for larger compositions; they were instead fully finished works in their own right. As a result, these drawings by the master were quickly circulated and discussed by numerous admirers, attaining considerable fame. Even the pope asked to see these sheets repeatedly. At the same time, the private and intimate nature of such gifts allowed the artist a degree of freedom in conceiving the imagery and composition.

A youth reclines upon a freestanding pedestal, resting his arms on a sphere and turning his torso sharply upwards. An angelic, winged figure plunges almost vertically downward towards him. It blows a trumpet, holding the instrument's bell not to the man's ear but instead against his forehead. During the Renaissance, and in the Neoplatonic philosophy of the time with which Michelangelo was well-versed, the forehead was regarded as the seat of the imagination. While these two foreground figures have been painstakingly finished and fully modelled, the shadowy, indistinct figures arranged behind them in a semicircle seem to emerge from a cloud. Several appear to personify various capital vices, from left to right: Gluttony, Lust, Greed, Wrath, Envy and Sloth; others are quotations from earlier works by Michelangelo.

The precise meaning of this complex, masterfully rendered drawing cannot be conclusively deciphered. Traditionally, it has been interpreted as an allegory of divine inspiration, associated since time immemorial with dreams, and as admonishing those ensnared in sin to aspire towards virtue. The drawing thus corresponds closely to the self-image and the lived experience of an artist who was tormented by self-doubt and predisposed to self-recrimination.

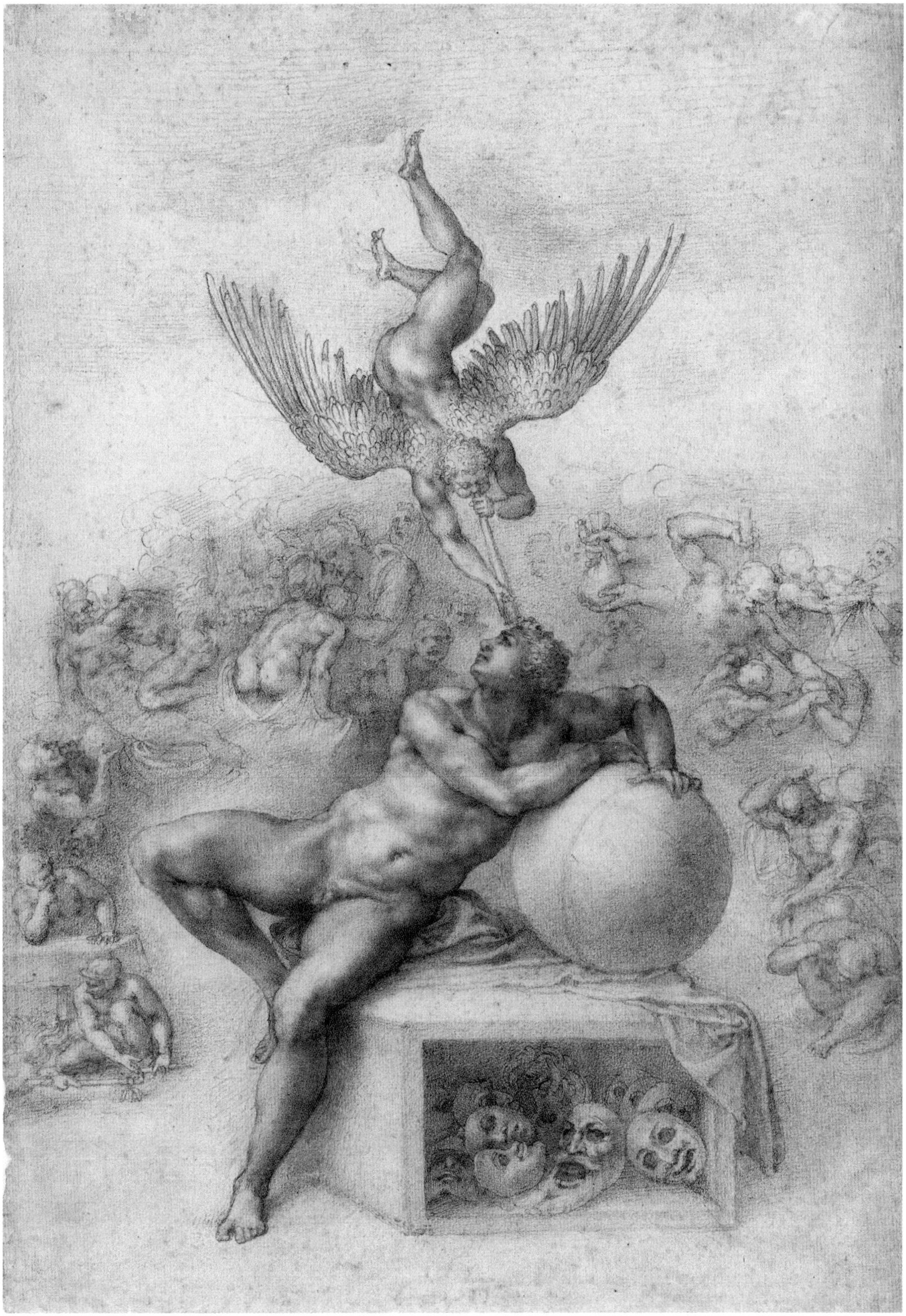

Il Sogno (*The Dream*), c. 1533, black chalk on laid paper,
39.8 × 28.1 cm (15 ⅝ × 11 in.), The Courtauld Gallery, London

GIOVANNI BATTISTA NALDINI
1535–1591

There are twin Gates of Sleep.
One, they say, is called the Gate of Horn
and it offers easy passage to all true shades.
The other glistens with ivory, radiant, flawless,
but through it the dead send false dreams up toward the sky.

VIRGIL, *AENEID*, BOOK 6 (29–19 BC)

Giovanni Battista Naldini's *Allegory of Dreams* is a component of an extraordinary and idiosyncratic space, the so-called *Studiolo* of Francesco I de' Medici, ruler and Grand Duke of Tuscany. This little room, part of Francesco's private apartments, could only be entered through his bedchamber and served as a place of retreat and a treasure chamber where the rarest and most precious objects were preserved. Altogether, adorning the walls of the *Studiolo* were forty-four paintings by thirty-one different artists, all produced under the artistic direction of Giorgio Vasari, known for his Mannerist paintings and architecture as well as for his encyclopaedic *Lives of the Most Excellent Painters, Sculptors and Architects*. Vasari devised the intricate decorative programme, which sets nature and human artifice into a variety of relationships, together with the scholar Vincenzo Borghini.

Allegory of Dreams is one of twenty oval paintings, each of which could be opened, with frames like doors, revealing the costly objects stored behind them in niches, each treasure related to the iconography of the respective image. All of the paintings feature the typical traits of Mannerism, the stylistic link between the Renaissance and the Baroque: an extraordinary richness of imagination, a dense profusion of visual forms and the capricious movements of the figures, along with the overall programme's rather strained erudition.

The painting depicts the realm of Somnus, the god of sleep, who lies in his bed in the background. He sends dreams out into the world through a pair of gateways: true dreams emerge from the one on the left, fashioned from horn, while false or illusory dreams emerge from the ivory gateway on the right. Naldini represents these dreams as tiny flying figures, streaming in a dense throng through these column-framed portals, led by two women who swing sceptres. A variety of interpretations have been proposed for the foreground figures. On the right, wearing a crescent moon in her hair and accompanied by an owl and a badger, is likely a personification of Night. Putti play nearby with pods of the opium poppy. The striking young woman at the centre of the image holds a transparent disk, probably a lens, used to distinguish true dreams, which foretell the future, from deceptive ones – a question of some urgency for the work's patron, whose preoccupation with astrology, alchemy and the interpretation of dreams is well-documented. Perhaps the niche behind the picture contained sleep-inducing preparations, precious optical lenses or certain crystals believed to have a calming effect on troubled dreams.

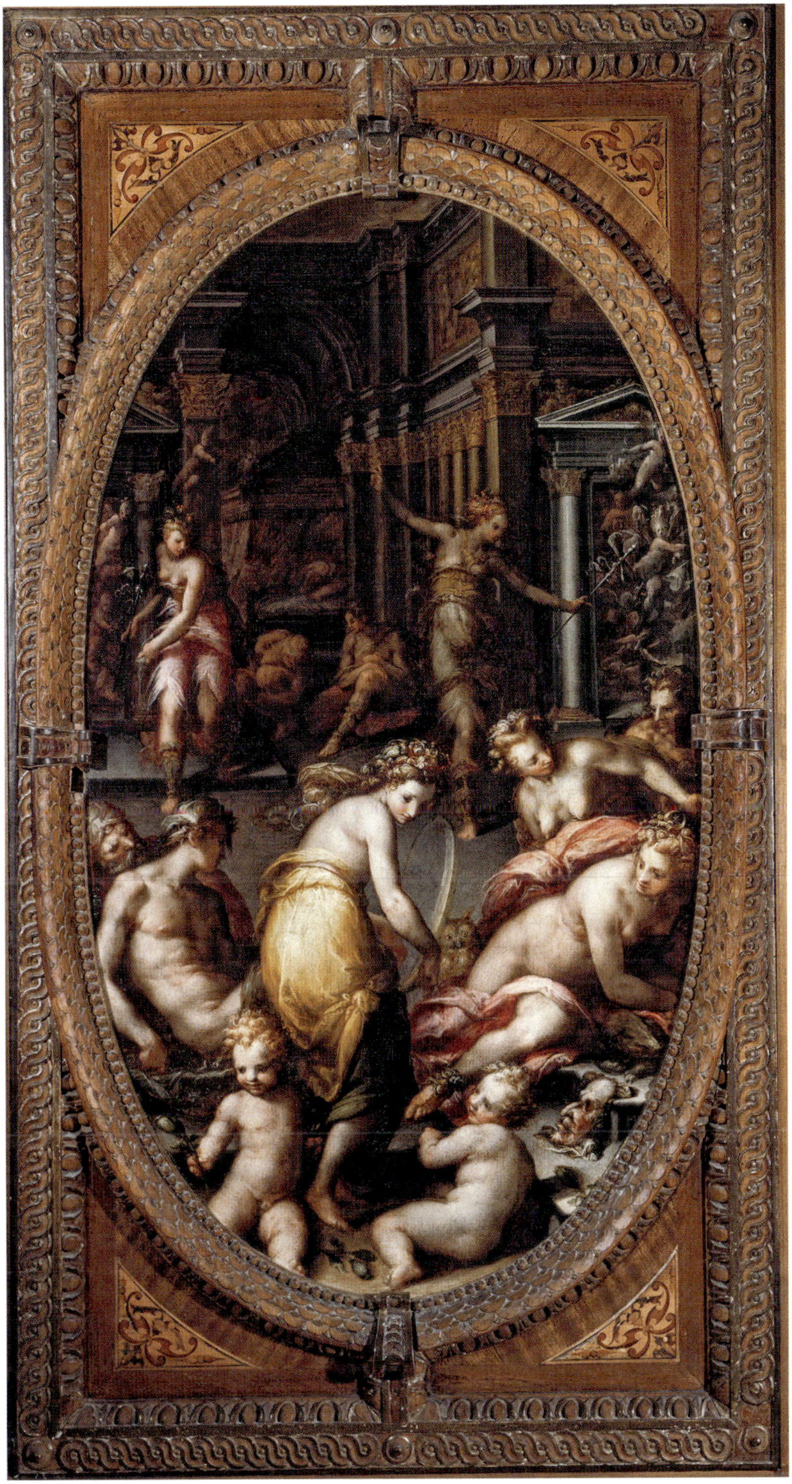

Allegory of Dreams, 1574, oil on slate, 151 × 89 cm (59 ½ × 35 in.),
Studiolo di Francesco I de' Medici, Palazzo Vecchio, Florence

REMBRANDT HARMENSZOON VAN RIJN
1606–1669

[...] an angel of the Lord appeared to Joseph in a dream.
'Get up', he said, 'take the child and his mother and escape to Egypt.'
[...] So he got up, took the child and his mother
during the night and left for Egypt.

MATTHEW 2:13–14

In a room that is shrouded in darkness, whose contours are only vaguely discernible, Joseph sits with a staff resting on his knee, immersed in a restless sleep. Alongside him, Mary lies reclined against a haystack, holding the baby Jesus. Along the right-hand edge of the picture, an ox gazes out directly at the viewer. All of these figures are indicated with just a few brushstrokes. From behind, enveloped in blinding white light, an angel lays a hand gently on Joseph's shoulder, gesturing with his left towards Mary and Child. Rembrandt depicts the moment when the dreaming Joseph receives divine instruction to escape Herod's wrath and the Slaughter of the Innocents in Bethlehem by fleeing with his family into Egypt. Visible on the left is the wall with the door through which Joseph, Mary and Child will exit the stable upon awakening.

The intense, evocative atmosphere of this painting arises from Rembrandt's characteristically masterful handling of light. A mysterious glow descends from above, seeming to seep through the ceiling, while at the same time radiating from the angel itself and diffusing through the scene as a whole, endowing it with drama, depth and intensity. Of course, this is no natural light, but rather divine luminosity that accompanies a miraculous apparition, dispersing gently throughout the room and playing around Rembrandt's figures, rendered with directness and simplicity. The charge given to Joseph comes from another world.

This is one of five dreams narrated in the first two chapters of the Gospel of Matthew in the context of the Christmas story. In the first, an angel announces to Joseph in a dream that Mary has conceived Jesus by the Holy Ghost; in the second, the Three Magi heed a warning received in a dream and avoid returning to King Herod after viewing the Christ Child. In the third dream, illustrated here by Rembrandt, the angel warns Joseph of Herod's evil intentions. In the fourth, which takes place in Egypt, an angel informs Joseph of Herod's death, while in the fifth, he is instructed to go to Nazareth. In contrast to so many equivocal and interpretively open dream visions, all five dreams convey clear and unambiguous divine commands to the protagonists, direct interventions that guide the course of events and thus bring about salvation in the world.

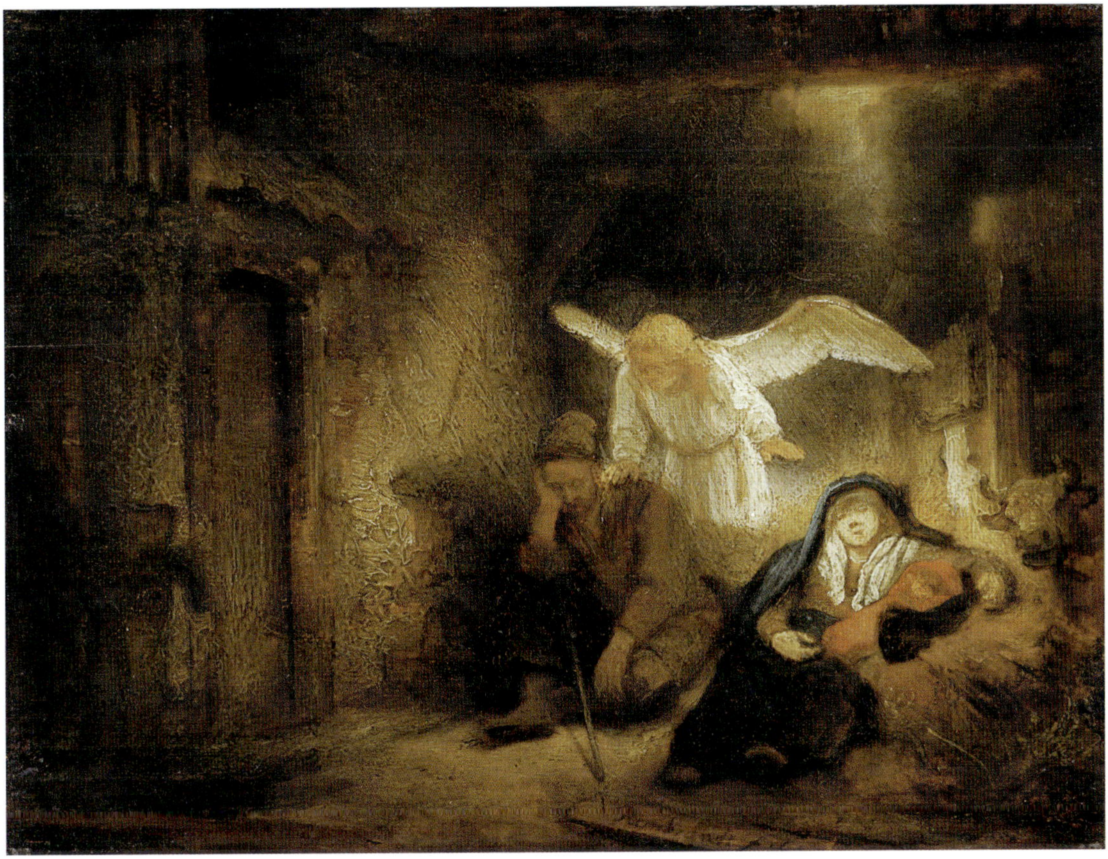

Joseph's Dream, 1645, oil on mahogany,
20.9 × 28 cm (8 ¼ × 11 in.), Staatliche Museen zu Berlin, Gemäldegalerie

JACOB JORDAENS

1593–1678

I have seen such a subject painted by Jordaens where a man lay in bed and dreamed. [...] The woman was painted from the back and done very beautifully in colours so that I as well as others considered the picture simply as a painting of a model to which the rest was added in order to complete the canvas.

GÉRARD DE LAIRESSE, *THE GREAT BOOK OF PAINTING* (1707)

Jacob Jordaens – the most renowned Flemish Baroque painter after Peter Paul Rubens and Anthony van Dyck – is both celebrated and notorious for his powerful imagery and effervescent delight in visual storytelling. Alongside his history paintings, his genre scenes were especially admired, with their striking immediacy drawn from everyday life; indeed, Jordaens never shrank from depicting the coarser aspects of human existence, with imagery that often verged on the grotesque. In the years after 1640, when the death of Rubens left him the most important painter in Antwerp, he accepted numerous large commissions from the Church, the aristocracy and the well-to-do middle classes, including a series of mythological paintings. His *Night Vision*, sometimes known as *Nocturnal Appearance*, is a wholly independent invention that did not rely upon a prior literary model. It departs significantly from traditional accounts of dreams and is based on a freely invented scenario rather than an established or familiar narrative.

The scene is plunged in nocturnal darkness, and the pale, murky light of an overcast moon enters through the window. As though infused with its own radiance, the masterfully executed female nude, seen from the rear, emerges from the shadows, a textbook example of a 'Rubenesque figure', reflecting the ideal of beauty in the Flemish Baroque. Surrounded by mist, the figure appears as the dream vision conjured by the man who lies in bed beneath a red baldachin, immersed in uneasy sleep, his hands stretched out in yearning, seeking to embrace his vision. Contributing to the scene's dramatic tension are an elderly woman and her male companion, shown bursting into the room through the door they have flung open in great haste. Her expression of shock and his curious gaze indicate that the spectral vision is perceptible to them as well. The light of the candle carried by them casts the gigantic shadow of a hand on the door, heightening the uncanny, menacing mood. The dream is about to end abruptly, however, since the swinging door has crashed into a footstool, sending a pewter jug and candlestick tumbling noisily to the floor.

We do not know what prompted Jordaens to create this extraordinary image, nor the identity of its original owner. Here, he merges the sensuous, robust corporeality so typical of the Flemish Baroque with the virtuosic rendering of darkness, light and shadow on a par with the technique perfected by Caravaggio.

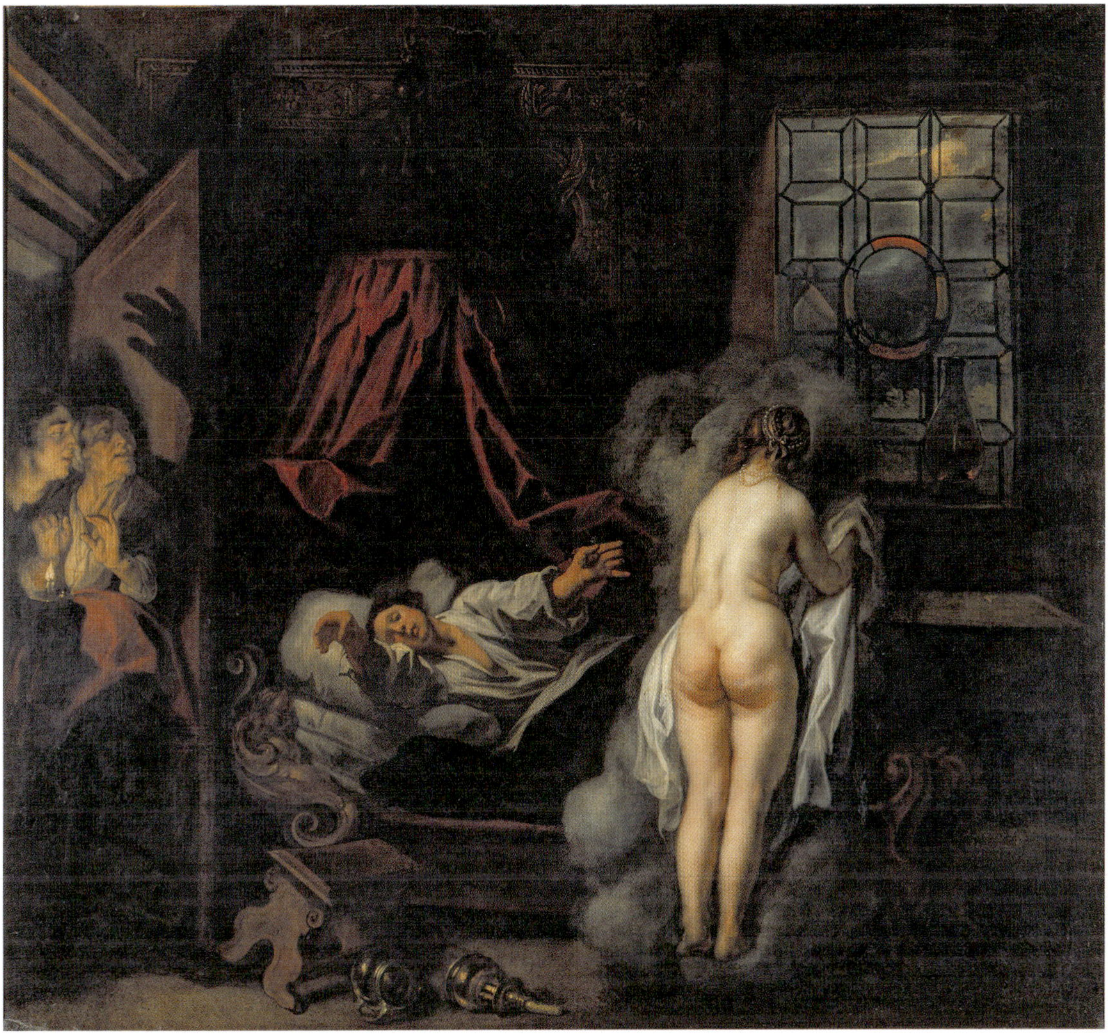

Night Vision, c. 1650, oil on canvas,
133 × 144 cm (52 ⅜ × 56 ¾ in.), Staatliches Museum Schwerin

JEAN-HONORÉ FRAGONARD
1732–1806

*Love and Sensual Delight lull the warrior to sleep
with the sweet illusion of pleasures.*

INSCRIPTION ON NICOLAS-FRANÇOIS REGNAULT'S 1791 ENGRAVING OF FRAGONARD'S PAINTING *THE WARRIOR'S DREAM OF LOVE*

A youthful, somewhat effeminate soldier dozes languidly on a divan, his head supported against his arm, a sword and abandoned at at his side. Two hounds sleep on a set of steps that form, like a pedestal, the lower edge of the picture. The diaphanous dream visions that hover above the reclining sleeper are rendered with virtuosity, ascending from the lower right to the upper left corner of the canvas. Light and shadow alternate, while a number of putti drift effortlessly through the diffuse space. Enthroned above, brightly illuminated and encircled by fluttering drapery, is a Venus-like, scantily clad female figure, her eyes concealed by a veil. She is the object of desire conjured by the warrior's dream. A diagonal beam of light traverses the image, linking the dream apparition and the dreamer. The play of the putti is equally fantastical: some observe the scene with interest, some appear to sleep, while others support the throne of clouds or convey symbols of love, such as a torch, flower petals and a goblet.

With its carefree elegance, dynamic composition, sensual intensity and frank eroticism, this image epitomizes the atmosphere of the late Rococo that prevailed during the second half of the eighteenth century. Here, Jean-Honoré Fragonard does not depict the stark contrast between the grim harshness of war and the tender delights of love, as artists of the previous century might have done; instead, he suffuses the entire image – given over to light-hearted pastimes and the cheerful enjoyment of life – with a light, cultivated sensuosity. Here he proves himself a grand master of an art designed to cater to the high society of the *ancien régime* in absolutist France, whose members seem to have lived in a world largely untouched by the travails of daily life, although its abrupt demise was already imminent. In the end, Fragonard would survive the French Revolution and its aftereffects largely unscathed thanks to the protection of the painter Jacques-Louis David, a direct participant in the upheavals of the era. Nevertheless, Fragonard proved unable, and unwilling, to adapt to the new, more sombre Neoclassical visual idiom then in vogue.

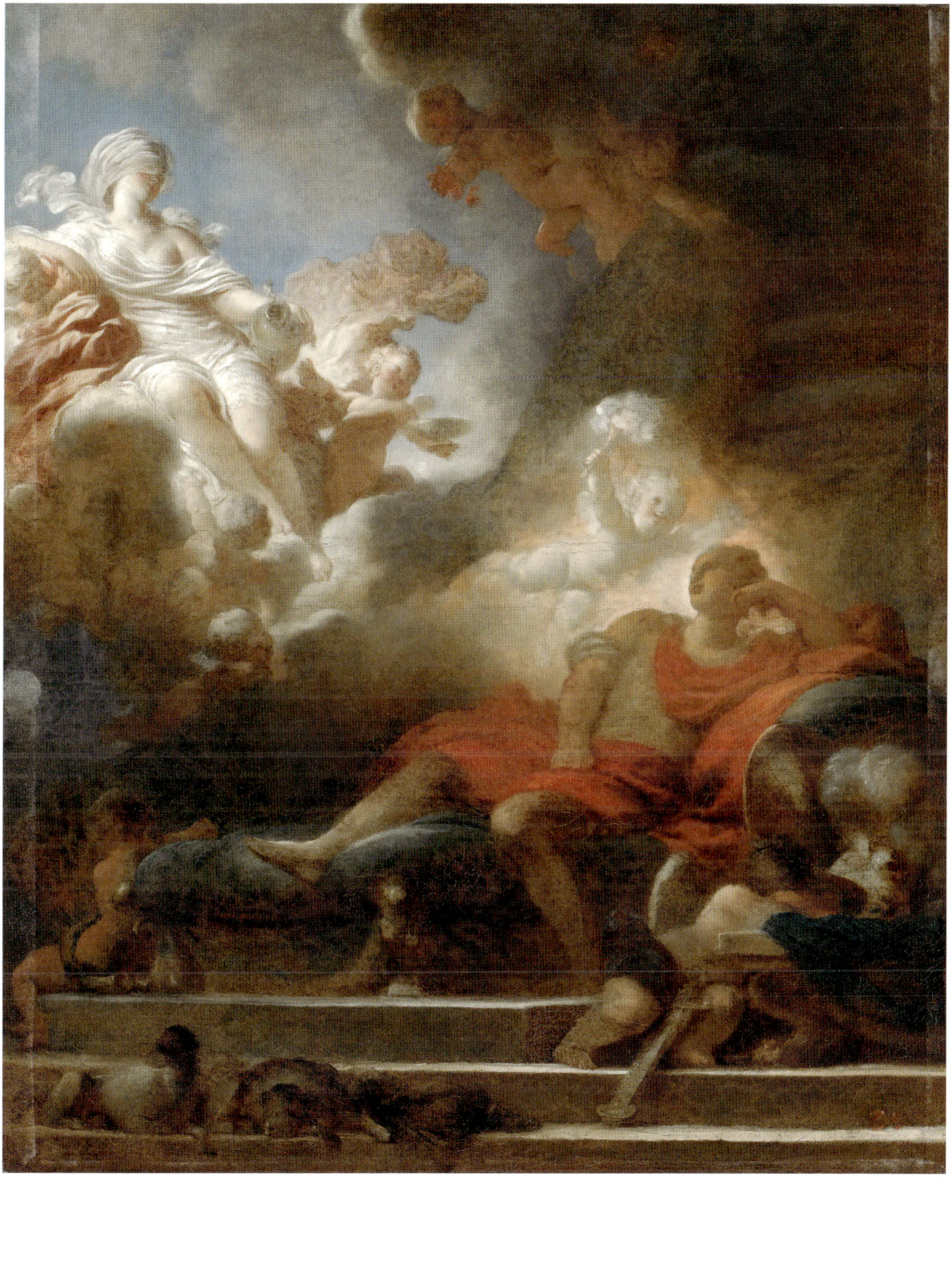

The Warrior's Dream of Love, c. 1780, oil on canvas,
79 × 67 cm (31⅛ × 26⅜ in.) Musée du Louvre, Paris

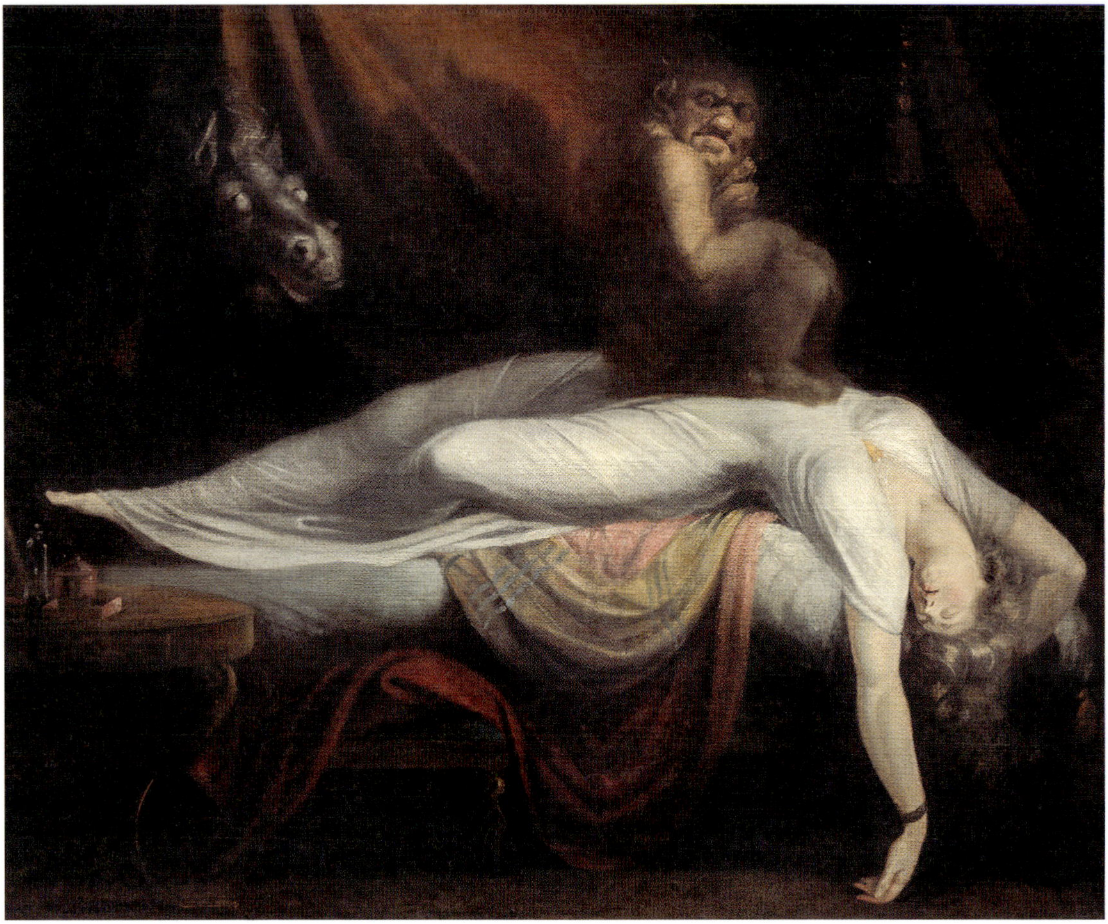

The Nightmare, 1781, oil on canvas,
101.7 × 127.1 cm (40 × 50 in.), Detroit Institute of Arts

HENRY FUSELI
1741–1825

One of the most unexplored regions of art are dreams [...]

HENRY FUSELI, APHORISM 231

The erudite artist Henry Fuseli (born Johann Heinrich Füssli) – originally a Reformed clergyman from Zurich – was a reclusive nonconformist. In 1765, having flouted the authorities in his hometown, he arrived in London through the intercession of the British ambassador at Berlin. In the English capital, his unconventional works and eccentric personality earned him a professorship and the office of Keeper at the Royal Academy, as well as the nickname 'the wild Swiss'.

With *The Nightmare* of 1781, arguably his most celebrated work, Fuseli fully lived up to his reputation. This true icon of Romanticism has become firmly embedded in our collective cultural memory as the quintessential image of night terrors.

A young woman lies asleep on a narrow bed, her upper body slipping downward towards the floor. The position of her arms, her bent leg and the tension in her right foot suggest that she is in the grips of a restless dream. Small wonder, for a demonic creature, grimacing menacingly, has settled on her stomach – the Nightmare, a figure from Nordic mythology, who fills with dread anyone he chooses to afflict. His phantom horse peers with glowing, mad eyes through the open curtain, its mane drifting mist-like in the darkness. The pallid, bluish-white coloration of the sleeping figure and the wan light that enters from the right bathe the scene in a spectral haze. The harsh contrasts between light and dark and the emphatic expressiveness of the gestures – both trademarks of Fuseli's work – heighten the scene's drama, endowing it with a theatrical, almost stage-like quality.

For the London public, accustomed to classical history painting and biblical motifs, this amalgam of fantasy, mythology, subtle eroticism and folk belief was radically new. Unsurprisingly, the picture was a source of fascination and excitement at its first presentation at the Royal Academy's annual summer exhibition in London in 1782. Exceptionally sensitive individuals were advised not to lay eyes on the painting. With its ghastly, disturbing atmosphere, *The Nightmare* soon came to symbolize Dark Romanticism – and would later come to emblematize the connection between dreams and the unconscious. Through engravings, the composition, of which Fuseli produced a number of painted versions, was soon disseminated throughout Europe. One such print hung above the desk in Sigmund Freud's study in Vienna.

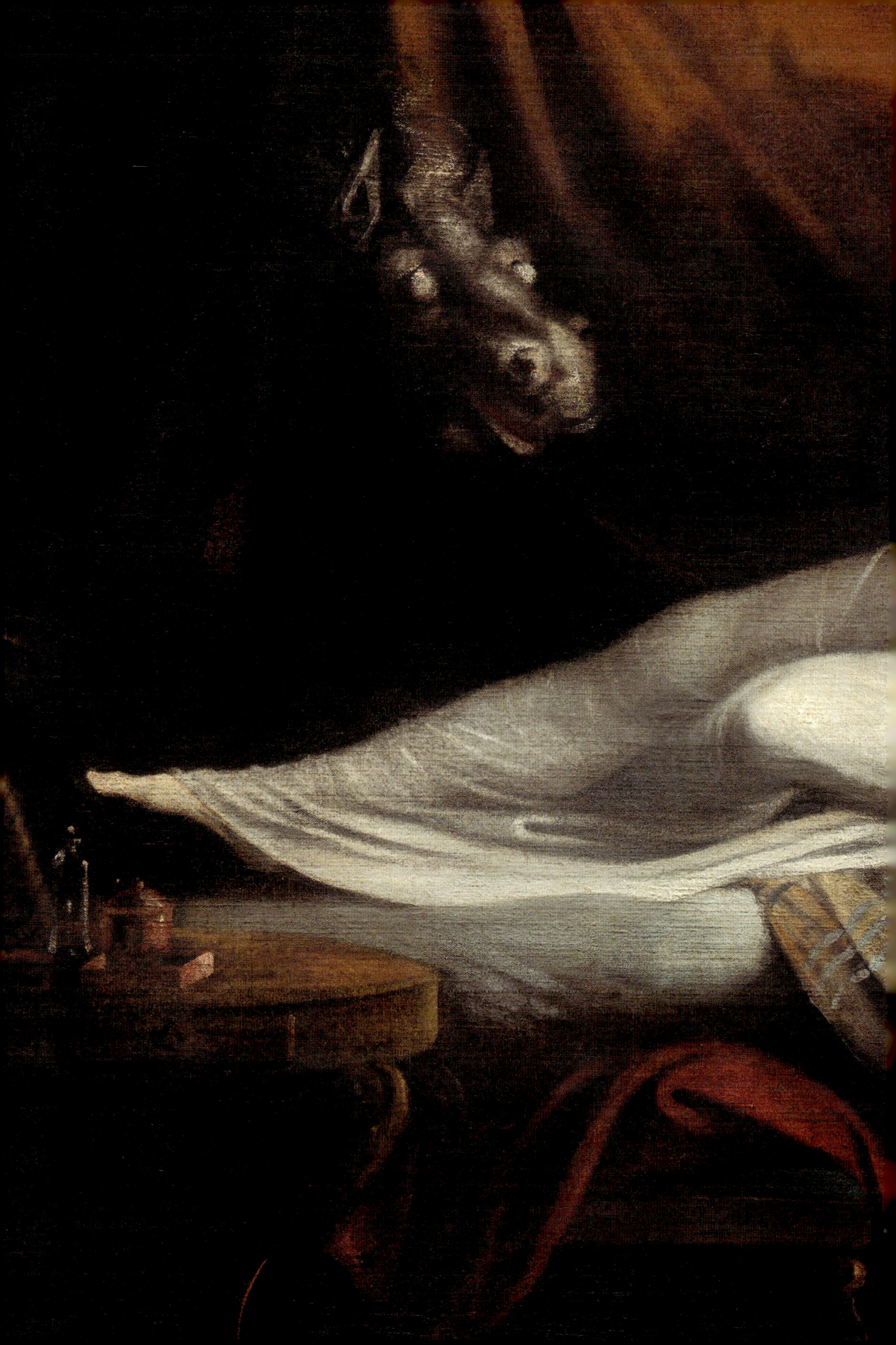

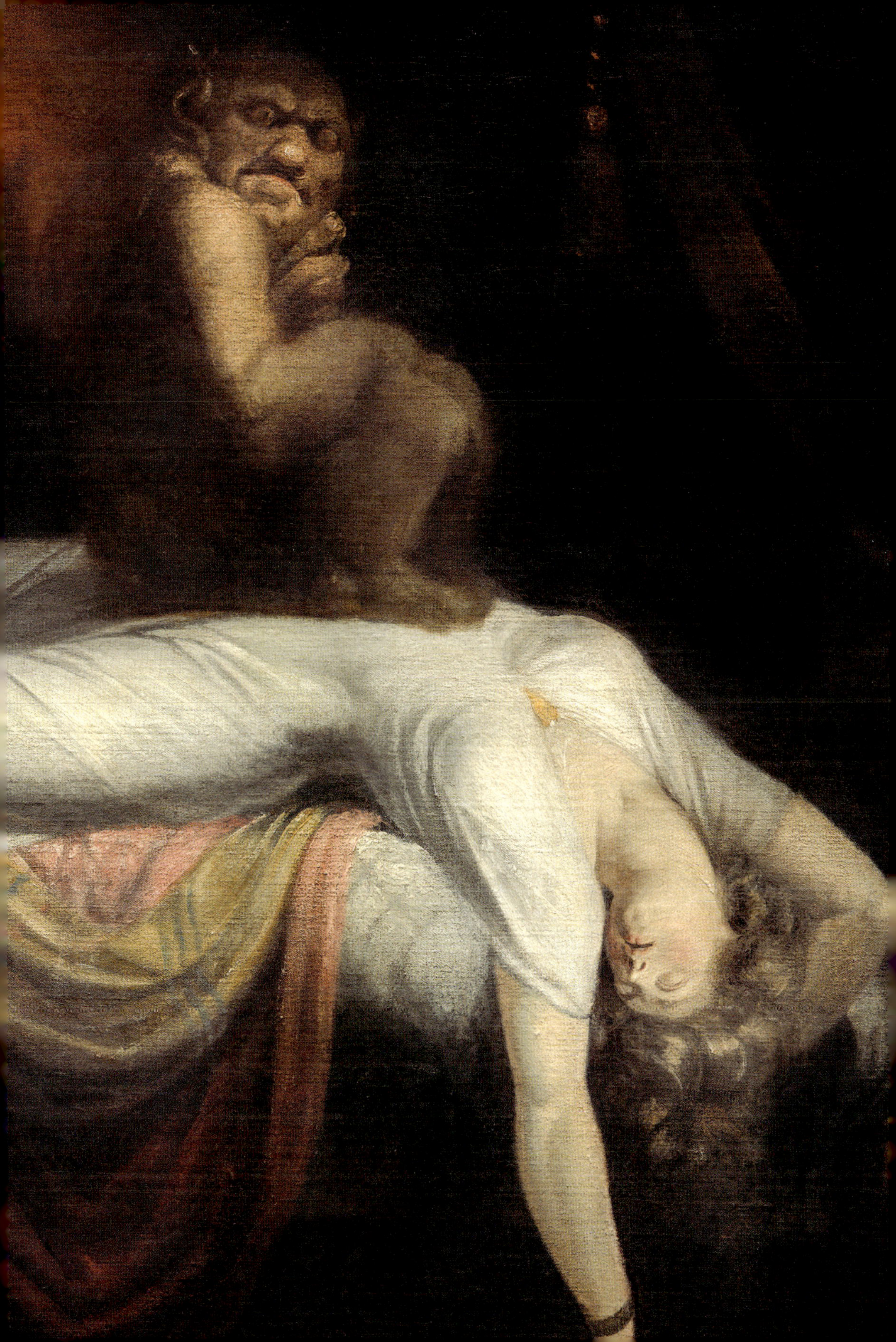

FRANCISCO DE GOYA
1746–1828

*Goya is always a great artist, often terrifying. […]
all the wild extravagances of dreams, all the hyperboles of
hallucinations, […] the sabbath of civilization!
Light and darkness play in and around these grotesque horrors.
What strange joviality!*

CHARLES BAUDELAIRE, 'SOME FOREIGN CARICATURES' (1857)

Francisco de Goya straddles the world of the Old Masters and the art of the nineteenth and twentieth centuries. His images reflect the vast historical convulsions that characterized his time. The late works in particular show him to be a subtle, profound, but also unflinching artist who pitilessly exposes and pillories the dark abysses of human nature.

No. 43 of his *Caprichos* – the celebrated print series depicting human folly, shortcomings and transgressions – is among the most frequently debated and variously interpreted works in the history of art. At the very threshold of modernism, the work's ambiguous, unfathomable imagery still retains its original urgency and immediacy.

This aquatint etching depicts the artist himself slumped over a table, evidently asleep, surrounded by numerous nocturnal creatures – owls, bats and a lynx. The title – *El sueño de la razón produce monstruos* – is positioned prominently within the image. The phrase is ambiguous, since *sueño* in Spanish can mean either 'sleep' or 'dream'. Two different interpretations are thus available to the viewer: when Reason sleeps, and irrational forces gain the upper hand, monsters appear, menacing humanity, society and the world. Or, alternatively: it is the very dreams dreamed by Reason, with its pure, cold rationality, that threaten to expel human qualities from the world; ultimately, it is an *excess* of rationality that unleashes monsters – inhuman forces. With impressive clarity, and precisely marking the turn of the nineteenth century, Goya presented humanity with a gloomy premonition of the dark side of modernity – and the ensuing centuries would provide numerous examples of both the sleep and the dream of reason. A perennial touchstone of debates about the dark side of progress, his forewarning of these twin dangers retains its full relevance. After more than two centuries, Goya's haunting image still serves as a quintessential emblem of the modern age.

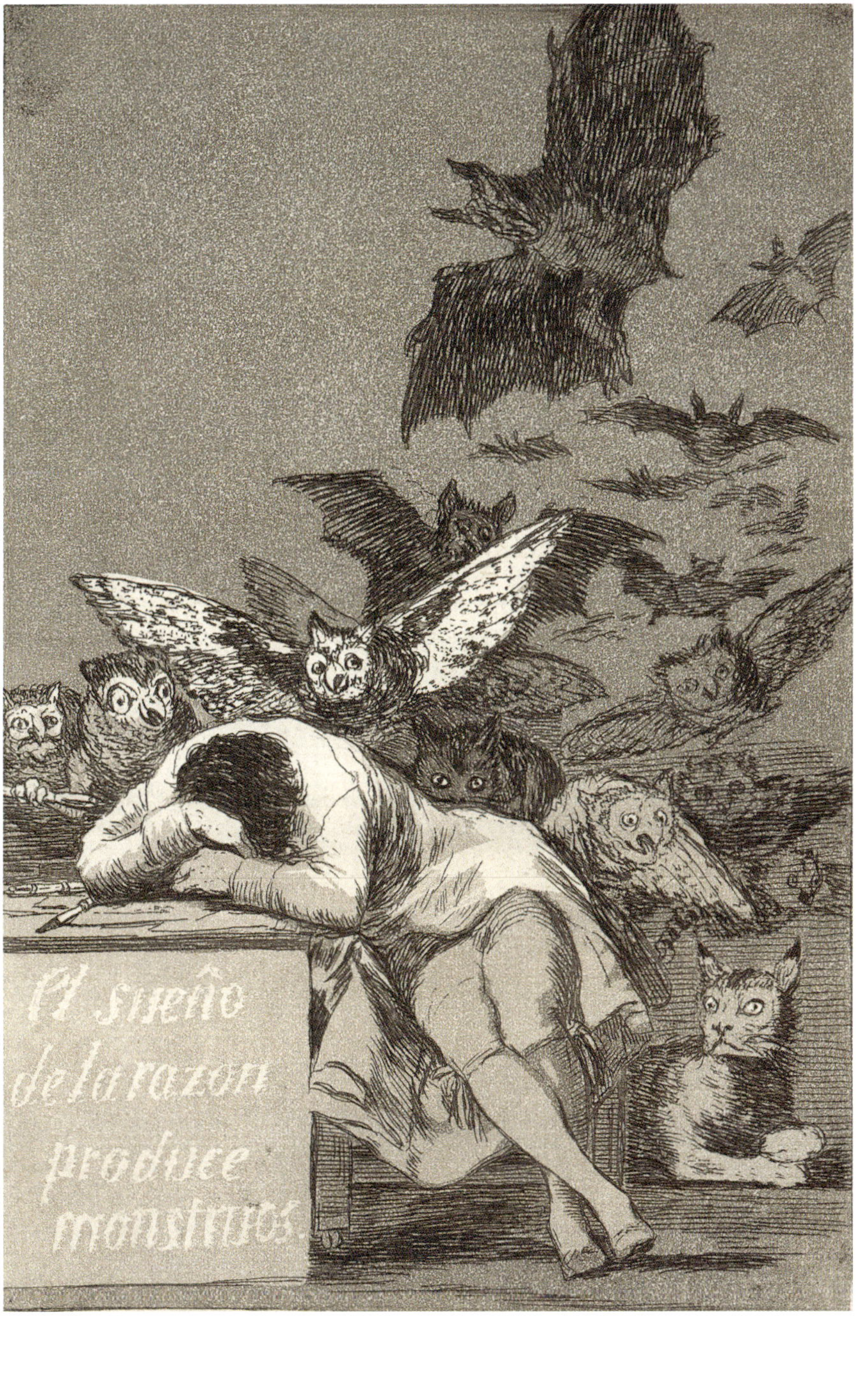

The Sleep of Reason Produces Monsters (or, less often, *The Dream of Reason Produces Monsters*), 1797–1799, aquatint etching on laid paper, platemark 21.8 × 15.2 cm (8 ⅝ × 6 in.)

JEAN-AUGUSTE-DOMINIQUE INGRES
1780–1867

Brooks, snow, heather, the steep mountain,
the solitary pine, the dark wood, the baying of a hound,
the cry of an eagle, the murmur of a brook,
the noise and the glow of the storm.
When the illusion fades as you finish reading,
it is as though you have not simply read of these things,
but have dreamt them yourself.

INGRES, NOTE ON OSSIAN (1812)

In the late eighteenth and early nineteenth centuries, the educated public was electrified by *The Poems of Ossian*, shrouded in legend and purportedly translations from Gaelic, said to originate in ancient Celtic times and attributed to the eponymous mythical bard. Known as the 'Homer of the North', the mysterious poet Ossian inspired a genuine euphoria that gripped many prominent figures of the time, including Johann Gottfried Herder, Johann Wolfgang von Goethe, William Blake and even Napoleon. It is said that the latter carried an edition of the poems with him everywhere, even into battle. For a long time, the controversy that soon emerged over their authenticity did little to dampen this enthusiasm. In fact, James Macpherson had not discovered and translated poems dating from the third century BC, as he claimed, but had largely composed them himself.

In 1810, at the high point of his power, Napoleon symbolically chose Rome as the 'second city' of the French Empire and the Quirinal Palace as his residence. The city's French governor commissioned the young Jean-Auguste-Dominique Ingres, then living in Rome, to execute a monumental ceiling painting for the bedchamber of the emperor, who personally selected the subject to be illustrated: the dream of Ossian. The choice of Ingres as the artist may also have been related to his own enthusiasm for the epic poet.

Ossian, asleep over his harp on rocky ground by the sea, dreams of the deceased protagonists of his poems, among them warriors, foes and kin. Set against the dark blue, starry sky, they hover above him as dream images, their pale, greyish coloration and irreal illumination marking them as otherworldly. To the right stands his son Oscar, holding a round shield and lance; to the left, his bearded father Fingal with a sceptre, beside a virtuosically staged pair of lovers – a warrior in armour and a nude beauty; at the centre is Starno, the hostile king from Scandinavia, his face barely discernible; all of whom are surrounded by further warriors and bards.

Unique within Ingres's oeuvre, this dreamy, fairy-tale composition – both a pivotal and pioneering work of early Romanticism – juxtaposes northern Celtic mythology with classical antiquity. It was never seen by Napoleon and was removed from the palace in 1815 after his fall. Ingres reacquired it in 1835, reworking and significantly altering it in the ensuing years. However, its singular, powerful pictorial invention, which circulated widely through engravings, continued to fascinate artists, including modernists such as Pablo Picasso and Juan Gris.

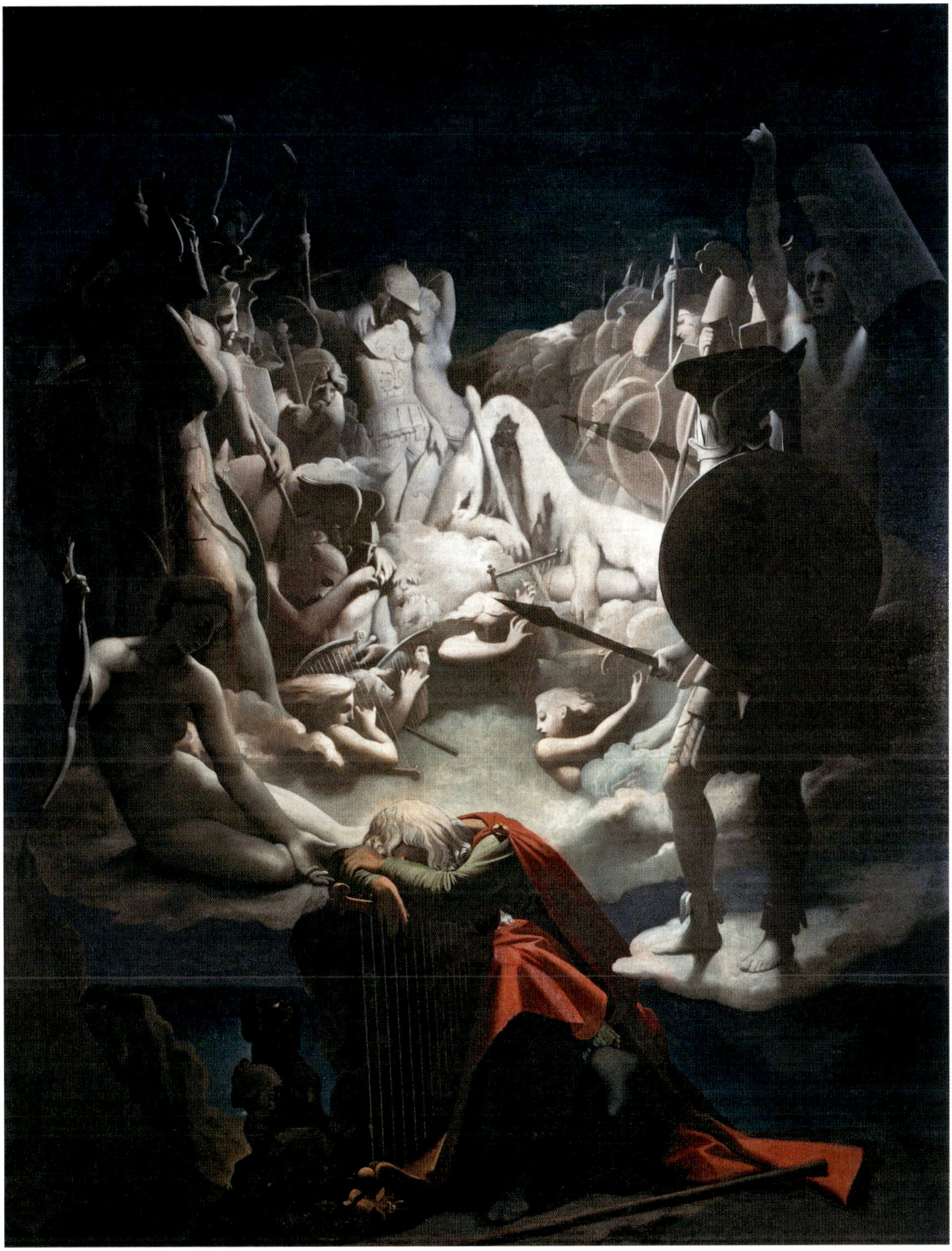

The Dream of Ossian, 1813, oil on canvas,
348 × 275 cm (137 × 108 ¼ in.), Musée Ingres Bourdelle, Montauban

KATSUSHIKA HOKUSAI
1760–1849

MAIDEN: Yes, it tingles now;
soon there will be no sensation at all left in my hips.
Ooooooh! Boundaries and borders gone!
I've vanished...!!!!!!

INSCRIPTION ON THE WOODBLOCK PRINT

With his extraordinary inventiveness, brilliant draughtsmanship and compositional ingenuity, Hokusai is one of the most dazzling creative figures in the history of art. He is best known for his colour woodblock prints in the Ukiyo-e genre, which during Japan's Edo period (1603–1868) increasingly focused on depictions of the pleasure quarters and sensual pastimes of the rising urban middle class.

This print is an example of what is known as shunga, characterized by its strongly erotic content. At the time these images were produced, Japanese attitudes towards sexuality were largely devoid of moralizing implications. It was regarded, quite simply and as a matter of course, as the pleasurable union of the sexes. Hokusai's shunga prints are among the most celebrated and widely disseminated images of their kind and, in their extreme directness, also among the most controversial.

Facing upwards, a nude woman – probably a pearl diver – reclines between two rocky outcroppings covered in vegetation, embraced by an enormous octopus. Its mouth is pressed between her spread legs, its tentacles eagerly exploring her body. A smaller octopus kisses the woman on the open mouth, her eyes nearly closed. The accompanying text, which fills the entire background, is quite explicit and leaves no doubt as to what is taking place. Hokusai depicts all the participants at the moment of sexual ecstasy and utmost satisfaction: the woman has nearly lost consciousness from the pleasure the sea creature gives her, evident in her arched back and her firm grip on one of the octopus's tentacles, and made unmistakably clear by the prolonged moans and cries – rendered phonetically – that run through the inscription.

Equally significant is the context in which this image originally appeared. It was part of the book *Kinoe no komatsu* (Young Pines), in which Hokusai published thirty shunga images in each of the three volumes. Each volume begins with a portrait of a courtesan, followed by seven full-page woodblock prints of a strongly sexual nature, in which the woman often assumes a dominant role, and concludes with a detailed drawing of the male and female genitalia of the protagonists introduced in the preceding section.

When this woodblock print surfaced in nineteenth-century Europe, reactions ranged from admiration for Hokusai's artistic gifts to rejection of the unsettling scene. Many artists were clearly influenced by the image, among them Pablo Picasso and Auguste Rodin.

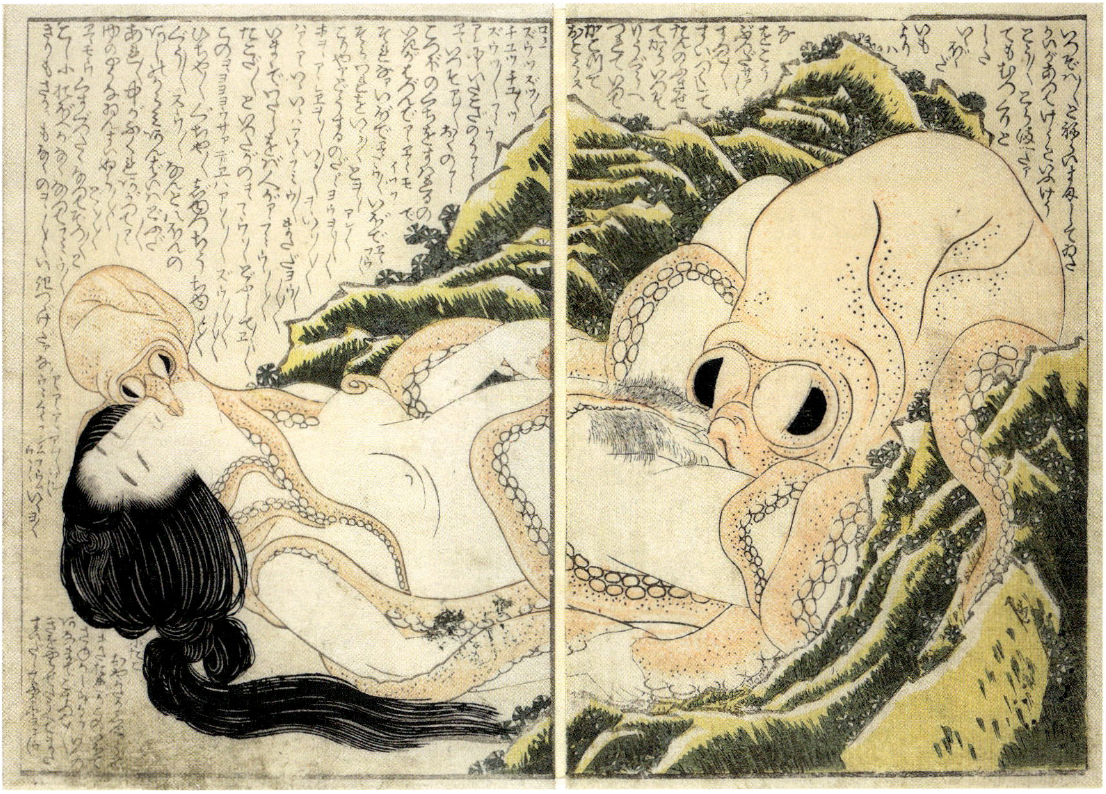

The Dream of the Fisherman's Wife (or *Diver and Two Octopuses*), 1814, colour woodblock print, 18.9 × 26.6 cm (7 ½ × 10 ½ in.)

CASPAR DAVID FRIEDRICH
1774–1840

The world becomes dream, the dream becomes world.

NOVALIS, *HEINRICH VON OFTERDINGEN*
(PUBLISHED POSTHUMOUSLY, 1802)

In the rather small painting *The Dreamer*, Caspar David Friedrich shows the tall, pointed arches of a decaying Gothic window, part of a medieval ruin. Through the two openings, we gaze out over a wide valley, already bathed in shadow, and above it, a sky illuminated by the setting sun. Two slender spruces rise upwards. On the window ledge to the right sits a man clad in black, who looks into the distance, apparently lost in thought.

As so often with Friedrich, this image is structured on two levels: visual and symbolic. In the foreground, and only dimly recognizable in the shadows of the ruins, are signs of decay: lifeless trees, moss and crumbling masonry. The dark, enclosed nature of the foreground contrasts with the luminous, airy vastness of the prospect that opens beyond the window. Like the glowing evening sky, the evergreen spruces can be interpreted as symbols of infinity. Mediating between these two levels is the figure of the man who leans against the ruined wall, set before the background almost like a silhouette – a variant of the figure seen from behind that plays such a decisive role in Friedrich's work. This dreamy, melancholic figure – which attracts the eye by breaking the picture's otherwise strict symmetry – enjoys an unobstructed and surely grand view that we can only imagine, as it remains hidden from us by the crumbling edifice.

In this painting, in a manner typical of Friedrich, the inner world of human emotion – in this case that of the dreamer – is made visible through the external world of nature. The ruins evoke a past that is irrevocably lost, while the radiance of the setting sun bathes meditative recollections of what has been in yearning and melancholy. In Romantic thought, the suprarational 'Ahndung' (premonition) experienced in an artwork surpasses all logical thought. In the warm glow of the evening sky, before these shattered ruins, the viewer is expected to perceive the spiritual in the material, the supersensuous in the sensuous, the infinite in the finite. The artist – as one of the elect – brings to light the essential being of the world, conjuring a distant echo, a symbol, of supra-individual, eternal truths. It is these qualities that make this painting, like so many others by Friedrich, a prototypical work of Romantic art.

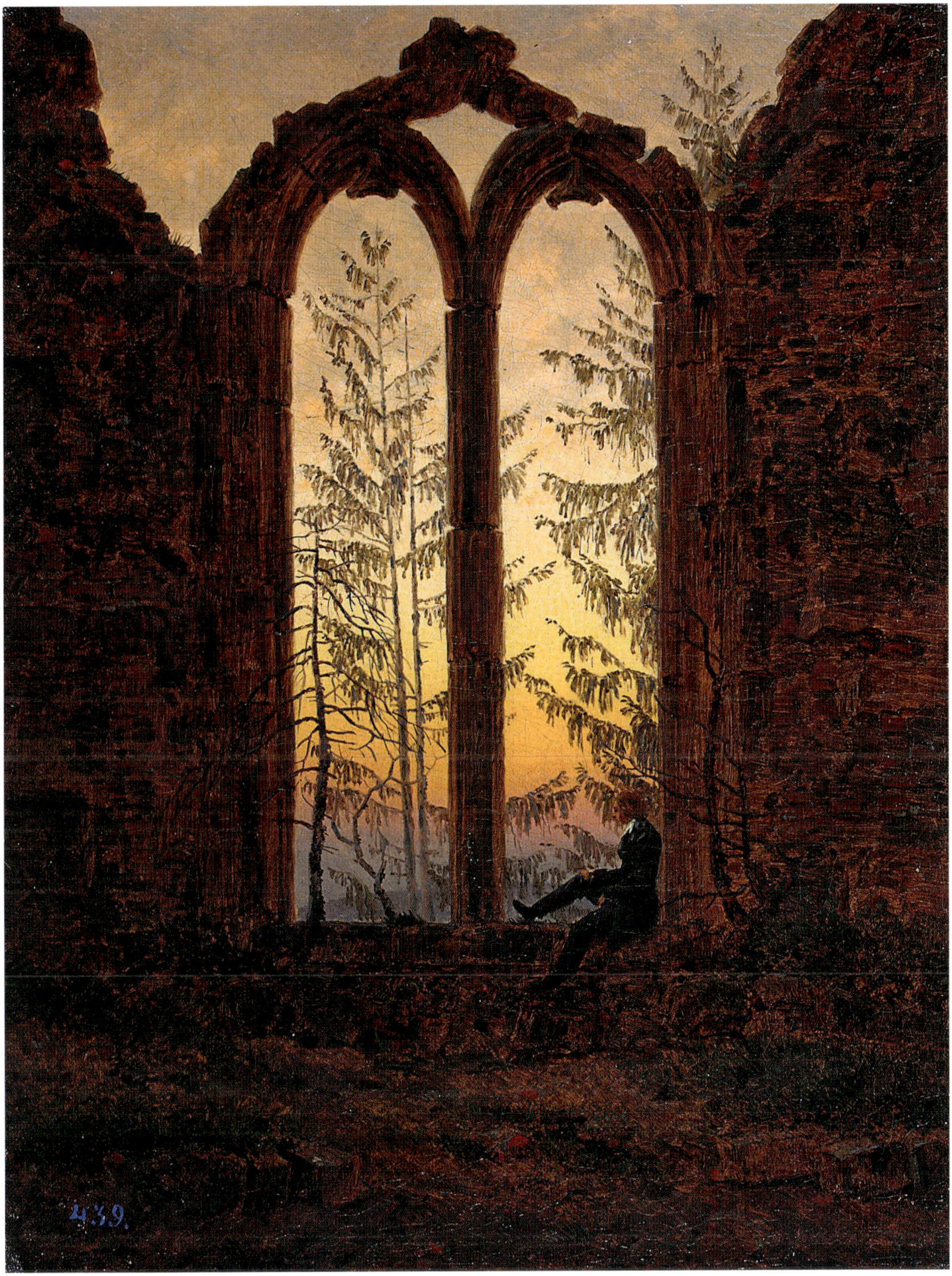

The Dreamer (Ruins of the Oybin Monastery), after 1835, oil on panel,
27 × 21 cm (10 ⅝ × 8 ¼ in.), The State Hermitage Museum, Saint Petersburg

MORITZ VON SCHWIND
1804–1871

Here is a reproduction of a picture by Schwind in the Schack Gallery in Munich, which shows how correctly the artist grasped the way in which dreams arise from the dominant situation. Its title is The Prisoner's Dream, *a dream whose content is bound to be his escape. It is a happy point that he is to escape through the window, for it is the stimulus of the light pouring in by the window that is putting an end to the prisoner's sleep.*

SIGMUND FREUD, *INTRODUCTORY LECTURES ON PSYCHOANALYSIS* (1916)

This early work by Moritz von Schwind depicts an unusual scene. In a somewhat dilapidated, presumably medieval prison cell, a ray of sunshine enters through a barred window, falling directly onto a prisoner's face. Reclining on bales of straw and a red cloak, he has made himself tolerably comfortable and now waits, arms folded, in enforced inactivity, as time passes. His yearning gaze follows the light through the bars into the open sky. Deprived of his freedom, he surrenders to a romantic, fairy-tale daydream. A group of dwarves has joined him in his cell, working diligently towards his liberation. Standing on the back of the dwarf king – identifiable through his crown, sceptre and long white beard – is a trio of additional dwarves, who visibly struggle to keep their balance. The uppermost figure holds a long file and is resolutely sawing through a window bar. Another dwarf dangles from the door of the cell. The comical awkwardness of the dwarves – which nonetheless leaves no doubt that they are capable of aiding the prisoner – contrasts with the elegant figure of the fairy or nymph hovering at the centre of the composition, who pours a beverage into a golden goblet, apparently to refresh those labouring for the dreamer's freedom.

This fantastical image belongs to a series of works that Schwind did not intend for the public, but painted for his own pleasure, referring to them as 'travel pictures', 'lyrical works' or 'occasional poems'. The content of these pictures is often difficult to determine precisely today, but many reflect the Romantic atmosphere found in the poetry and prose of the time, for example in the works of Ludwig Tieck, a writer of fairy tales. Not long before, between 1833 and 1834, Schwind had painted the 'Tieck Room' in the palatial Munich Residenz with scenes drawn from the author's tales and fairy stories. Stylistically, this dream image exemplifies Schwind's highly characteristic approach: strong contours and a homogeneous use of colour guide the viewer into a fanciful, often grotesque world of the imagination. Schwind retained this visual idiom far into old age, long after the art of painting had taken very different directions in its search for new forms.

In the early twentieth century, *The Prisoner's Dream* attracted increased attention when Sigmund Freud discussed it explicitly in his *Introductory Lectures on Psychoanalysis* and even included an illustration of the painting as the frontispiece in the corresponding volume of his collected works.

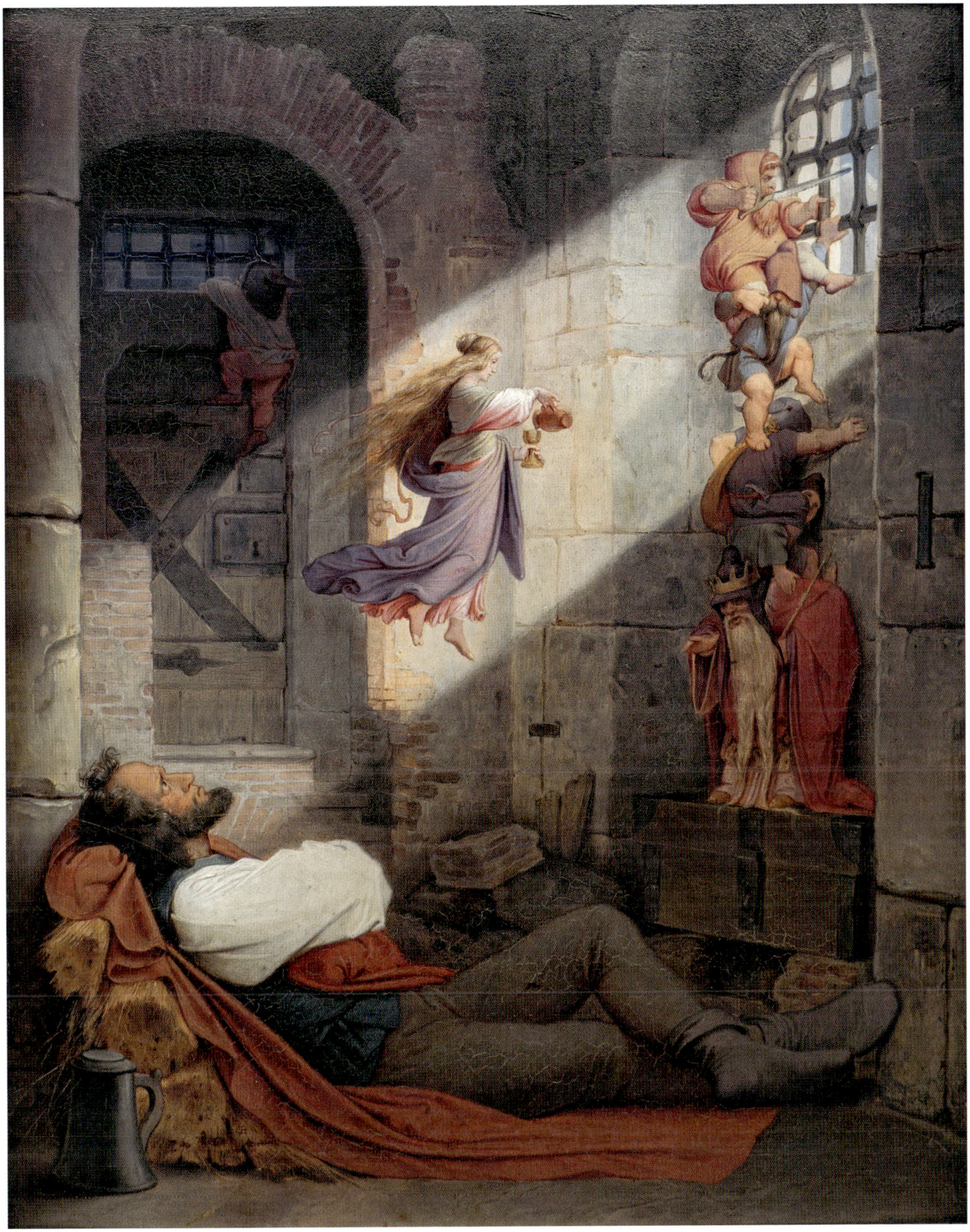

The Prisoner's Dream, 1836, oil on cardboard,
53 × 42.5 cm (20 ⅞ × 16 ¾ in.), Bayerische Staatsgemäldesammlungen – Schack Collection, Munich

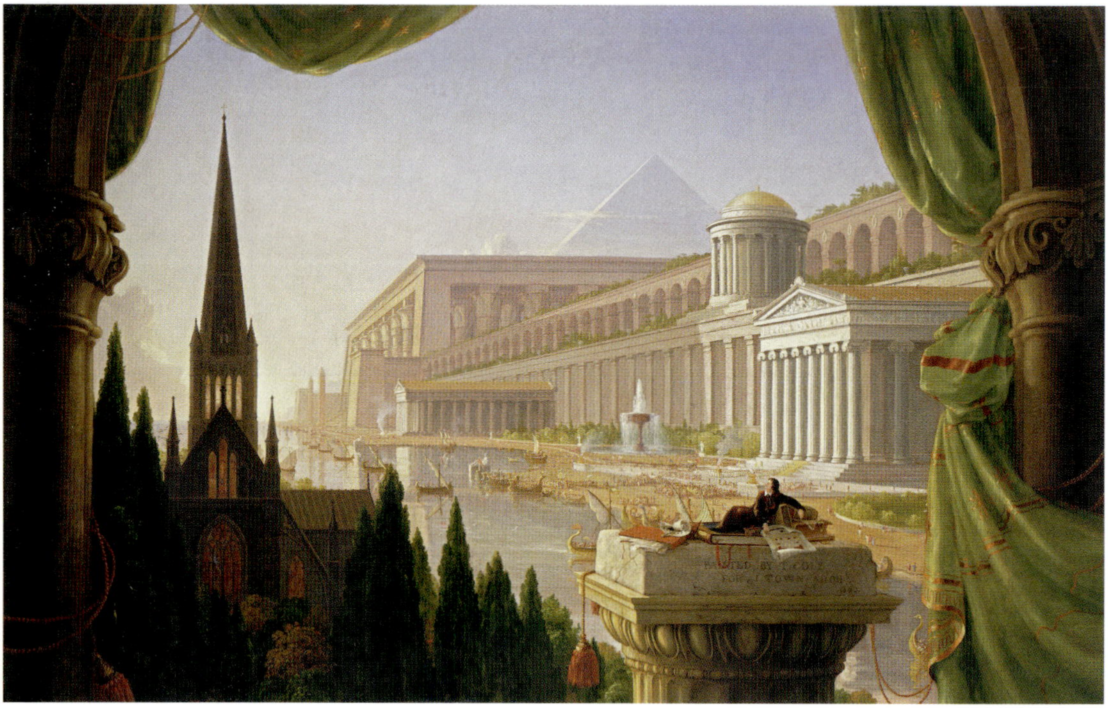

The Architect's Dream, 1840, oil on canvas,
134.6 × 213.5 cm (53 × 84 in.), Toledo Museum of Art, Ohio

THOMAS COLE
1801–1848

If the imagination is shackled, and nothing is described but what we see, seldom will anything truly great be produced either in Painting or Poetry.

THOMAS COLE, LETTER TO ROBERT GILMORE (1825)

Born in England and an early émigré to the United States, Thomas Cole was the founder and key representative of the Hudson River School, a group of American landscape painters who were active in the mid-nineteenth century. With *The Architect's Dream*, Cole created an image embodying Romantic notions of inspiration, poetry, art and history.

Framed by a pair of columns from a medieval round-arched window, the viewer's gaze follows a series of buildings set along a river embankment, receding diagonally towards the vanishing point. Everything is bathed in the gleaming light of the late afternoon sun. Crowds of people gather before the temples, rows of columns and arcades, the small scale of the figures serving to underscore the monumental dimensions of the structures. What is imagined here is nothing less than the history of architecture itself, from the pyramid looming above everything else in the hazy distance, by way of Egyptian and Greek temples, to a splendid Roman building, in front of which a procession holding banners halts at white steps among sacrificial altars. The watercourse that runs through the image thus becomes a river of time, reflecting the achievements of antiquity. To the left, on the opposite bank of the river, a Gothic cathedral rises in shadow, surrounded by a dense wood. Only the stained glass windows of the tower are illuminated by the light of the sun. Here, Mediterranean antiquity and northern European Gothic architecture appear as ideal images, the two primary references for the historicist architecture of Romanticism.

But Cole's painting involves a further dimension as well. In the right foreground, set on a massive capital, the architect himself reclines on a stack of tomes, texts and plans, his eyes closed and his head tilted back. His dream is embodied in the scene behind him. Visualized here is a central idea of Romanticism: art does not emerge solely through deliberation, calculation, historical knowledge, surveying and copying. Equally indispensable is the individual creator, who draws inspiration from the unconscious, from the realm of dreams.

The pragmatic environment of America in the 1840s may not have been especially receptive to this poetic conception of architecture. Cole executed the painting on commission from the highly sophisticated architect Ithiel Town, a leading representative of the first generation of professional architects in the United States and the creator of numerous historicist buildings in the Greek Revival and Neo-Gothic styles. When Town saw the painting for the first time, he rejected it outright, feeling that he had been misunderstood, if not actually deceived. Evidently, he could perceive no connection between his everyday activities, shaped by acquired knowledge, technical expertise and skill in negotiation, and Cole's Romantic conception of the artist as an isolated, dreaming visionary.

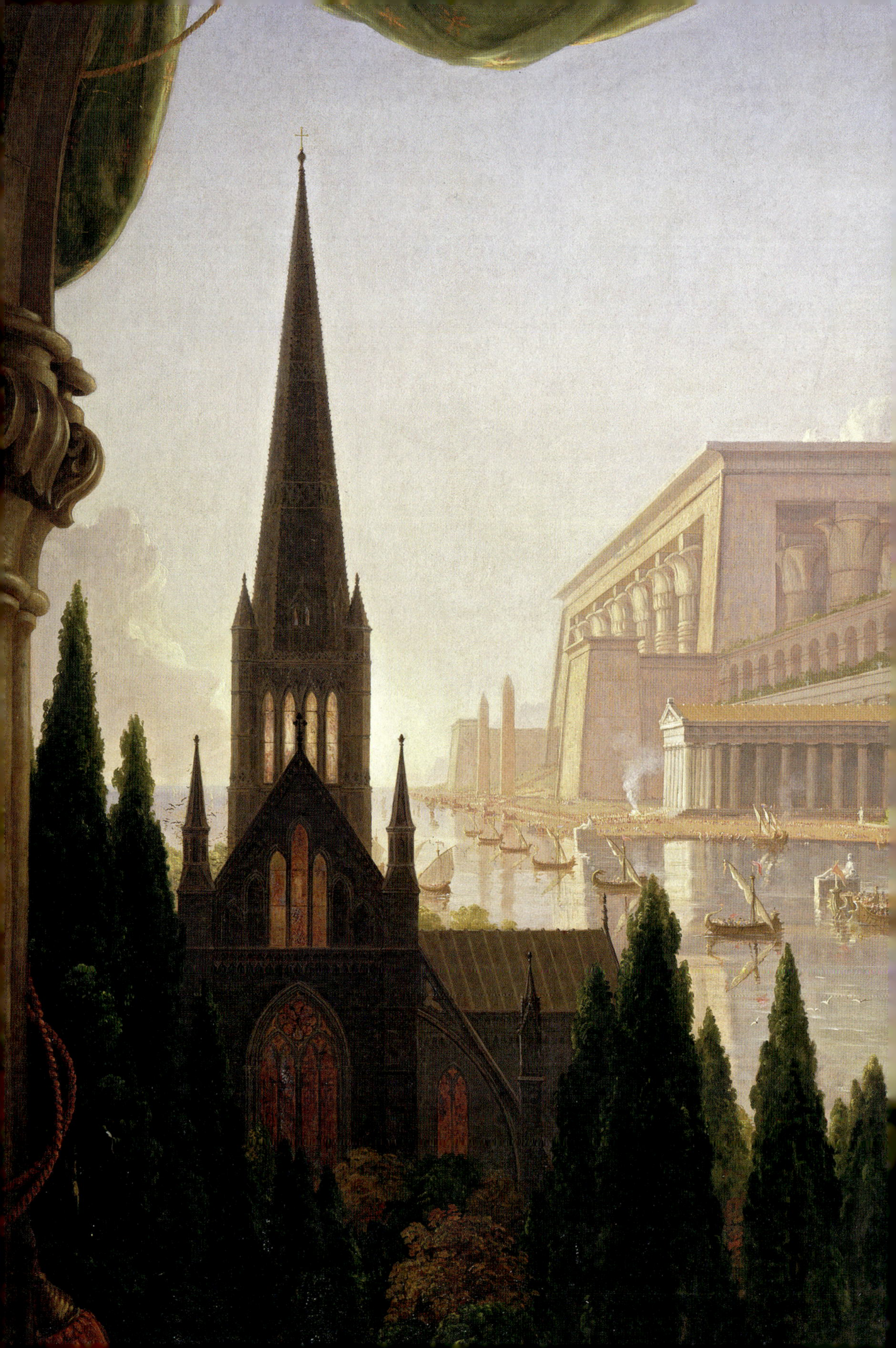

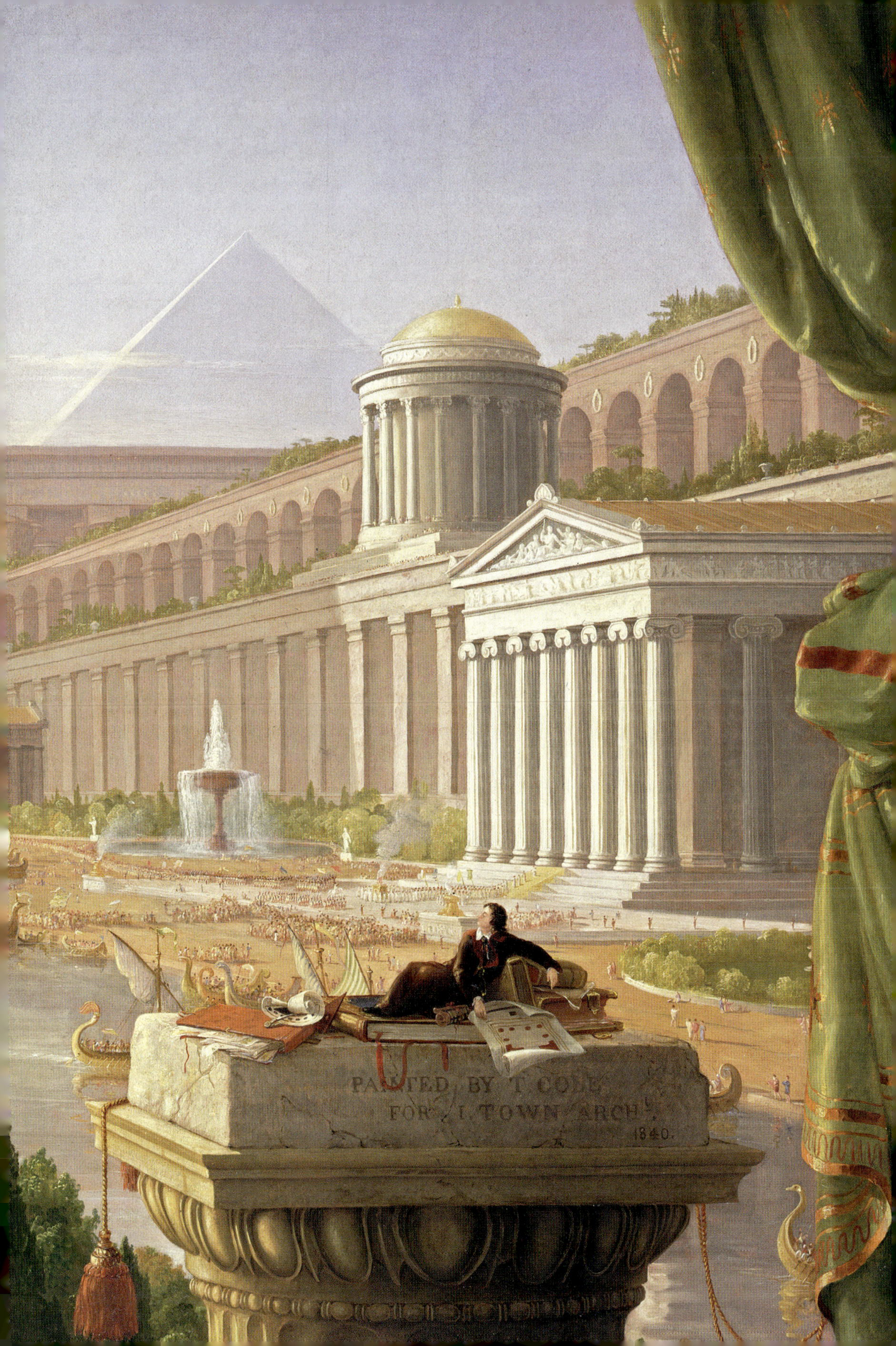
BY T. COLE
FOR I. TOWN ARCH
1840.

ODILON REDON
1840–1916

My drawings inspire, *and are not to be defined. They do not determine anything. Like music, they take us into the ambiguous world of the indeterminate.*

ODILON REDON, JOURNAL ENTRY (1894)

Unquestionably, Odilon Redon was one of the most unusual artists of the late nineteenth century. Although a contemporary of the Impressionists, he embarked on a distinctly individual artistic path, one that renders his work virtually unclassifiable, even though he participated in the eighth and final Impressionist exhibition in 1886, contributing fifteen works. His aim was not to display the serene shimmer of light and colour, nor to render impressions of the real world on canvas, but instead to immerse himself in the abysses of the unconscious, in the shadow realms of the soul. In his sombre *noirs* (works in black), charcoal drawings that earned him a reputation among both artists and writers, he captured bizarre and unreal images on paper, mysterious, dreamlike visions that inspired his friends to call him the 'prince du rêve' (prince of dreams). He exerted a particularly powerful influence on the subsequent younger generation of Symbolists, on the artists' group known as the Nabis and on the Surrealists, who regarded him as a visionary forerunner.

In the last quarter of the nineteenth century, hoping to reach a larger audience and fearing that his works might otherwise fade away unseen in the portfolios of a few connoisseurs, he began producing and publishing lithographs in large numbers and in rapid succession, both singly and in series. His very first, and perhaps most important, series was titled *Dans le rêve* (*In the Dream*). The ten plates, marked by a virtuosic command of the printing technique, present a loosely connected series of fantastical motifs, most of which had already been realized as charcoal drawings and which arose from his explorations of the vast field of the unconscious and its obscure sources of inspiration.

The disembodied head that hovers above a body of water in Plate VI serves as an emblem of the un-, pre- and non-conscious, while the solitary eye of *Vision* suggests an exceptional capacity to perceive the subjective, the inner and the non-objective. Both arise from the world of dreams, of somnambulism and of hallucination. Redon's fame spread rapidly, particularly after 1884, when the fashionable and much-lauded author Joris-Karl Huysmans published the novel *À rebours* (*Against the Grain*), in which Redon is discussed in an extended passage. Redon's style underwent another rapid shift around the turn of the century, now in the direction of luminous colour and heightened abstraction.

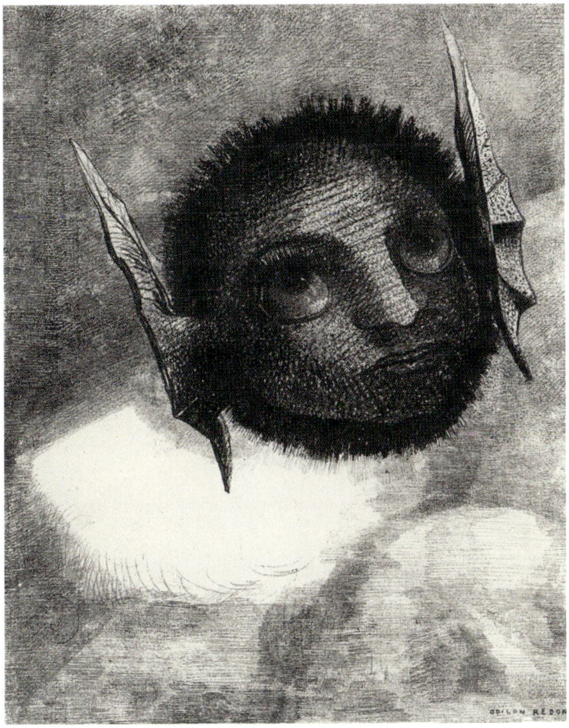

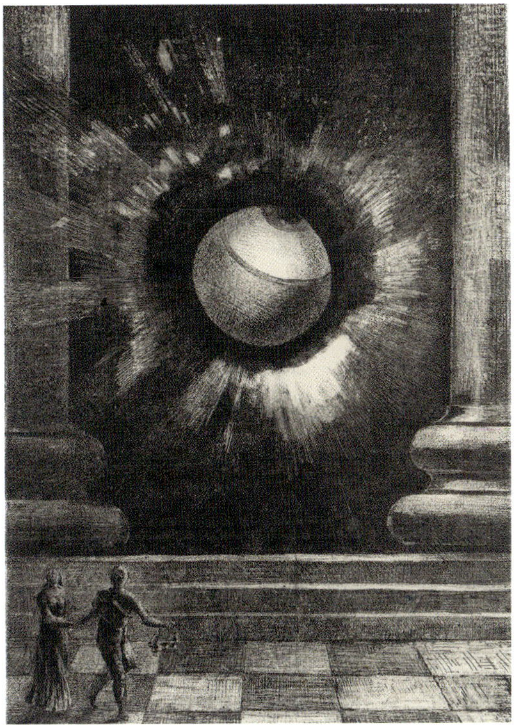

Dans le rêve (*In the Dream*), 1879: *VI Gnome*, lithograph,
27.2 × 22.0 cm (10 ¾ × 8 ⅝ in.); *VIII Vision*, lithograph, 27.4 × 19.8 cm (10 ¾ × 7 ¾ in.),
Bibliothèque nationale de France, Paris

PIERRE PUVIS DE CHAVANNES

1824–1898

It would be as intrusive as it would be pointless to seek an overly precise meaning in a composition that the master doubtless intended to be just that: poetry drifting through a dream [...]

MARIUS VACHON, *PUVIS DE CHAVANNES: A MASTER OF HIS TIME* (1900)

Pierre Puvis de Chavannes – who had exhibited regularly at the Paris Salon since the 1850s – enjoyed the height of his fame during the final decades of the nineteenth century. Credited by many critics with reviving history painting, he was seen by some as the first modern painter. More than five hundred guests attended a banquet in his honour marking his seventieth birthday, among them many of the leading French artists, poets and intellectuals of the time. Puvis was known in particular for his imposing, large-format murals, commissioned by the state, including those for the Hôtel de Ville, the Grand Amphithéâtre of the Sorbonne and the Panthéon in Paris, which established his reputation as a precursor of Symbolism.

When *The Dream* was first exhibited at the Salon des Artistes Français in 1883, it was accompanied by a brief catalogue explanation: 'In his sleep, he sees Love, Glory and Wealth appear before him.' A young man lies fast asleep at the foot of a tree; by his side, tied to a stick, is a small bundle. With subtlety, the positioning of his head and arms betrays the uneasy restlessness of a dreamer. A trio of hovering women, set against the starry night sky, descend upon him from the right. The first strews roses, emblem of Love; the second presents a laurel wreath, symbol of Glory; the third tosses gold coins, signifying Wealth. The surrounding landscape is rendered with stark simplicity and consists largely of delicately graded, loosely applied planes of colour. The uniform, chalky tones and restricted chromatic spectrum create a tranquil harmony of the pictorial elements, illuminated only by beams of pale moonlight. Through the inanimate stiffness of the figures and their classically styled robes, which seem untouched by even the slightest breeze despite their flight, this painting takes on a monumental and timeless serenity characteristic of Puvis de Chavannes. The simple compositional rhythm and use of colour fuse the otherwise isolated elements of the picture into a harmonious equilibrium – a dreamy counter-image to the breakneck technological and industrial progress and fast-paced bustle of the French metropolis shortly before the turn of the century.

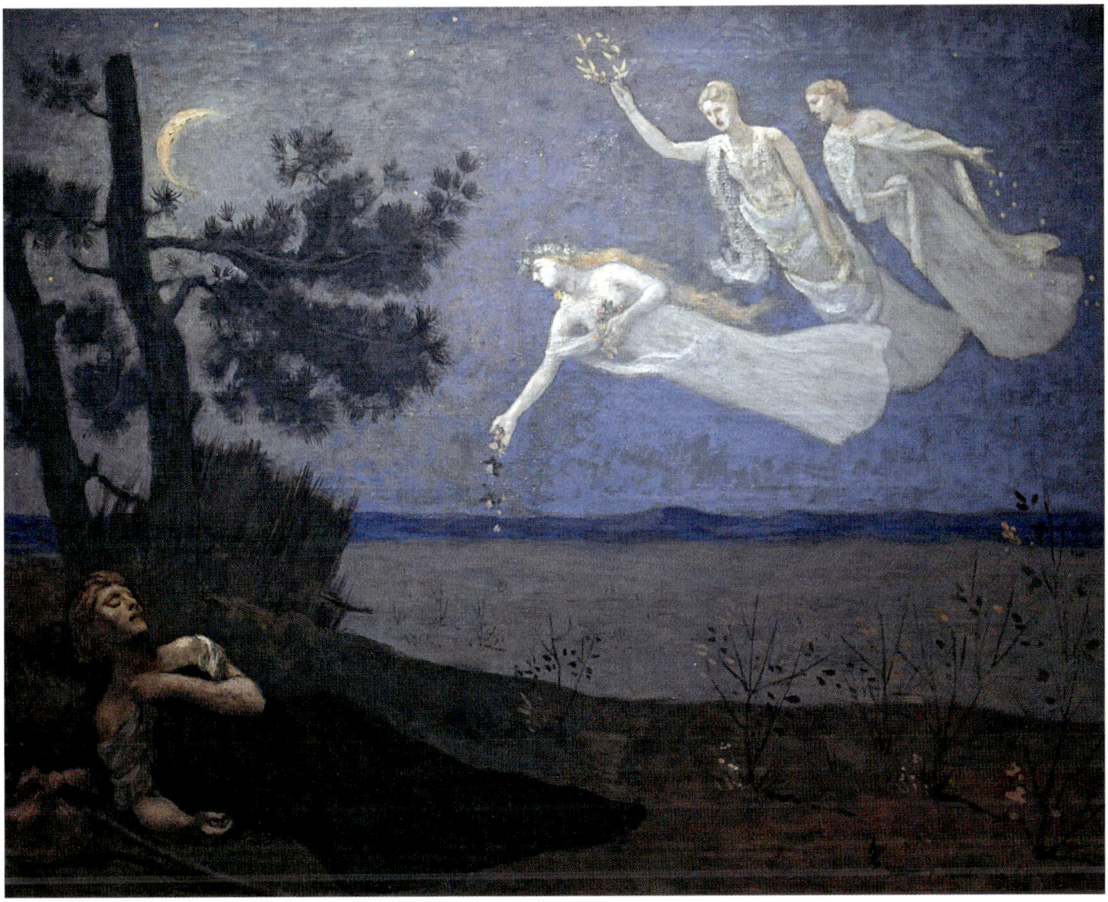

The Dream, 1883, oil on canvas,
82 × 102 cm (32 ¼ × 40 ⅛ in.), Musée d'Orsay, Paris

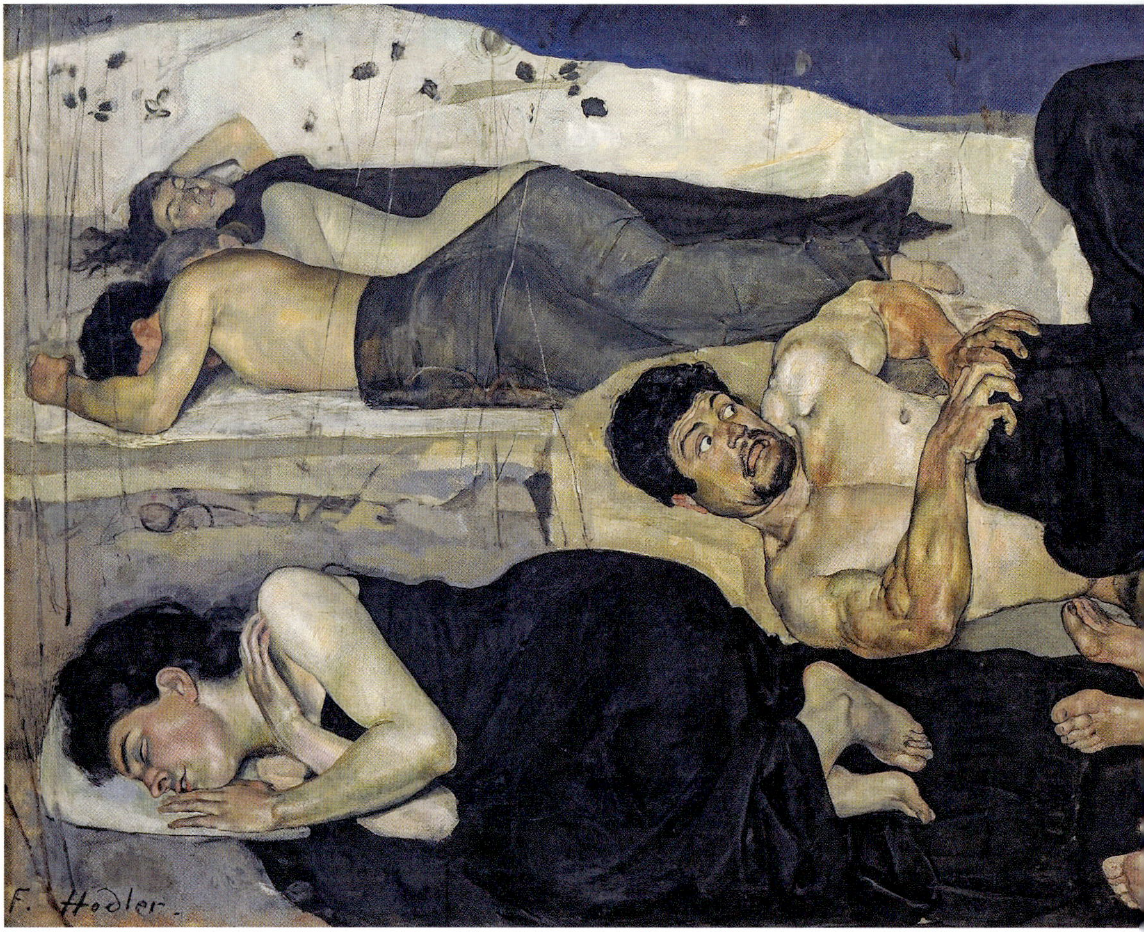

FERDINAND HODLER
1853–1918

Many are those who lie down peacefully of an evening and do not wake the next morning.

INSCRIPTION ON THE ORIGINAL FRAME OF THE PAINTING *THE NIGHT* (1890)

It took Ferdinand Hodler several months to complete *The Night*, working – contrary to his customary approach – directly on the canvas without extensive preparatory work, an effort that, in his own words, 'cost him an inordinate amount of time' and 'nearly caused him to collapse'. The extraordinarily large painting suddenly achieved widespread attention in February 1891 when the Geneva Council of State decided to exclude it from a municipal art exhibition on moral grounds. Hodler, who was still living in poverty at the time, seized the opportunity to spark a controversy that played out in the press. He exhibited the work in rooms he rented himself, and with such resounding success that he not only attracted throngs of visitors but also earned enough from admission fees to be able to spend a period in Paris, then the epicentre of the art world. There, *The Night* was accepted for exhibition at the Salon du Champ-de-Mars, marking his long yearned-for breakthrough as an artist.

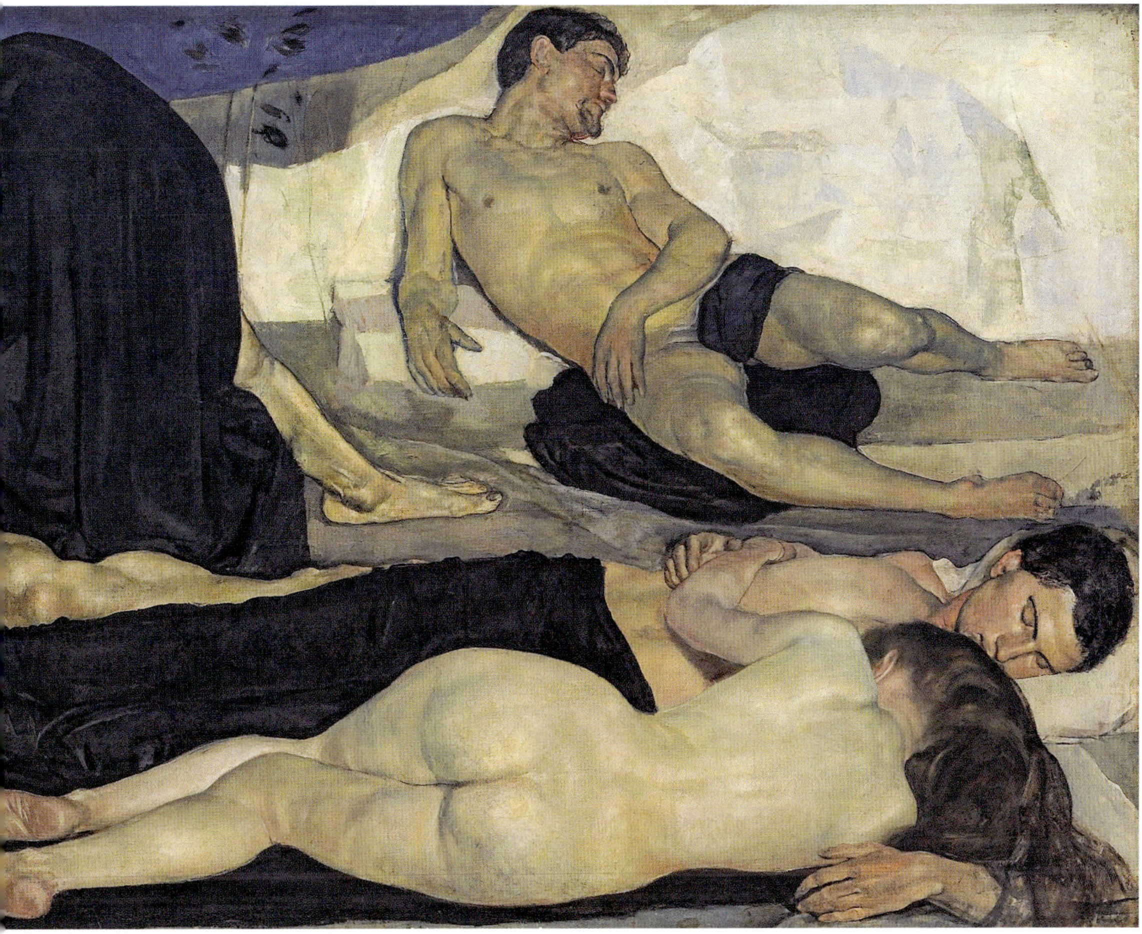

In a monumental, bleak landscape, a number of women and men lie asleep on the stony ground, the figures in the foreground almost life-sized. Tightly framed by the composition, they extend nearly to the edges of the canvas. The scene is bathed in a pale, eerie light. At the centre, one man has suddenly started from sleep, his face contorted with fear, his arms tensed and hands raised in a defensive posture; a terrifying figure sits upon him, wholly shrouded in black: a nightmarish vision. This dramatic situation contrasts sharply with the relaxed tranquillity of the other figures. The startled man is utterly alone with his experience. Hodler gave the terrorized figure his own facial features. The woman seen in the left-hand foreground is Augustine Dupin, the mother of his son Hector, while the masterfully executed nude on the right, seen from the rear, depicts Bertha Stucki-Hodler, with whom he had been married since 1889. During work on the painting, he would go on to separate from both. This image thus became an emblem of the artist's oppressive, despairing emotional world, of the loneliness, abandonment and isolation of a struggling individual, surrounded by others who, detached and indifferent, continue to sleep beside him. Hodler himself considered *The Night* his central work, and it is still regarded as one of the most important and celebrated paintings of Symbolism.

The Night, 1890, oil on canvas, 116.5 × 299 cm (45 ⅞ × 117 ¾ in.), Kunstmuseum Bern

EDVARD MUNCH
1863–1944

In the pale nights, the forms of nature have fantastical shapes.
Stones lie like trolls down by the beach.
They move.

EDVARD MUNCH, NOTEBOOK (1890–1892)

Edvard Munch was a master of both inner experience and the art of landscape. His works were shaped by his emotional world; within them, human existence and the realm of nature merge, giving rise to an intensely expressive atmosphere. His recurring themes are love, anxiety, jealousy, loneliness, sorrow and death. Munch assembled a number of central images to form his so-called 'Frieze of Life', which he characterized as 'the poetry of life, love and death', a project he never fully completed. In its earliest conception, the cycle was to open with *A Summer Night's Dream: The Voice*.

Standing alone in a forest landscape in a plain white dress is a young woman, her hands folded behind her back, her pose and facial expression suggesting nervous expectancy. Her large eyes are directed outwards, fixed directly on us, the viewer. Arranged around and behind her in an almost ornamental pattern is a group of nine trees; at the centre of the picture, the moon is reflected in the water, forming a tall column that extends almost to the shoreline – a striking motif that recurs throughout Munch's work. The forest floor, the shore and the fjord are rendered as broad, homogeneous planes of colour, forming a powerful horizontal contrast to the numerous vertical elements. Drifting along on the water is a small boat; floating above like clouds in the blue sky are the lightly indicated branches of the trees.

The setting is the coastline of the Oslofjord near Åsgårdstrand, a motif Munch returned to frequently from the 1880s until the end of his life and a place intimately bound up with his biography. In an understated way, the image captures a young girl's nascent romantic feelings, emotions that oscillate between yearning anticipation and shy reluctance. Her gaze expresses searching, contemplative intensity, but also the fear of future disappointment and sorrow. The overall mood – very much in keeping with Munch's own inner life – is one of deep melancholy. This image has often been associated with Milly Thaulow, the artist's first love – an attachment that was never fulfilled and a disappointed dream that would mark his relationships with women for the rest of his life.

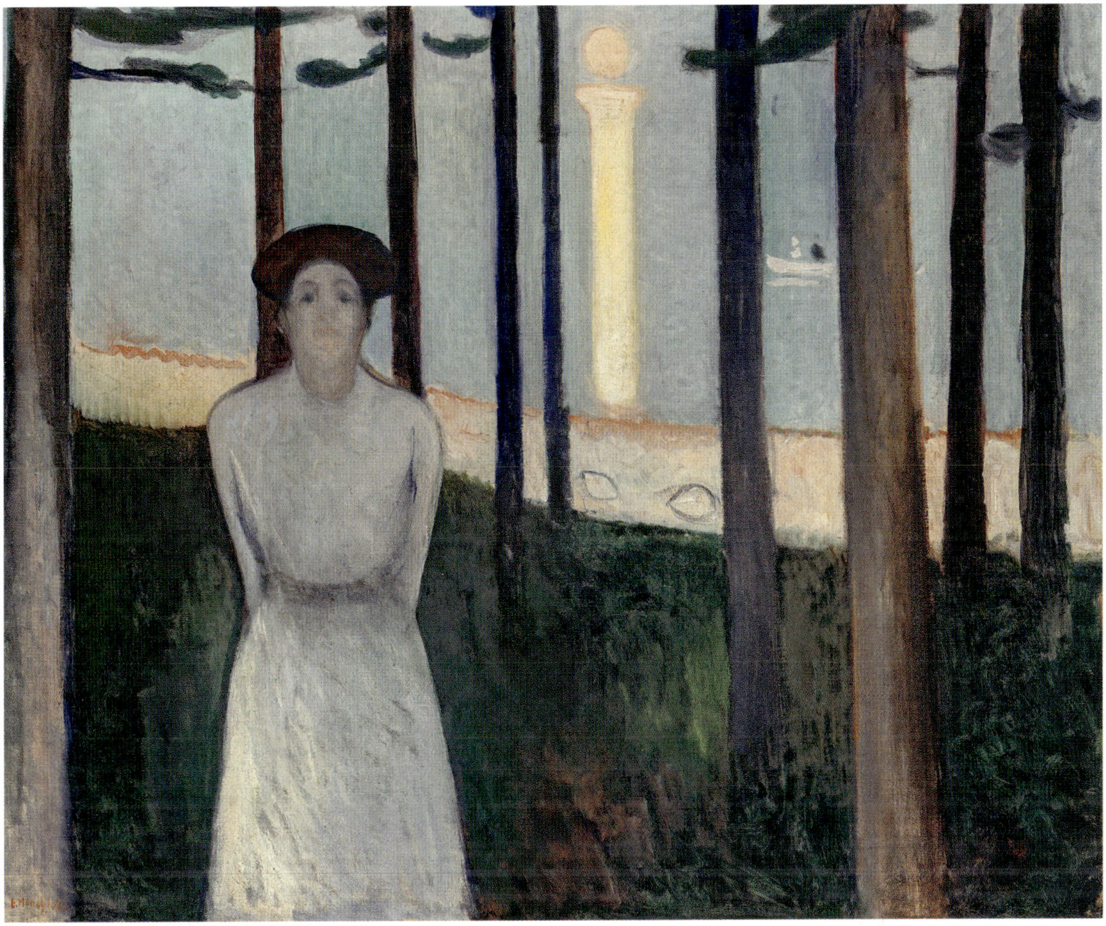

A Summer Night's Dream: The Voice, 1893, oil on canvas, 87.9 × 108 cm (34 ⅝ × 42 ½ in.), Museum of Fine Arts, Boston, Ernest Wadsworth Longfellow Fund

EDWARD BURNE-JONES
1833–1898

I mean by a picture a beautiful, romantic dream of something that never was, never will be – in a light better than any light that ever shone – in a land no one can define or remember, only desire.

EDWARD BURNE-JONES, LETTER TO A FRIEND (1872)

Since at least the twelfth century, the vast and multifarious body of legends about King Arthur has been firmly embedded in Europe's cultural memory. It was quite by chance, however, that two students at Oxford, namely Edward Burne-Jones and William Morris – a founding figure of the Arts and Crafts Movement – came across Thomas Malory's *Le Morte d'Arthur*, a Middle English version of the legend dating from around 1470, which became a source of continual fascination throughout their lives. Both artists would repeatedly take up themes from Arthurian legend in their works, in particular the quest for the Holy Grail by the Knights of the Round Table.

Lancelot at the Chapel of the Holy Grail illustrates a scene of dramatic failure at the very threshold of the long-sought goal. At a crossroads, after a long journey and numerous adventures, Lancelot du Lac discovers a chapel from which an unearthly light emanates, but which he cannot enter. Exhausted, he lies down in front of its door and falls asleep. In a half-dreaming state, he witnesses the healing of a knight by the Grail. His companion interprets Lancelot's inability to awaken as a sign of his sinfulness – of his erotic attachments to Guinevere, the king's wife. When Lancelot finally awakens, a voice commands him to abandon the holy place.

Characteristically, Burne-Jones adopts an austere composition containing just a few isolated, statuesque figures in the foreground. Exhausted, his sword held only loosely in one hand, Lancelot leans back against a fountain; the lifeless, eerie tree in the background, from which his shield hangs, is a symbol and harbinger of his failure. In the doorway of the chapel, from which the radiance of the Holy Grail emanates, stands an angel, startled and troubled, who will tell the knight of his unworthiness when he awakens. In the background, above drifting banks of fog, a sinister wood appears; the nocturnal gloom reflects Lancelot's plight. The image exhibits many characteristic features of Pre-Raphaelite art, a movement marked by nostalgia for the medieval world, the veneration of Italian pre- and early Renaissance art, and a Romantic turn towards nature, along with its mystical exaltation.

This painting is a variation on a design for a series of large tapestries depicting the search for the Holy Grail that Burne-Jones realized in collaboration with Morris for Stanmore Hall in Middlesex beginning in 1890. Reproduced several times and shown at the Exposition Universelle of Paris in 1900, they contributed significantly to Burne-Jones's posthumous fame.

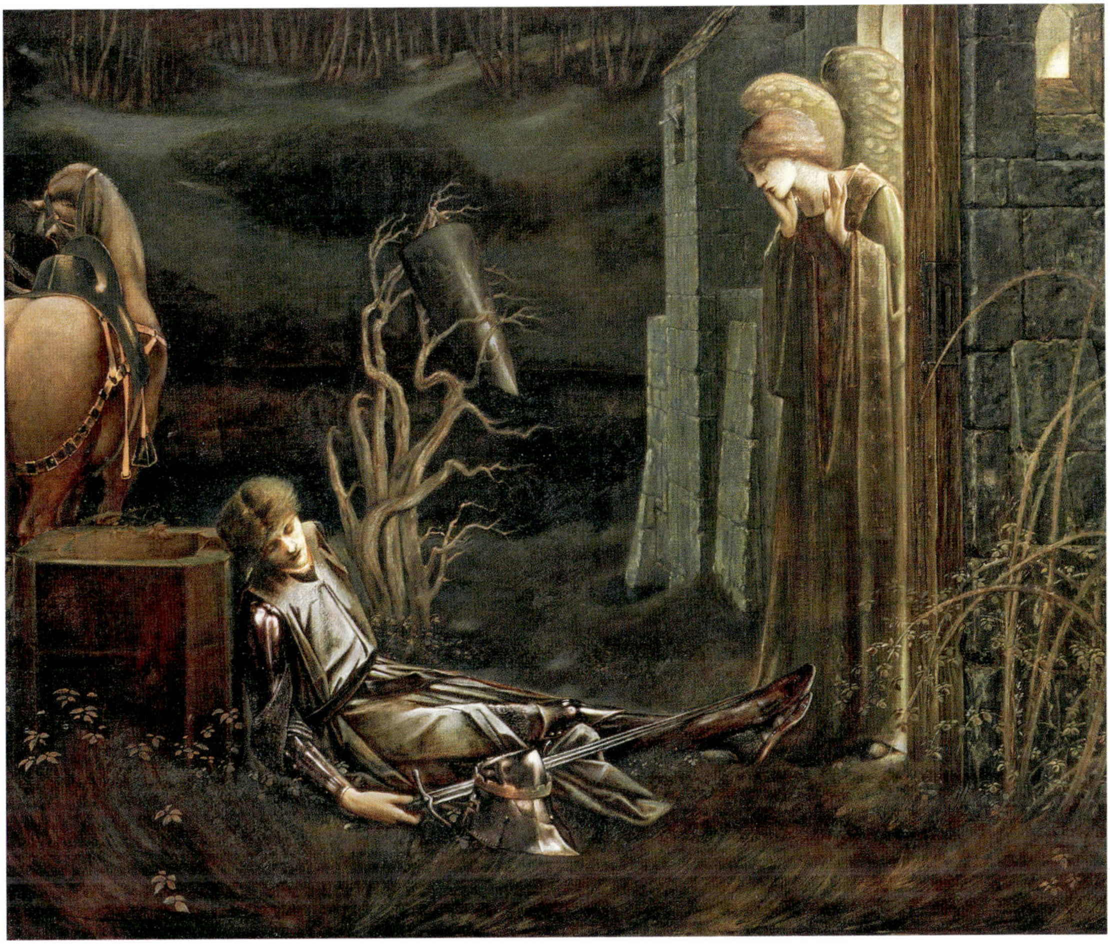

Lancelot at the Chapel of the Holy Grail, 1896, oil on canvas,
138.5 × 169.8 cm (54 ½ × 66 ⅞ in.), Southampton City Art Gallery

HENRI ROUSSEAU
1844–1910

Having fallen into a gentle sleep
Yadwigha, in a dream,
Heard the sounds of a musette
Played by a benevolent magician.
While the moon shone down
Upon the flowers, the green trees,
The wild serpents listened to
The instrument's merry tunes.

HENRI ROUSSEAU, POEM TO ACCOMPANY THE PAINTING *THE DREAM* (1910)

Henri Rousseau's final large-format painting, *The Dream*, is regarded as the culmination of his celebrated jungle pictures, and thus a central achievement of his highly influential oeuvre. Amidst the dense vegetation of a primeval forest, a nude woman reclines on a red upholstered settee, surrounded by gigantic stylized blossoms, and gazes out at the natural world before her. The luminous green that extends across the entire picture seems almost to contain its own light source, and makes an overpowering impression, like the exceptionally large composition itself, which measures a full three metres (almost ten feet) in width. Only gradually does the viewer become aware of the various creatures in the painting: birds, monkeys, an elephant that is almost concealed by the tangled undergrowth, a serpent, visible along the lower right of the picture's edge, and a pair of lions that gaze out with wide-open eyes. Standing near the centre is a figure holding a flute, whose dark skin almost merges with the vegetation, while the colourfully striped skirt marks the most vivid area of colour in the painting. Hovering above everything – despite the blue sky – is a full, round moon. Everything exudes the agreeable, dreamy atmosphere of a tranquil, exotic idyll – an image of longing that contrasts sharply with the bustling metropolis of Paris around the turn of the twentieth century, beyond whose immediate surroundings Rousseau never actually ventured.

In the poem that accompanies this work, Rousseau explains, as he would later do to friends, that the reclining woman, whose name is Yadwigha and of whom nothing further is known, is dreaming. What is revealed here is the content of her dream, and its depiction confronts us with a seemingly surreal scenario. As so often with Rousseau, his imagery cannot be conclusively defined or interpreted, and instead remains enigmatic – which doubtless accounts, at least partially, for the undiminished fascination with his works to this day. In 1910, when Rousseau exhibited his recently finished canvas at the Salon des Indépendants, it became a source of controversy, and his art was once again rejected by conservative critics. But the work of this autodidact had already received a degree of recognition and become an important reference and source of inspiration, in particular for the circle of avant-garde artists grouped around Pablo Picasso, Fernand Léger, Henri Matisse and Robert Delaunay. The mysterious and magical quality of his pictures embodies the rediscovery of fantasy in early Modernism.

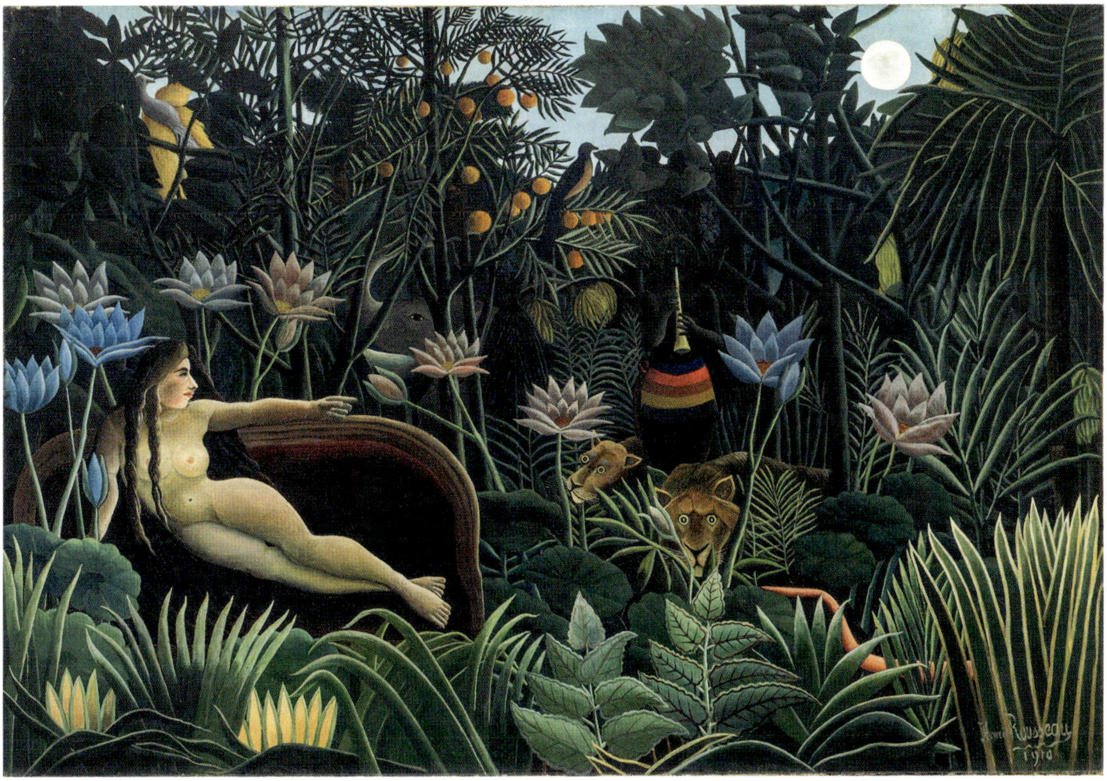

The Dream, 1910, oil on canvas,
204.5 × 298.5 cm (80 ½ × 117 ½ in.), The Museum of Modern Art (MoMA), New York

FRANZ MARC
1880–1916

*Art is nothing but the expression of our dream;
the more we surrender to it the closer we get
to the inner truth of things, our dream-life, the true life
that scorns questions and does not see them.*

FRANZ MARC, LETTER TO MARIA FRANCK (1907)

When the poet Else Lasker-Schüler experienced financial difficulties after her divorce from the art dealer and publisher Herwarth Walden, Karl Kraus called for contributions in his magazine *Die Fackel* (The Torch). Franz Marc – who was bound to the poet by a close friendship that also gave rise to their celebrated correspondence, published by Lasker-Schüler herself – contributed the painting *Dream*, which he intended to sell at a private auction he himself organized in Munich. A diminutive inscription along the lower left reads 'Dedicated to the Prince of Thebes', referring to the poet herself, who had adopted this fantastical persona and fashioned from it a dreamlike alter ego.

At the time this painting was created, Marc – having drawn inspiration from Paul Gauguin and Vincent van Gogh, along with Fauvism, Cubism and Futurism – had renounced the academic approach characteristic of his youth, instead developing an abstract style dominated by flat planes and powerful colours. Slightly earlier, in 1912, he had published the almanac *Der Blaue Reiter* (The Blue Rider) together with Wassily Kandinsky. The artists associated with this legendary publication were among the key figures who helped drive the development of twentieth-century Modernism.

Animal life is the principal element in Marc's paintings, with an emphasis not on the external forms of the depicted creatures, but instead on their essential natures, which he sought to grasp through a continual process of empathy. For Marc, animals symbolized purity, innocence and a primordial life in harmony with nature, with which they appear to merge seamlessly in his images. Often, he presents the viewer with a dreamlike utopia, a kind of paradise, where forms and colours no longer reflect reality, and instead express the essence of life itself.

Along the lower edge of the picture, wrapped in voluminous robes and lying on the red earth, we see a dreaming figure whose black, medium-length hair is reminiscent of Lasker-Schüler's bob cut and evokes her imaginary artist persona, the Prince of Thebes. The landscape is assembled from plants and stereometric rock formations in primary colours. In the upper right, where the paint application is thinner and the imagery thus seems more evanescent and weightless, a pair of elephants enters the picture from the right. Together with the pale, crystalline architecture against which they are set, they seem to be part of the dream. Typically for Marc, the intertwining of animal and human figures with the natural environment generates a unified, rhythmically animated interplay of form and colour.

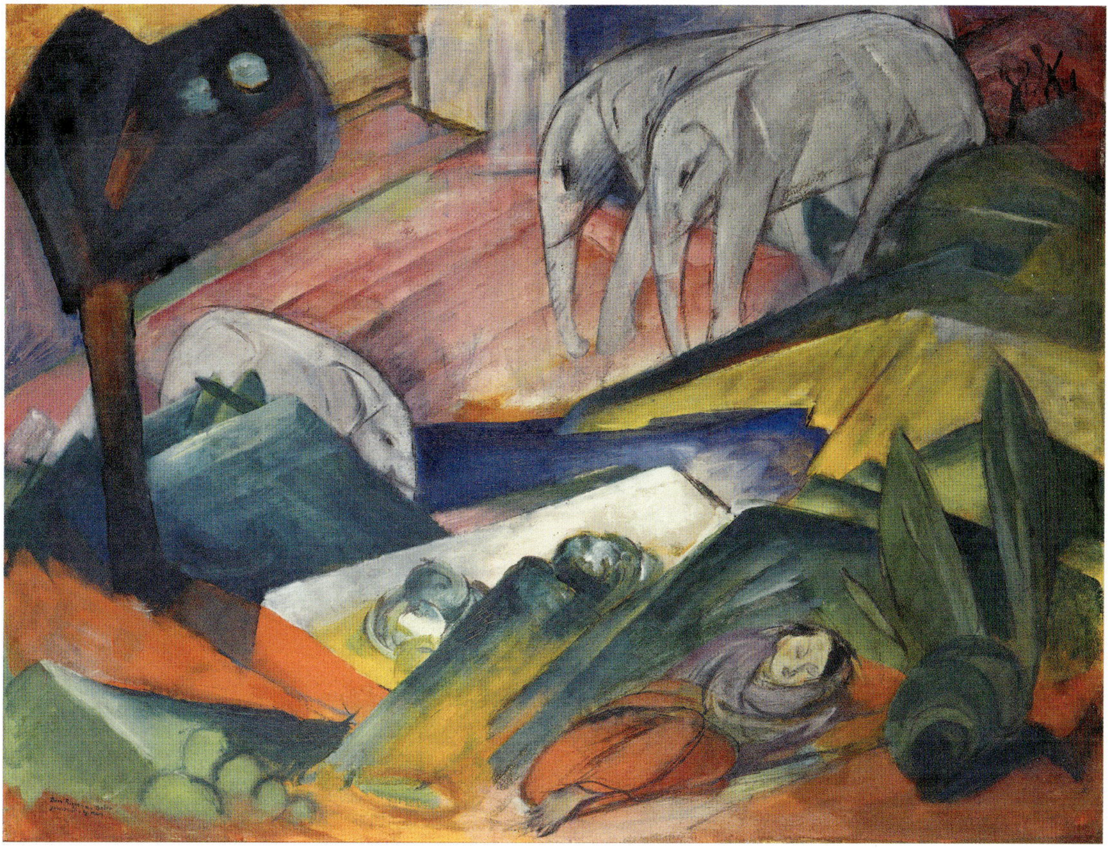

Dream, 1913, oil on cardboard, with an intermediate layer of glue-impregnated fabric, mounted on plywood, 76 × 101 cm (29 ⅞ × 39 ¾ in.), Kunstmuseum Bern

GIORGIO DE CHIRICO
1888–1978

The painting of de Chirico is not painting in the sense that the word is used today. One could define it as a dream writing.

ARDENGO SOFFICI, 'SOFFICI IN MILAN' (1914)

Giorgio de Chirico's early works all seem to emerge from the world of dreams. Not because they depict fantastical creatures or supernatural events, but because of their singular conjunction of ordinary objects with extraordinary spaces. Rigorously constructed arcades and façades, isolated objects, disconcerting perspectives and menacing shadows combine to create an oppressive sense of solitude, immobility and emptiness of the kind often encountered in dreams.

In the images of his early phase, as a leading figure of so-called *pittura metafisica* (metaphysical painting) – a movement he helped to found and of which he was a key protagonist – de Chirico repeatedly employed the same enigmatic ciphers. The painting *The Double Dream of Spring* displays several of these in exemplary fashion, and does so on multiple levels.

The pictorial structure is intricately layered. Suspended at the centre of the image in the extreme foreground and mounted on a post that runs vertically through the composition is a painted panel with a narrow frame. Visible in this picture-within-a-picture are arcaded structures; to the right in the distance stands a cylindrical tower; beneath it, swallowed up by the vast space, are two tiny figures; below them the draped legs of a celebrated antique sculpture of Ariadne; a vessel set on a pedestal; an old-fashioned locomotive; and the rear view of a sculpture – all elements found within de Chirico's well-established iconography and recurring in his earlier and later paintings alike. An equally unreal scene unfolds behind the panel. A male figure wearing a morning coat, his back to the viewer, gazes upwards into a monochrome blue sky. Behind an arcade that lies in shadow, the enormous head of a mannequin gazes out at the landscape. These are the two dreamers of spring. On the right, scattered across an almost endless landscape bathed in the low spring sun and receding into a distant snow-clad mountain range, are diminutive figures casting long shadows.

For the young Surrealists working in Paris, among them Max Ernst, Salvador Dalí, René Magritte and André Breton, de Chirico's strangely elusive, unreal images were revelatory, and they soon adopted his dreamlike juxtaposition of fragments of reality as a method for their own work. From 1919 onwards, de Chirico himself turned away from his early style, and continued into grand old age producing works inspired by the masters of the Renaissance and Baroque, none of which, however, would attain the fame or influence of his dream images.

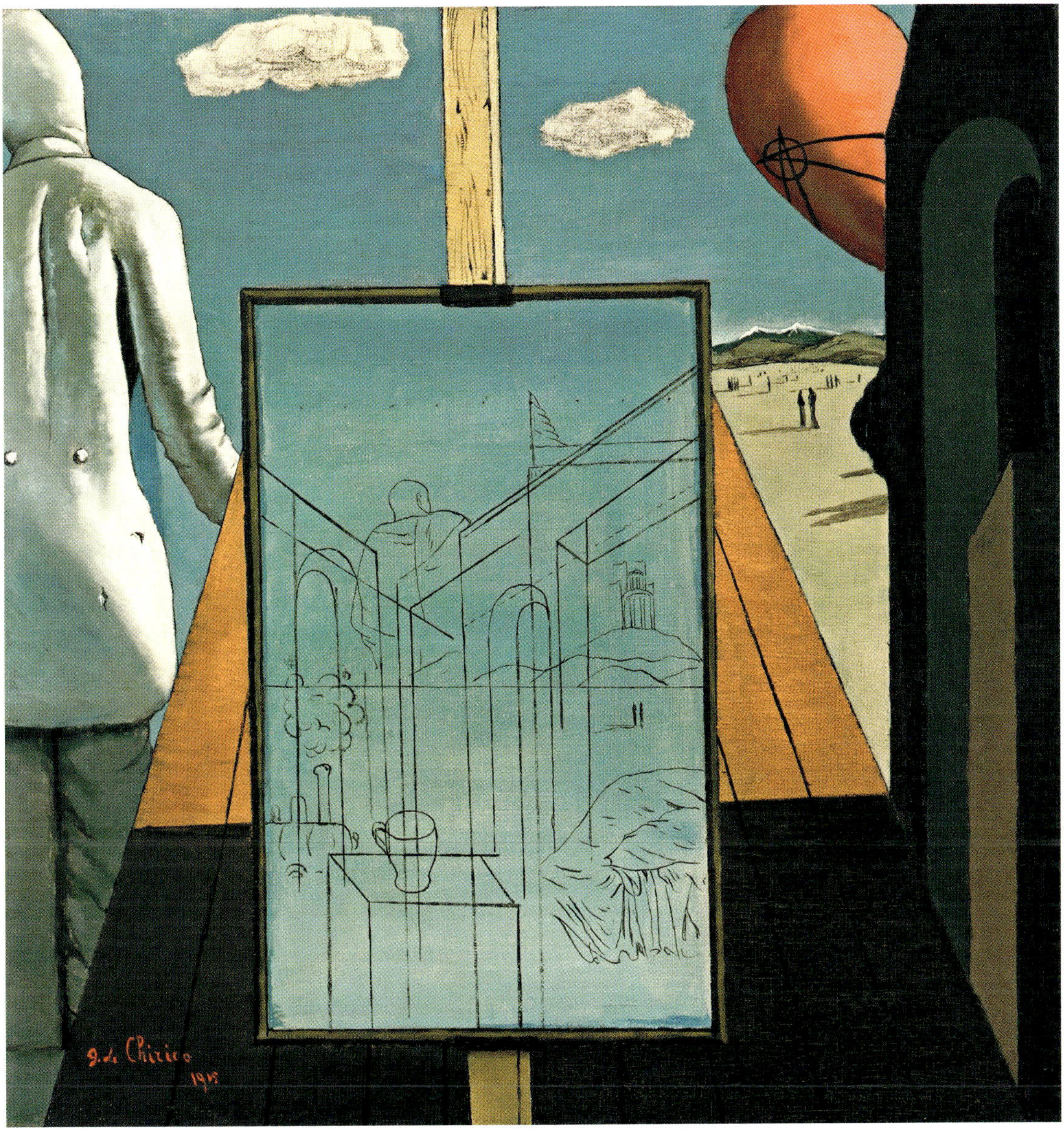

The Double Dream of Spring, 1915, oil on canvas,
56.2 × 54.3 cm (22 ⅛ × 21 ⅜ in.), The Museum of Modern Art (MoMA), New York

PAUL KLEE
1879–1940

His buildings, too, are dreams enchanted into crystalline form.

THEODOR DÄUBLER ON PAUL KLEE (1918)

Paul Klee – an inspired, idiosyncratic maverick who is difficult to categorize in relation to the numerous 'isms' of twentieth-century art – produced this watercolour after his appointment to the Bauhaus in Weimar, having just begun his now-legendary teaching activities at the school.

A constellation of architectural forms rises from the lower edge of the sheet – towers, windows, stone walls and gables are recognizable. Consisting of multiple silhouettes of individual structures, this imaginary urban cluster – a key motif that appears frequently throughout Klee's oeuvre – builds upwards in staggered layers. It is accompanied by vegetal forms, most noticeably a tree-like figure, with its multiple blossoms, on the lower right. Bird-shaped clouds float across the sky, while triangles suggest a soaring mountain range; the sun and moon can also be discerned. The sheet as a whole is permeated by the interweaving of delicate bluish-green and pinkish-violet in the most finely nuanced shades and gradations. Darker areas give the forms clear contours, endowing the sheet with a powerfully graphic, even ornamental character. Everything is radically abstract, yet at the same time clearly perceptible in its palpable presence.

Through its angular forms and the pronounced gradation of its edges in a subtly modulated range of colour tones, the dream world conjured by Klee appears strikingly crystalline and vitreous in character. At the Bauhaus in its early years, crystalline domes, glass palaces and cosmic architecture gave rise to utopian architectural visions that were presented with expressive and quasi-religious intensity – before the school quickly shifted towards the technical and rationally oriented design style that has since become world-famous. With his fragile, seemingly delicate dream vision, Klee gave form to the avant-garde zeitgeist as it still prevailed in 1921.

In 1937, Klee's watercolour, then part of the Staatliche Kunstsammlungen in Weimar, was confiscated by the National Socialist commission of the Reich Ministry of Public Enlightenment and Propaganda and denounced as 'degenerate'. With the aim of raising foreign currency, it was dispatched to the New York branch of gallerist Karl Buchholz, where it was sold. After various detours, it entered the collection of the Galerie Berggruen & Cie in Paris in 1966. It then changed hands several times until, in 1993, it was acquired for a second time by Heinz Berggruen.

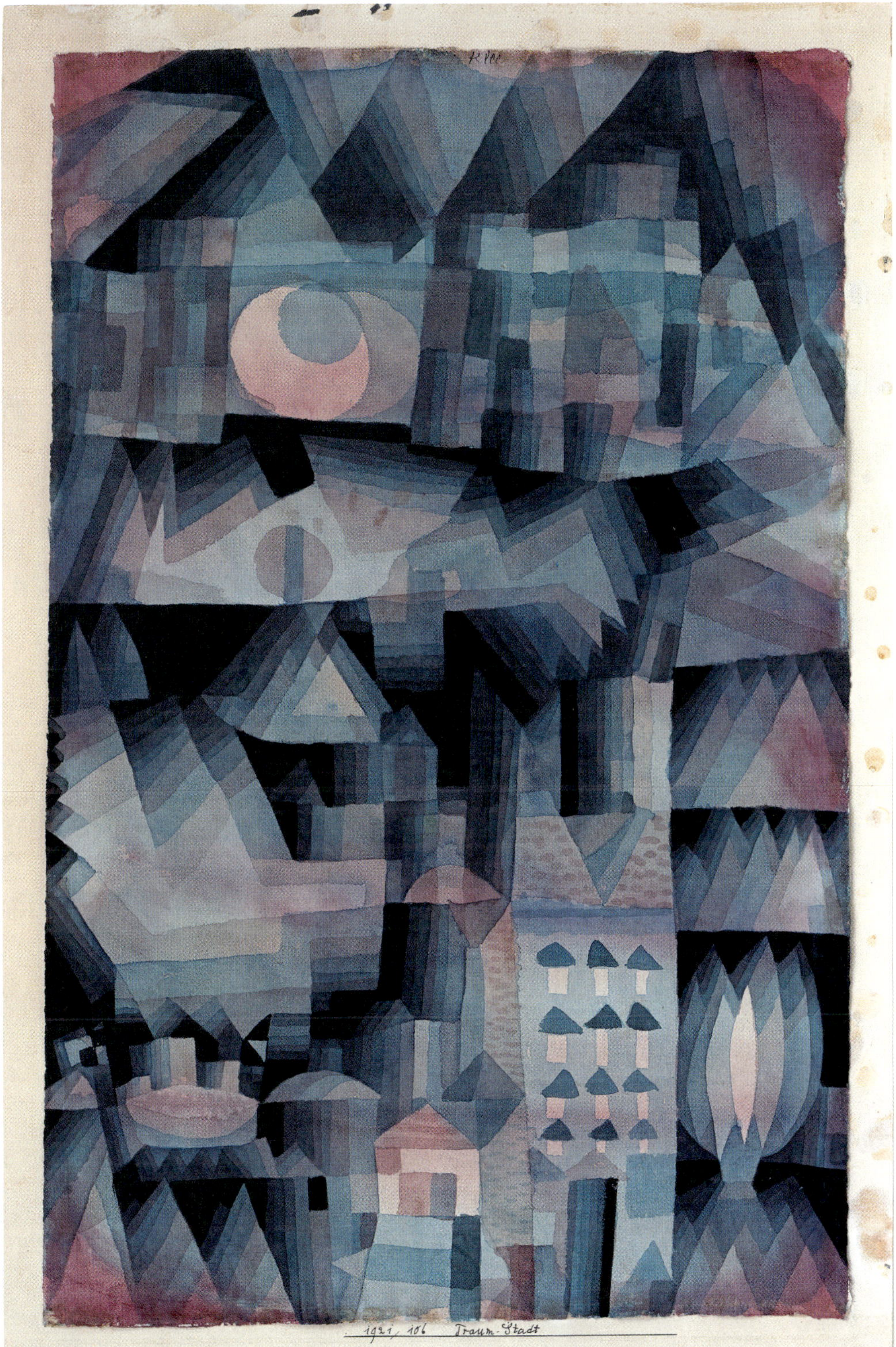

Dream City, 1921, watercolour on paper, laid down on board,
47.5 × 31 cm (18 ¾ × 12 ¼ in.), Staatliche Museen zu Berlin, Nationalgalerie, Sammlung Berggruen

MAX ERNST
1891–1976

The collage technique is the systematic exploitation of the accidentally or deliberately provoked encounter of two or more intrinsically unrelated realities on a seemingly incongruous plane – and the spark of poetry that leaps across the gap as these two realities approach.

MAX ERNST, 'BIOGRAPHICAL NOTES: TISSUE OF TRUTH – TISSUE OF LIES' (1959)

In 1918, after four years of military service, completely disillusioned and appalled by the madness of war, the autodidact Max Ernst abandoned his studies in the humanities to become an artist – he would go on to be a central figure in both Dada and Surrealism. Ernst cofounded the Dada group in Cologne, aligning himself with a movement that relied on chance, irony, absurdity and rebellion, and sought the radical destruction of bourgeois conventions and established culture. In 1922, he moved to Paris, where he soon became associated with the Surrealists, whose preoccupation with the unconscious and the world of dreams and fantasy increasingly defined his work. One of his best-known and most characteristic paintings, displaying the traits of both Dada and Surrealism, is *Two Children Are Threatened by a Nightingale*, dating from 1924 and representing a high point of his collage technique.

A red wooden gate leans against a simple wooden picture frame, guiding the eye deep into the pictorial space: beneath the radiant blue sky that covers most of the image, a disquieting scene unfolds. A girl has drawn a large knife and appears intent on attacking the tiny bird seen hovering directly above the blade. A second girl lies outstretched on the grass, apparently unconscious. On the right, a man stands on the roof of a toy house pasted onto the picture plane, holding another child in his arms and hurrying to reach an alarm button mounted on the picture frame, presumably to escape the threat. A long wall recedes into the background, where a triumphal arch, a tower and a dome emerge faintly in the distance. The title written in French – *2 enfants sont menacés par un rossignol* – is inscribed along the lower edge of the painted surface like a commentary.

The combination of an idyllic landscape, classical perspective and a traditional figural arrangement with absurd content and objects inserted as in a collage gives the image an irrational, grotesque, oppressively ominous mood – like a bizarre dream vision. In fact, Ernst traced this image back to a fever dream he experienced as a child during a bout of measles.

In retrospect, Ernst described the work as a kind of farewell to the Dadaist collage technique. Shortly thereafter, with his development of frottage (a drawing technique involving rubbing pencil or charcoal over a sheet of paper placed against a textured surface) and grattage (a technique involving the scraping away of wet paint), Ernst's work took a new turn that would have a profound impact on the development of art in the twentieth century.

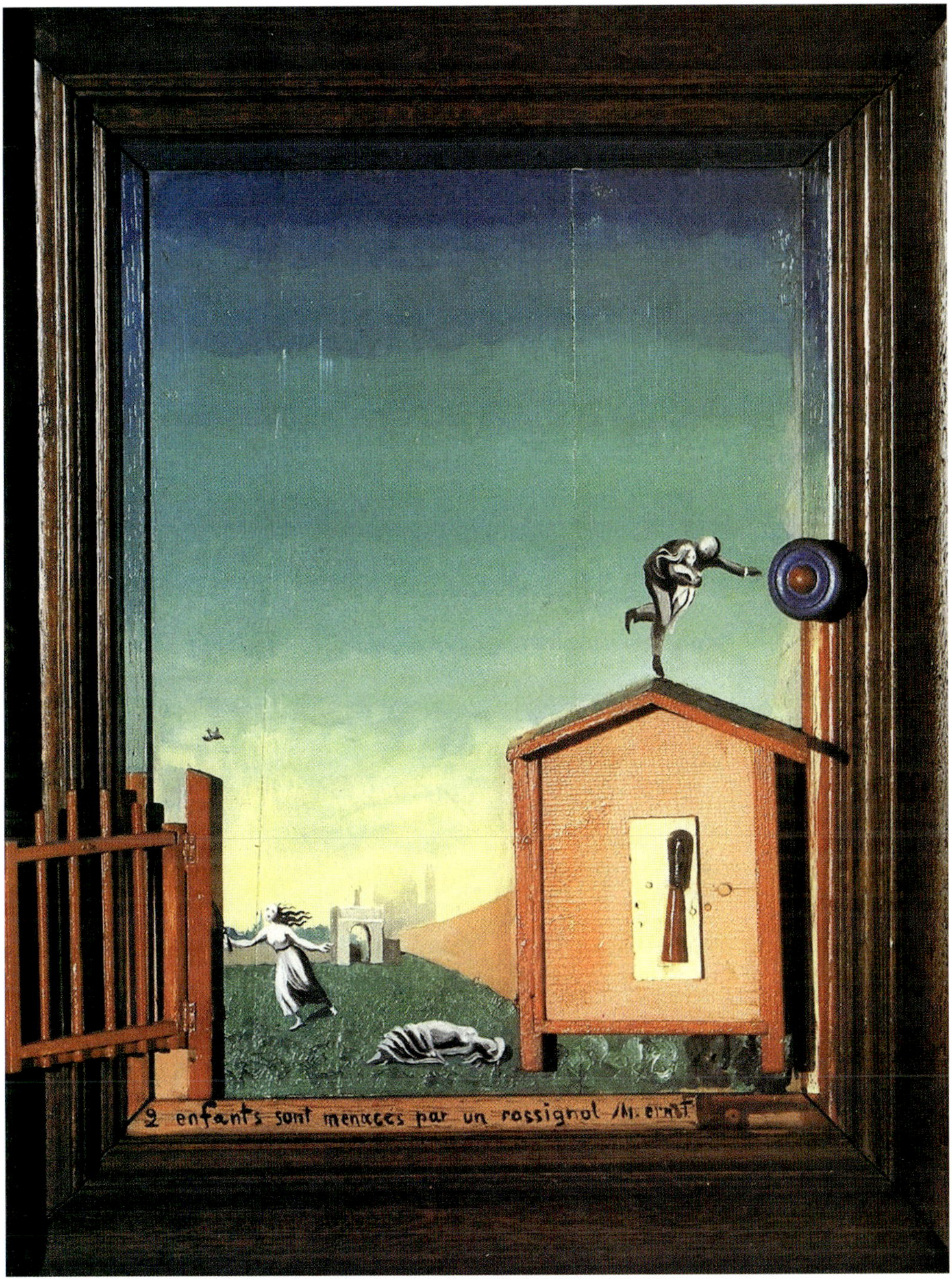

Two Children Are Threatened by a Nightingale, 1924, oil with painted wood elements
and cut-and-pasted printed paper on wood with wood frame,
69.8 × 57.1 × 11.4 cm (27 ½ × 22 ½ × 4 ½ in.), The Museum of Modern Art (MoMA), New York

WASSILY KANDINSKY

1866–1944

Of course, every phenomenon of the external and of the inner world can be given linear expression – a kind of translation.

WASSILY KANDINSKY,
POINT AND LINE TO PLANE (1926)

Wassily Kandinsky was one of the decisive pioneers of abstract art. A cofounder of the artists' group Der Blaue Reiter (The Blue Rider) and an instructor and deputy director at the Bauhaus, he was among the leading artistic figures of the twentieth century, and his influence was far-reaching. Through his oeuvre, the path from representation to total abstraction can be traced with particular clarity – partly because, during his career, he accompanied his work with publications and theoretical writings. Over the course of his development, the union of opposites plays an essential role: deliberation and intuition, reason and emotion, and later, more concrete formal qualities such as horizontal and vertical, straight and curved, undulating and geometric, stiff and loose, warm and cold, and line and point. It is through the contrapuntal interlocking of these elements that eloquent, harmonious compositions emerge.

In his celebrated essay *Point and Line to Plane*, published in 1926 as the ninth volume in the 'Bauhausbücher' (Bauhaus Books) series, Kandinsky developed a systematic grammar of individual formal elements and their combinations, presented point by point in textbook style, yet the text remains difficult to follow, even opaque. The volume concludes with its sole colour illustration, a reproduction of *Little Dream in Red*, accompanied by a schematic diagram of the composition. This reflects the high esteem in which the artist held this painting, which he gave to his wife Nina.

In fact, the painting appears to be a kind of didactic preparation for his theoretical writings. The intersecting rounded and angular lines, the interpenetrating diagonals and circles, the triply repeated curves, and the quadrilaterals and coloured planes are the individual design elements discussed in his text. Their arrangement and contrast generate tension and dynamism, and their combined effect is intended to produce a harmonious whole. Typical of his works from the Bauhaus years is the dominance of precise geometric forms, executed by Kandinsky with compass and ruler – an abstract language that, despite the artist's seemingly objective explanations, ultimately eludes rational understanding. Yet present in this image, however obliquely, is a faint trace of figuration: the striking half-circle at the centre of the composition and its superstructure echo a symbol often used by Kandinsky: a ship intersected by three diagonals – its oars.

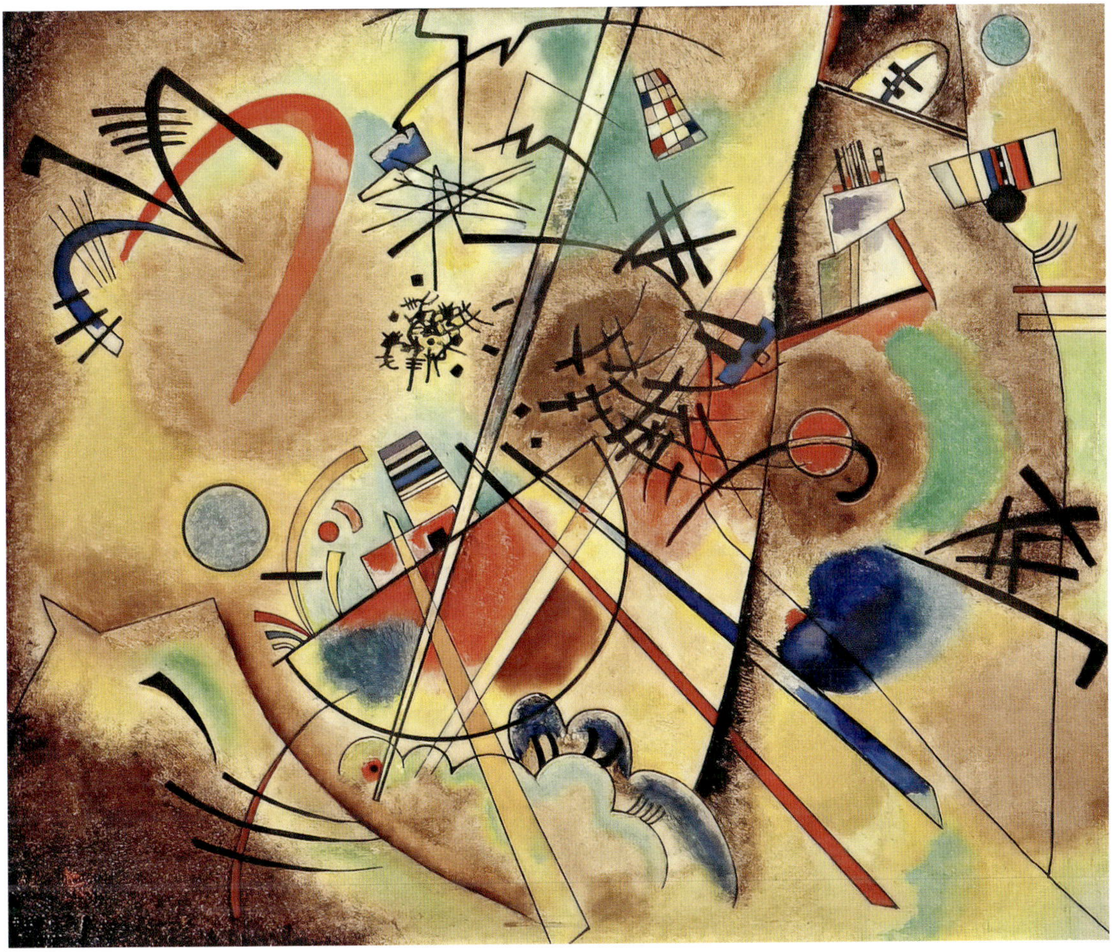

Little Dream in Red, 1925, oil on board,
35.5 × 41.2 cm (14 × 16 ¼ in.), Kunstmuseum, Bern

JOAN MIRÓ
1893–1983

I began gradually to work away from the realism I had practiced […], until, in 1925, I was drawing almost entirely from hallucinations. At the time I was living on a few dried figs a day. I was too proud to ask my colleagues for help. Hunger was a great source of these hallucinations. I would sit for long periods looking at the bare walls of my studio trying to capture these shapes on paper or burlap.

JOAN MIRÓ, IN CONVERSATION WITH JAMES JOHNSON SWEENEY (1948)

In 1920, when the young Catalan artist Joan Miró moved from Barcelona to Paris, he quickly immersed himself in the city's vibrant creative milieu. He was attracted in particular to the slowly emerging Surrealist group, and his studio in Rue Blomet quickly became a meeting point for the avant-garde writers whose works inspired him. His images moved progressively away from a representational idiom and towards a fantastical dance of forms and symbols, until, in 1925, he abandoned all visual conventions and surrendered in his idiosyncratic and uncompromising way to the dictates of the unconscious. The paintings produced during this period, from 1925 to 1927, are known as 'dream paintings'. These works do not, however, depict dream experiences or visions, but instead involve an attempt to relinquish conscious control, indeed to immerse oneself in the realm of the unconscious and to translate its contents into imagery without the intervention of reason or logic – for example, through deliberately induced hallucinations.

In *The Birth of the World*, isolated shapes and lines float before a nebulous, wholly undefined background, created by streaking, pouring and spraying paint onto the irregularly primed canvas. Individual objects are still recognizable – a bird or dragon, a balloon, a human figure with a white head – yet they remain isolated, without logical context, competing for attention with the blurred smudges, stains and traces of colour Miró spread across the vast surface of the canvas, which measures two and a half metres (almost three yards) in height. This picture is an attempt to capture an experience welling up from the artist's unconscious. Miró spoke of 'a sort of genesis', and his poet friends gave the painting the lyrical title *The Birth of the World*.

However, Miró's process of making the 'dream paintings' was by no means as spontaneous as it might appear. He began by recording the forms and associations experienced in moments of hallucinatory intensity in sketches, while the subsequent elaboration in paint was developed step by step with great care. The motifs – initially summoned intuitively, beyond the rational – were then reworked consciously and transformed into an ensemble of highly suggestive forms.

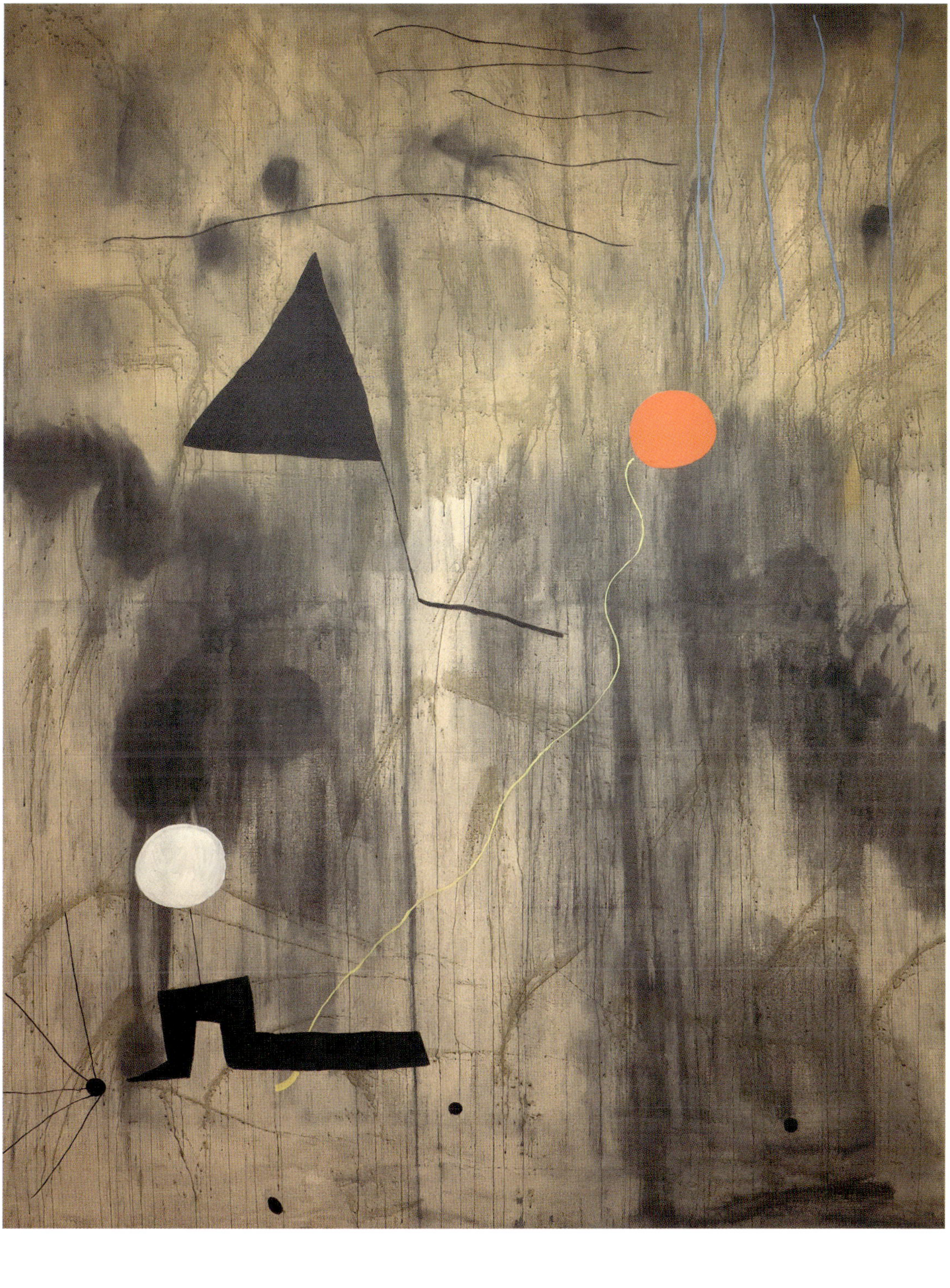

The Birth of the World, 1925, oil on canvas,
250.8 × 200 cm (98 ¾ × 78 ¾ in.), The Museum of Modern Art (MoMA), New York

RENÉ MAGRITTE
1898–1967

An object is not so attached to its name that one cannot find another that suits it better.

RENÉ MAGRITTE, 'WORDS AND IMAGES' (1929)

Four objects are depicted against a dark background within a frame divided into four sections, reminiscent of a window: a bag, a half-open pocketknife, a leaf and a sponge. What at first appears to be a playful, innocuous, even banal appropriation of a children's primer reveals, on closer inspection, a surprising and disorienting feature. The words inscribed somewhat awkwardly in cursive below the objects do not correspond to the illustrations: the bag bears the legend 'the sky', the pocketknife is labelled 'the bird', the leaf is titled 'the table' and the sponge – almost as one might ironically expect – is captioned 'the sponge'.

Underlying the strangeness of this constructed arrangement, which ultimately breaks with every convention through its element of surprise, are complex reflections on linguistics and the philosophy of language, ideas repeatedly expressed by René Magritte himself. He believed that a spoken word or a visual image did not correspond to the object itself, and was instead accepted as a convention, a socially determined agreement and a sign designed to facilitate communication. Magritte draws attention to this through his collage-style distortions, at the same time opening the door to wide-ranging associations and intellectual games: the juxtaposition of bag and sky, for example, might suggest air travel; while leaf and table could evoke a wooden table; and the sponge, in turn, may point to wiping away the inscriptions from this surface resembling a blackboard. Magritte pursued such word-object shifts further by repeating the same compositional idea in multiple versions, always with different objects and lexical terms. For him, this practice was entirely legitimate, since it was not the execution itself, but instead the underlying premise and the conceptual framework, that constituted the essential artistic contribution. *La Clef des songes* (*The Key to Dreams*), sometimes titled *The Interpretation of Dreams*, thereby calls the classical conception of art into question.

This picture represents a distinct tendency within Surrealist art, one that assembles fragments of the world within a strict compositional structure and dispenses with all that is fantastical. A key source of inspiration for these so-called 'word-pictures' may have been the numerous dream books that appeared in large editions in the nineteenth and early twentieth centuries, which explained dream visions in the manner of a lexicon, drawing on Egyptian hieroglyphics, often presenting four or six objects per page in square boxes, each with a caption. This not only explains the painting's title, but also establishes the artist's reference to a 'mystery' around which, according to his own statements, all of his pictures revolve.

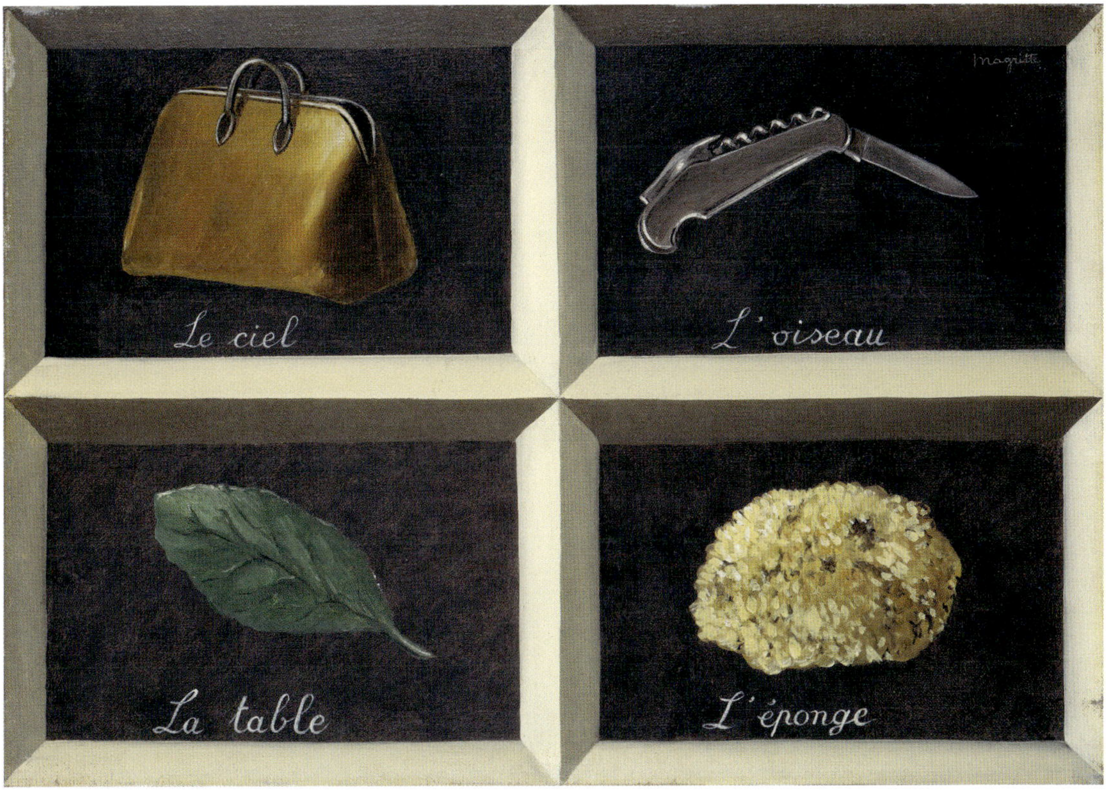

La Clef des songes (*The Key to Dreams*), 1927, oil on canvas,
38 × 53 cm (15 × 20 ⅞ in.), Pinakothek der Moderne, Munich

PABLO PICASSO
1881–1973

In the end, there is only love.
However it may be.

PABLO PICASSO IN CONVERSATION
WITH TÉRIADE (1932)

Like many paintings by Pablo Picasso, *Le Rêve* (*The Dream*) displays distinctly autobiographical traits. In 1927, he met Marie-Thérèse Walter – then just seventeen years old – in the Galeries Lafayette in Paris. She soon became his model, as well as his secret lover. In 1932, a decisive year for his creative development, when Picasso was preparing his first major retrospective for the Parisian Galerie Georges Petit, he produced a substantial series of works portraying Marie-Thérèse, then twenty-two years old. Their relationship served as an escape from his increasingly difficult marriage with Olga Khokhlova, but also a vital source of artistic inspiration.

The best-known work from this period, arguably, is *Le Rêve*, said to have been executed in his Parisian studio in a single afternoon in January 1932. It displays the combination, so typical of Picasso at that time, of surreal imagery, lyrical chromatic harmonies and the Cubist fragmentation of outward appearances. At the same time, it is permeated by powerful erotic overtones.

Seated in the red and yellow armchair that appears in many paintings by Picasso, we see a young woman, her head tilted to one side and her eyes closed. The straps of her dress have slid downwards, exposing her left breast. All of the composition's lines curve sensually. The head is divided in half; the upper portion of her face is devoid of realistic traits, and can even be read as an erect penis, perhaps that of the artist himself. In her lap, her hands join to form a vulva. Here, we witness a fantasy of raw sexuality dreamed by the fifty-year-old artist. When the painting was shown as part of the exhibition at the Galerie Georges Petit, Picasso's relationship with Marie-Thérèse came to light as well. But only in October 1935, when their child was born, did Olga separate from her husband and Picasso began living openly with Marie-Thérèse.

Le Rêve is famous not only for its artistic quality, but also for its provenance. In 1997, it was sold at Christie's for $48.4 million, the sixth highest price ever paid for a painting up to that time. In 2001, it was sold to real estate developer Steve Wynn for an estimated $60 million. In 2006, shortly before offering the painting for $139 million, he accidentally damaged it with his elbow, causing the sale to fall through and triggering a spectacular insurance lawsuit. In March 2013, the newly restored painting found a new owner, this time for $155 million – making it one of the most expensive paintings of all time.

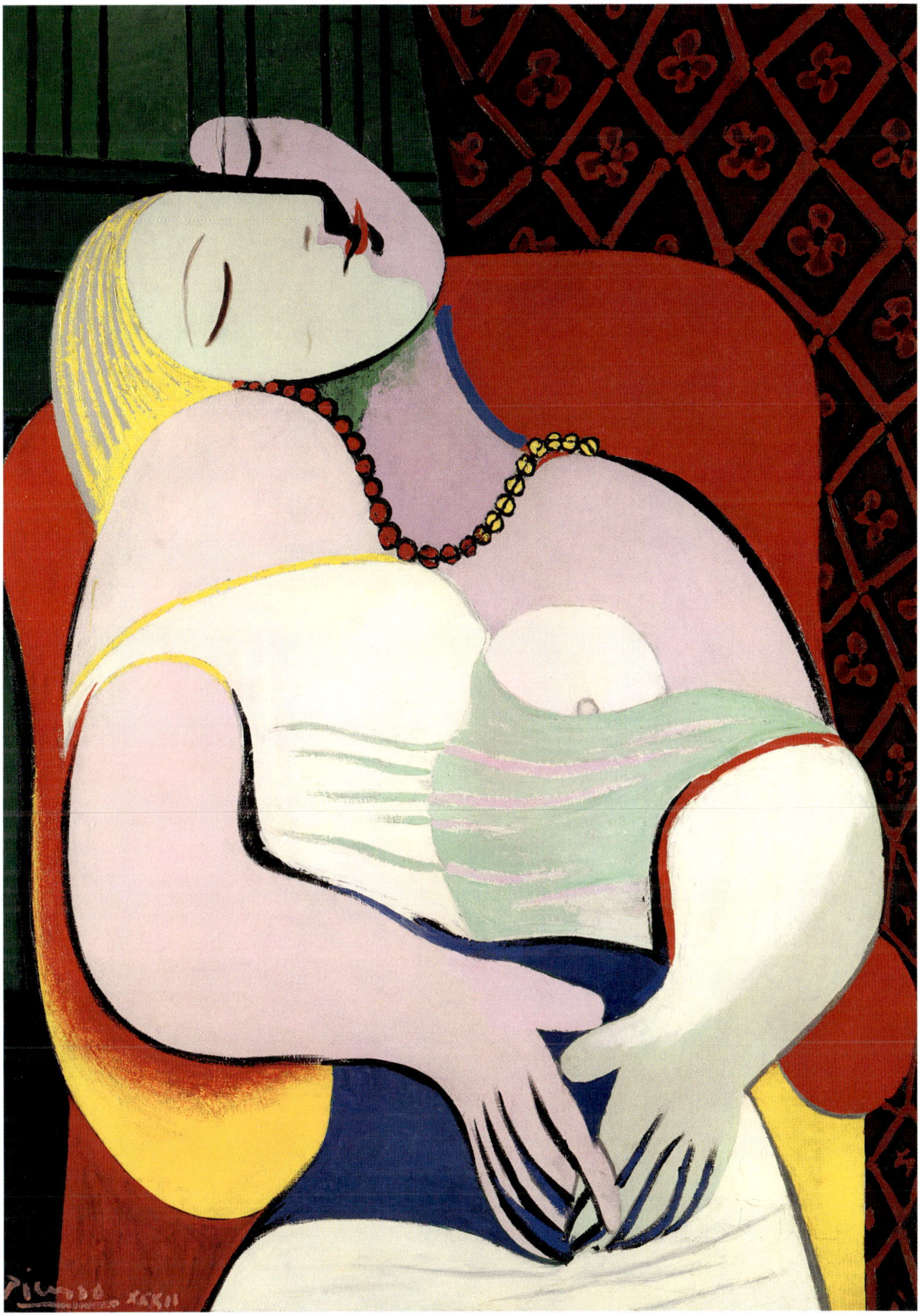

Le Rêve (*The Dream*), 1832, oil on canvas,
130 × 97 cm (51 ⅛ × 38 ¼ in.), Private Collection

HENRI MATISSE
1869–1954

What I dream of is an art of balance, of purity and serenity, devoid of troubling or depressing subject matter, an art which could be for every mental worker [...] a soothing, calming influence on the mind, something like a good armchair which provides relaxation from physical fatigue.

HENRI MATISSE, 'NOTES OF A PAINTER' (1908)

Devoid of extraneous detail but invested with overwhelming presence, this painting shows a female nude lying fast asleep on a blue quilt. The image is dominated by two large areas of colour: first, by the sleeping figure, in a range of softly modulated pink tones, and second, by the blue expanse of the fabric, with its checked pattern. The woman, defined by only a few dark contours, whose serene expression and gentle smile suggest a pleasant dream, almost fills the entire composition. She rests her head gently on her arms, and this triangle formed by her face, arms and the blue background creates a tranquil, balanced composition and her striking, distinctive pose.

Throughout his life, Henri Matisse – perhaps alongside Pablo Picasso the most important artist of the first half of the twentieth century – searched for an immediacy of expression that springs directly from the image, an effect he sought above all in the medium of colour itself. Essential to his artistic strategy was the reduction of both the pictorial content and compositional structure to a basic core that would allow the combinations of colour and their intensity to achieve greater force and impact. In *The Dream*, this ambition is achieved through the harmony of blue and pink, and through a subtle interplay of lines that fuses the entire image into a single visual arabesque, one that can be grasped at a glance. In this sense, the picture represents an important preliminary step towards Matisse's late work and anticipates his famous cut-outs.

The woman depicted is Lydia Delectorskaya, who modelled frequently for Matisse from 1935 onwards. For this artist, an encounter with a new model was always a source of novel motifs, and he devoted considerable time, through close observation, to finding the pose that best corresponded to the sitter's natural bearing. Shortly before this picture was made, Matisse began photographically documenting key successive stages in the development of his painting, which he often radically reworked in the process. This procedure soon became an important means in his pursuit of perfection, as it allowed him to reflect on and control the development of the work, and to correct it when it began to move in the wrong direction. Six such photographs have survived for *The Dream*, and they are a key to understanding his working method.

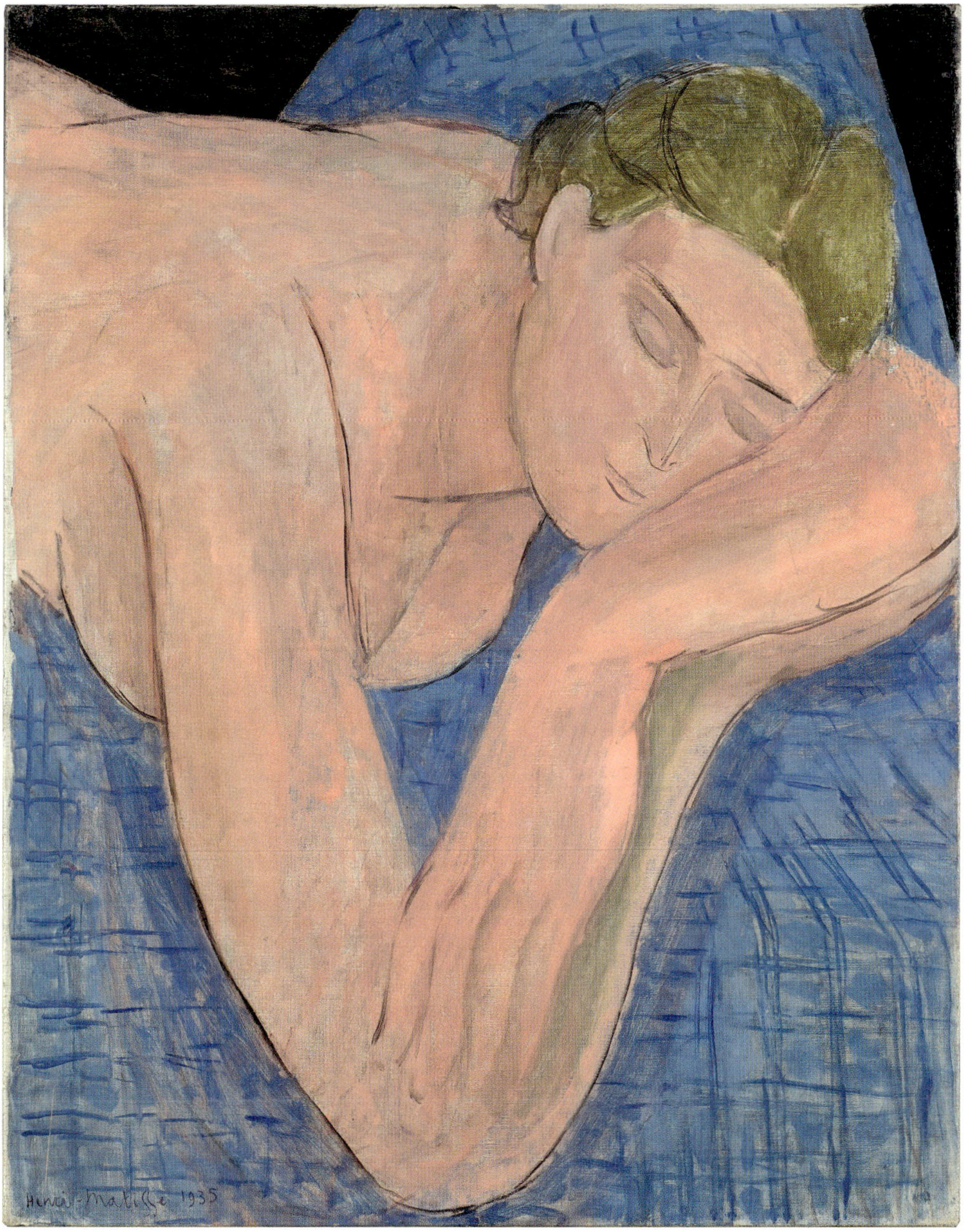

The Dream, 1935, oil on canvas,
81 × 65 cm (31 ⅞ × 25 ⅝ in.), Musée national d'art moderne, Centre Pompidou, Paris

MARC CHAGALL
1887–1985

The essential thing is art, painting, a painting different from the painting everyone does.

MARC CHAGALL,
IN HIS AUTOBIOGRAPHY *MY LIFE* (1923)

Among artists, it is perhaps Marc Chagall – already nicknamed 'le poète' (the poet) by his Parisian friends in the 1910s – who is most closely associated with the world of dreams. Many of his works take the form of fantastical dreams, with a strangely nostalgic and joyous mood in which one readily loses oneself. These images are assembled from a curious combination of seemingly unrelated motifs, contradicting all sense of reality and the logic of the familiar. Indeed, these peculiar scenes are often overlaid by a magical glow of colour, distancing them further from mundane reality and heightening their emotional intensity to the extreme.

An old-fashioned bed hovers in front of a town of wooden houses immersed in nocturnal darkness. A pair of lovers sit on the bed's edge, leaning towards one another in a tender embrace. The distinctive light of this section, echoed in its colour, sets it apart from the reality of the rest of the image. Beside the bed stands a small wooden table, on which a blue vase holds a bouquet of blue flowers; on the right, a rooster hovers, seeming to watch the couple. Behind the bird rises a conspicuous building with a tall, narrow door, above which hangs a sign bearing the Russian word for 'shop'. An angel flies diagonally downwards, following the line of the roofs and the street, making gestures of blessing and assent. On the upper right, at the edge of town, a domed building intensifies the image's spiritual and mystical character.

In different combinations, all of these motifs recur throughout Chagall's oeuvre. These highly personal symbols, fragments of memory, are combined into a distinctly individual network of meanings. The town is Vitebsk, where Chagall spent his childhood and which he transformed into a place of enduring longing. The floating couple represents Chagall and his beloved wife Bella. The rooster appears frequently alongside lovers but also alludes to the simple peasant life of Vitebsk, while the narrow house behind the bird is where Chagall himself once worked as a sign painter.

The tranquil, gentle mood and the seemingly nostalgic, untroubled evocation of childhood memories, however, are deceptive. In the narrow strip of sky above the horizon, dark storm clouds are already gathering. Chagall sensed the growing threat. In 1939, the National Socialists unleashed the Second World War, and Chagall, a Jewish painter, was soon confronted with flight, expulsion, fear and grave hardship, not for the first time in his life. Far from being merely an image of cherished memories, *The Dream* appears to express a desire for safety and shelter in dark times. It thus becomes a moving artistic document shaped by a moment of existential danger.

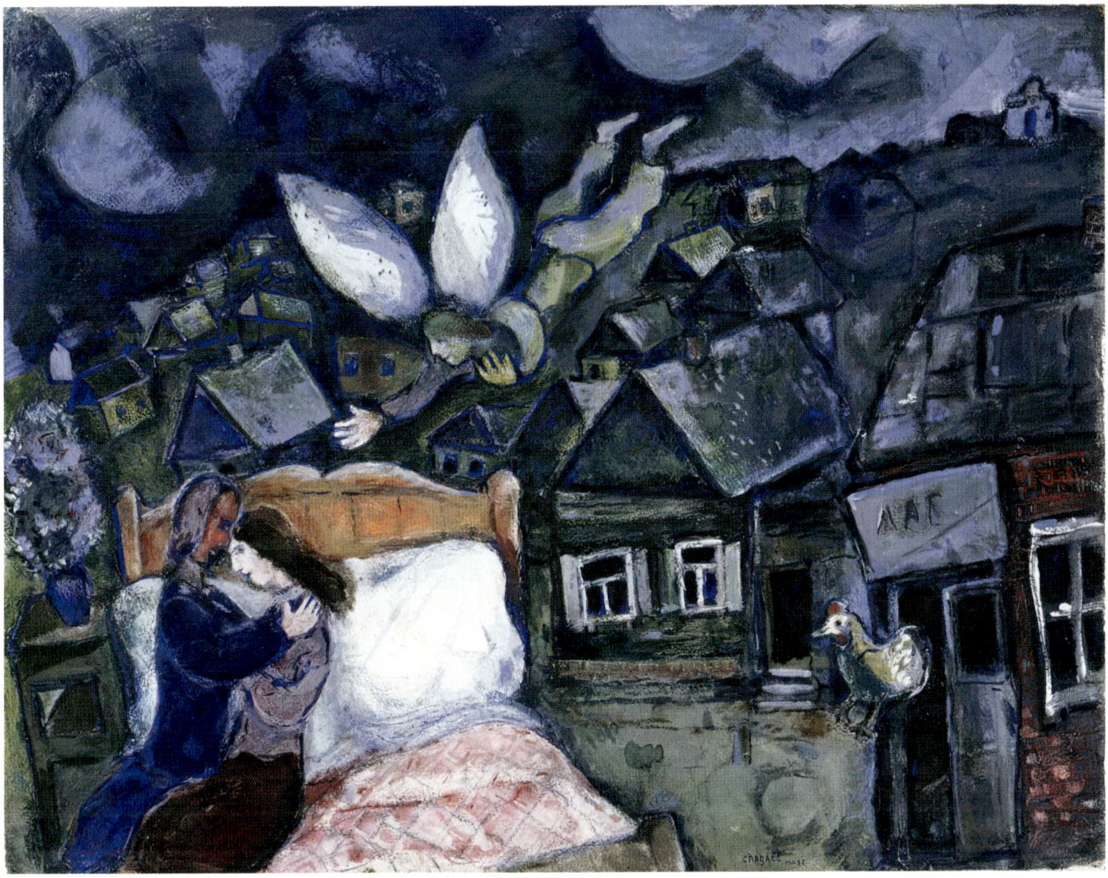

The Dream, 1939, opaque and transparent watercolour and pastel on paper, 52.2 × 67.9 cm (20 ½ × 26 ¾ in.), The Phillips Collection, Washington, DC

FRIDA KAHLO
1907–1954

Since my themes have always been my sensations, my states of mind, and the deep reactions that life has been causing inside me, I've frequently materialized all that into portraits of myself, which were the most sincere and real thing that I could do to express how I felt about myself and what was in front of me.

FRIDA KAHLO, LETTER TO CARLOS CHÁVEZ (1939)

Frida Kahlo has become an icon of the twentieth century through her artistic achievements, her public persona and her extraordinary biography. Her striking, distinctive face, which she depicted in dozens of self-portraits, is as familiar as that of any other artist. It has become a pictorial symbol found the world over.

In her work, Frida Kahlo fuses pre-Columbian Mexican, surrealist, political and biographical elements into a wholly distinctive visual language. Throughout her life, she endured severe physical suffering. An early bout of polio, and the prolonged confinement to bed that followed, caused her right leg to be shorter than her left. While at the age of eighteen, she was so badly injured in a bus accident that she was forced to undergo repeated operations and long periods of hospitalization for the rest of her life.

Dominating this image from 1940 is the bed from which Kahlo was at times compelled to paint. It hovers in front of a sky filled with clouds while the artist lies in it, sleeping peacefully, her head resting on a pair of pillows and turned to one side. A climbing plant spreads across the golden bedspread, a symbol of vitality, but also a kind of fetter that binds her body. Stretched above her, mirroring her pose is a skeleton. Entwined with dynamite, it holds a bouquet of flowers, while its head lies on a pair of pillows, like the artist's. It appears to watch over Kahlo and evokes the ever-present possibility of death; the flowers allude to the Mexican religious tradition of the *Día de los Muertos*, the day of remembrance for the dead – not, however, in an atmosphere of anxiety and sorrow, but in a spirit of joy and celebration.

When Kahlo painted this picture, she was at a turning point in her life. In autumn 1939, she separated from her husband Diego Rivera, only to remarry him less than a year later, while her health steadily deteriorated. For her, the threat of death was neither abstract nor remote, but an intimate and constant presence. Here, Kahlo transformed her daily confrontation with pain and mortality into an almost lyrical scene. The bed, entirely detached from reality, becomes a metaphysical stage upon which she appears, exposed and vulnerable. This painting is one of her most subtle yet radical self-portraits. In November 2025, it was sold at auction for $54.7 million, making it the most expensive work of art by a woman sold up to that point.

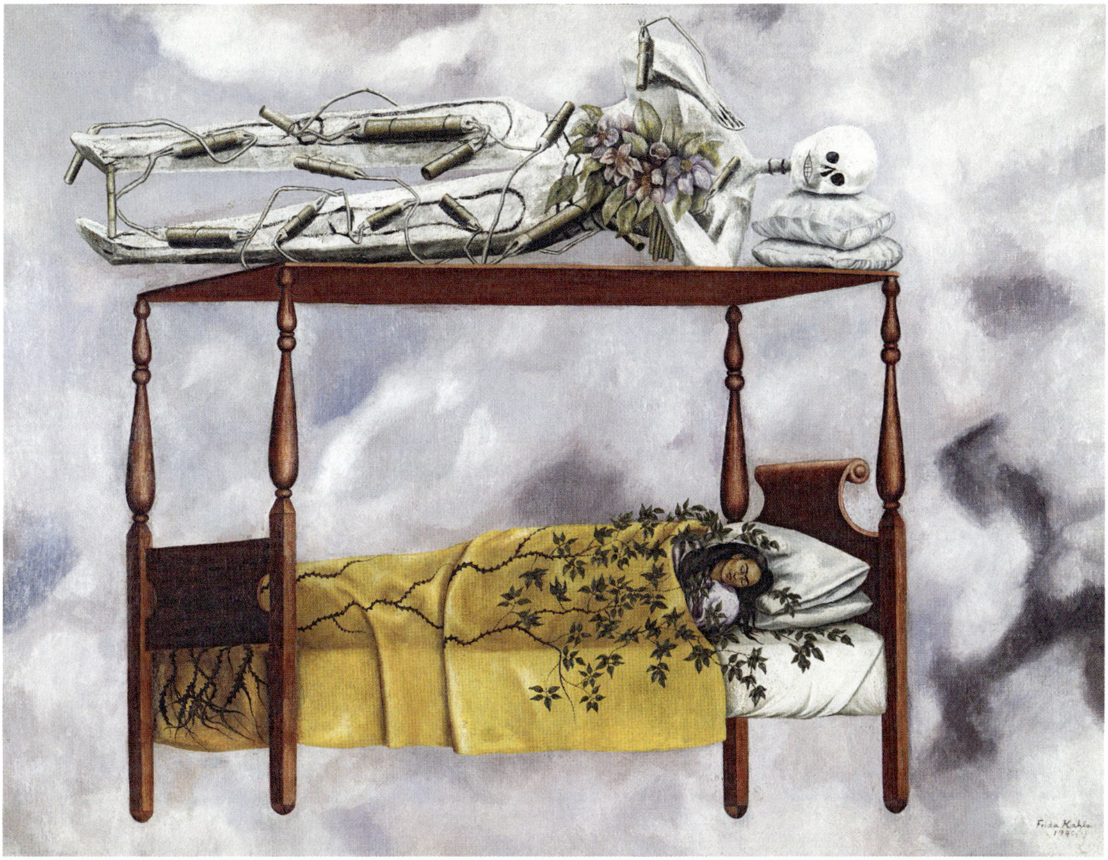

The Dream (The Bed), 1940, oil on canvas,
74 × 98 cm (29 ⅛ × 38 ⅝ in.), Private Collection

MAX BECKMANN
1884–1950

Now, we'll dream together […]. This is my attempt to deceive the demons that lurk around us.

MAX BECKMANN, LETTER TO HIS SECOND WIFE, MATHILDE 'QUAPPI' BECKMANN (1925)

Max Beckmann is one of the great loners of art history. Especially after his emigration from Nazi Germany to Amsterdam, his imagery is often highly cryptic and difficult to decipher. It remains, to a large extent, puzzling, even impenetrable – as is the case, for example, with *Dream of Monte Carlo*, finished in 1943 during the German Occupation and amid the turmoil of war.

The image illustrated here draws on a visit by the artist to the Casino de Monte-Carlo during a stay on the French Riviera. As sketching in the Casino itself was forbidden, Beckmann covertly produced nine rapid pencil and ink drawings, studies of heads and figural types, some of which he incorporated into the painting. Work on the composition dragged on from autumn 1939 until late March 1943, and evidently proved difficult for Beckmann.

The scene opens onto an ornate room. Three women play cards in the foreground; the two fashionably clad younger women have exposed their breasts, while the older woman, her pale face etched with concern, uses her right arm to embrace a small child who carries a wooden sword. This trio forms a central compositional triangle around which the other figures are arranged. In the background, we see two menacing croupiers; their card paddles, ordinary tools of the trade, have been transformed into weapons. Standing behind them are two hooded figures that appear to hold spherical bombs in their hands. On the far left, only partially visible in the picture, stands a man wearing a suit and holding a long candle; seated on the right, on a low step, is another croupier with a roulette rake, whose face is twisted into a grotesque grimace. He peers at the cards of the woman in front of him, who reclines lasciviously across the game table, holding the ace of spades – a symbol of death, melancholy and suffering. The scene is set against elaborate columns, wall hangings and the Casino's gilded portal.

Beckmann's ominous image – whose powerful planes of colour, hard black contours and skewed spatial relationships arising from disparate vanishing points, give rise to a disturbing, agitated atmosphere – has been variously interpreted: as a critique of the false luxury and illusory nature of the casino; as an allegory in which the three women embody the 'ages of life'; or as an encoded commentary on the National Socialist regime, with some of the figures tentatively identified as real people involved in the Nazis' organized art theft. Ultimately, the picture remains enigmatic, in keeping with both the nature of dreams and Beckmann's artistic strategy.

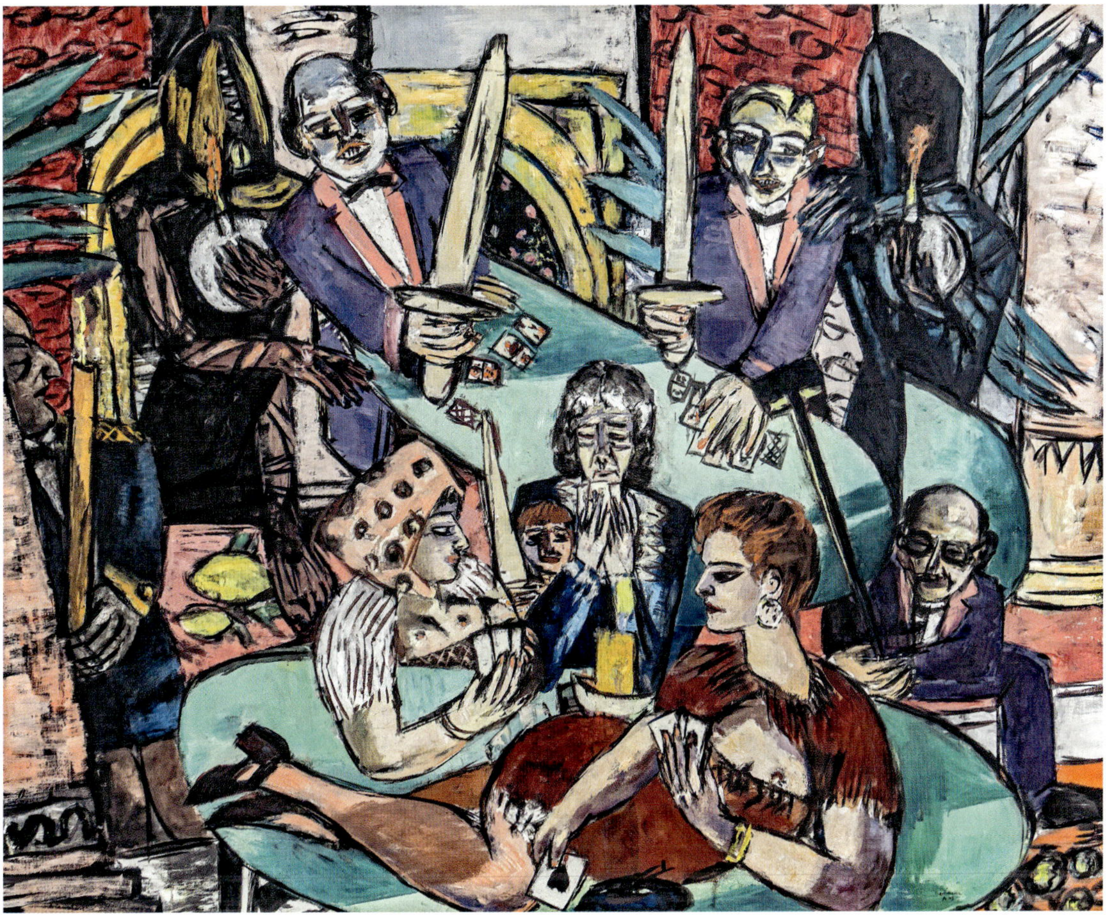

Dream of Monte Carlo, 1939–1943, oil on canvas,
160 × 200 cm (63 × 78 ¾ in.), Staatsgalerie Stuttgart

SALVADOR DALÍ
1904–1989

In the end, it will finally be officially recognized that reality as we have baptized it is a greater illusion than the dream world.

SALVADOR DALÍ, IN CONVERSATION WITH ANDRÉ PARINAUD (1973)

During his time in the United States, which lasted from 1941 until 1948, Salvador Dalí – probably the best-known artist among the Surrealists – produced few paintings, as he was primarily occupied with exhibitions, film projects, illustrations and the writing of books. This relatively small-format painting – measuring only 51 × 41 cm, just over two square feet – with its unwieldy title is, however, among his most memorable and celebrated works.

Hovering above a tranquil, minimalist coastal landscape is the nude body of Gala, Dalí's sleeping wife and muse. Arching over her from the left is a wild, surreal assemblage of figures: leaping from a giant half-opened pomegranate is an orange-coloured fish, from whose gaping mouth a tiger springs and in turn pursues a second tiger. The pair of felines are evidently about to pounce on the naked Gala; meanwhile, forming the terminus of this series of elements is a rifle with a bayonet whose tip seems poised to pierce the body of the sleeping figure. This curious scene is explained by the title and by the small pomegranate that hovers below the female figure, around which a bee flies. In 1962, Dalí explained that with this picture, he succeeded for the first time in visually expressing Sigmund Freud's discovery that the scenario of a seemingly extended dream may in fact be the result of a brief, chance event that causes the sleeper to awaken. The real buzzing of a bee engenders the dream image of a stabbing bayonet, whose sting is about to rouse the dreamer abruptly from her sleep. Throughout his life, Dalí was inspired and impressed by the work of Sigmund Freud, and in 1938, the artist sought out the psychoanalyst in his London exile, an encounter about which Freud himself reported favourably.

Unfurled across each of his 'hand-painted dream photographs', as Dalí liked to call his works, is a dense web of symbols that lends itself to a variety of interpretations. Gala, for example, is depicted in the traditional, highly erotic pose of Venus. The two water droplets seen hovering below her (Venus is believed to have emerged from the sea), along with the heart-shaped shadow of the smaller pomegranate, suggests the same association. The tigers – whose black and yellow coats mirror the texture and coloration of the bee – stand for aggressive sexual drive. The surreal, dreamlike figure of a pale, long-legged elephant strides across the sea in the background, fully detached from the scene in the foreground and bearing an obelisk on its back; it alludes directly to a sculpture by the Baroque sculptor and architect Gian Lorenzo Bernini in the Piazza della Minerva in Rome. Dalí's little picture is a striking example of the Surrealist attempt to blur the boundaries between dream and reality, inner and outer worlds.

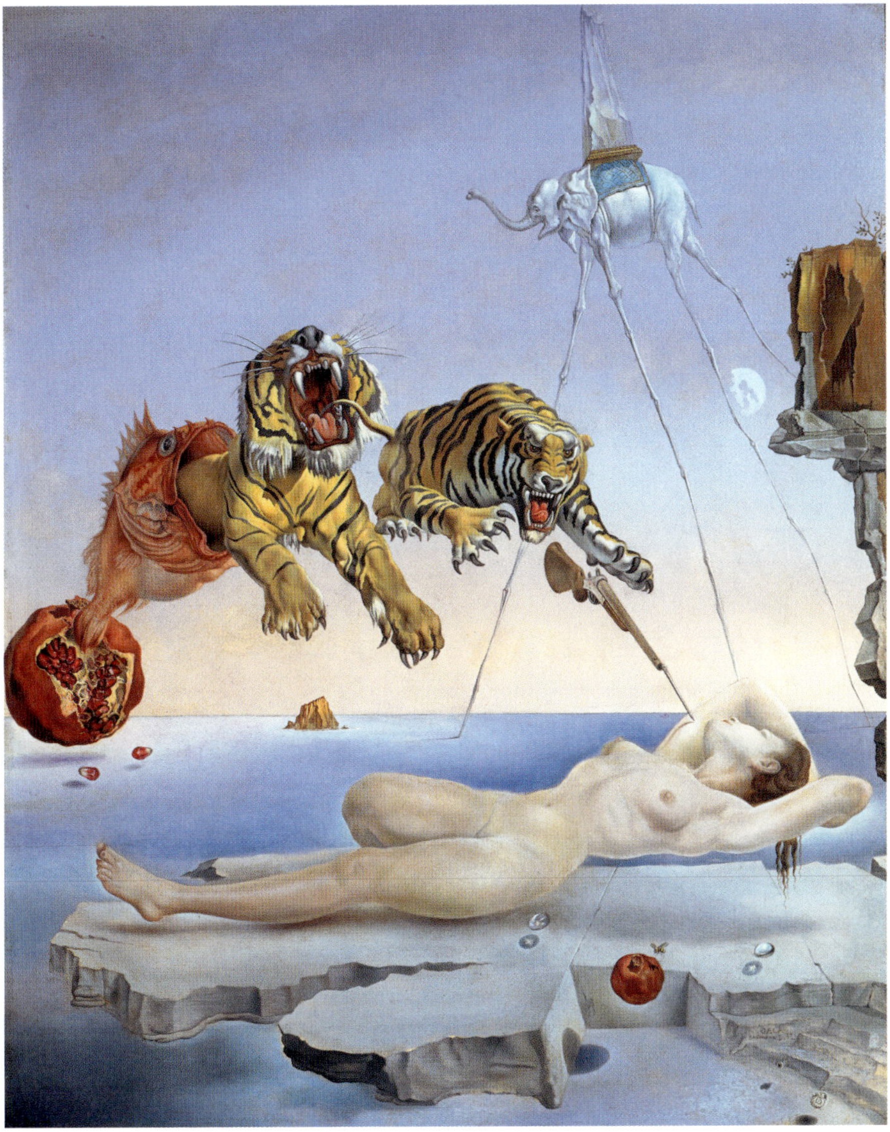

Dream Caused by the Flight of a Bee around a Pomegranate a Second before Awakening, 1944, oil on panel, 51 × 41 cm (20 ⅛ × 16 ⅛ in.), Museo Nacional Thyssen-Bornemisza, Madrid

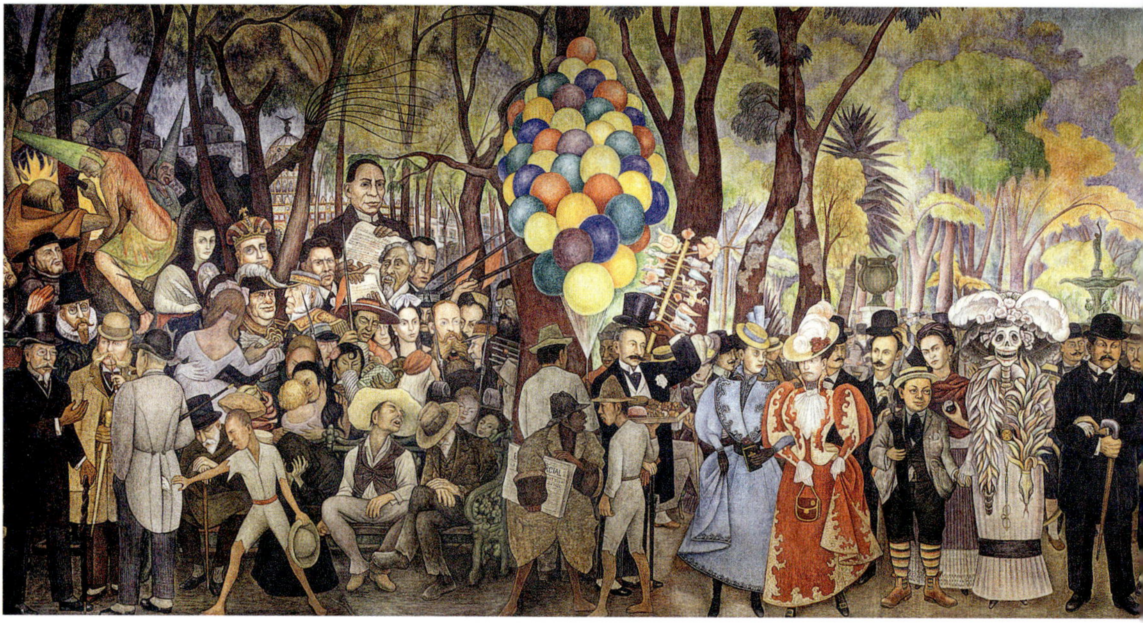

DIEGO RIVERA
1886–1957

The whole work is made up of memories from my life, from my childhood and my youth, and spans the period from 1895 to 1910. The characters along the path, they all dream, some while asleep on benches, others while strolling along chatting.

DIEGO RIVERA, IN CONVERSATION WITH ALARDO PRATS (1948)

Alameda Central, located in the historic centre of Mexico City, is a square, green space that was laid out as early as 1592 by the Spanish viceroy. In 1946, Diego Rivera received a commission to execute a wall mural in the dining room of the Hotel del Prado, located in the park grounds. Rivera was already a celebrated artist, not least for his murals, some created in Mexico, some in the United States – large-format wall paintings executed in his distinctive visual language, which had already influenced artistic developments internationally. He conceived this dream painting as a view of the Alameda park, in such a way that it reflects the history of his homeland, Mexico.

As a child, Rivera often visited the park with his parents, so he included himself among the central group of figures as a nine-year-old boy who has hidden a frog and a snake in his waistcoat pockets. The fantastical figure standing next to him, an elegantly clad female skeleton wearing a feathered hat and a feathered serpent around her neck, holds out her hand to him. She is Calavera Catrina, a figure deeply rooted in Mexican folk traditions,

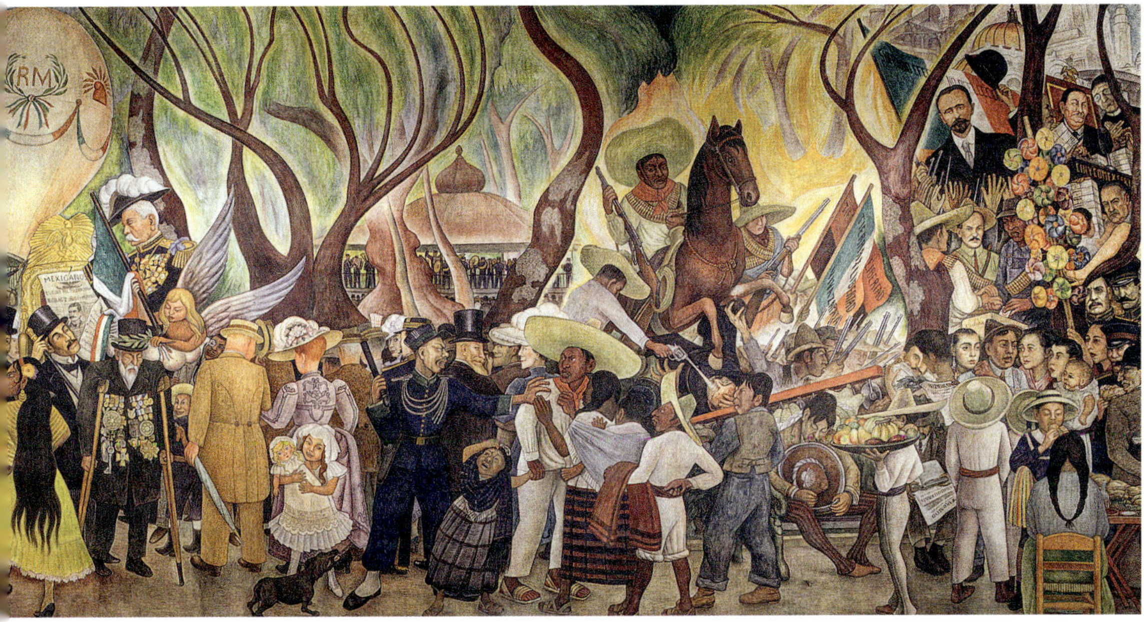

who is ubiquitous during one of the most important Mexican religious holidays, the *Día de los Muertos*. Standing behind the young Diego and resting her right hand on his shoulder is the artist Frida Kahlo, his famous wife, who was actually twenty-one years his junior. Around the central group unfolds a wild, colourful throng with a wide array of figures and personalities, from beggars to pickpockets, prostitutes and police officers, as well as presidents, ecclesiastics, military officials, artists and intellectuals – all of whom left their mark on Mexican society. Historical events of exceptional significance are also depicted, including the burning stakes of the Inquisition, colonial wars and bourgeois revolutions – a dream vision assembled from childhood memories, national legends, fantasies and accounts drawn from history books.

During his lifetime, Rivera was a controversial figure; his activism as a Communist was both admired and detested. When the work was unveiled and the hotel was to be inaugurated, Archbishop Martínez refused to bless the building because the mural contained an image of Ignacio Ramírez, a liberal nineteenth-century reformer and hero of the young Rivera, who holds up a sheet of paper bearing the inscription 'Dios no existe' (God does not exist). A group of students stormed the hall, scratching the inscription from the mural, though Rivera restored it that same night. The hotel management, mindful of tourists from the United States, covered the mural with a movable wall, displaying it only to special guests. In 1986, after the Hotel del Prado was badly damaged by an earthquake, the mural was moved to a specially built museum.

Dream of a Sunday Afternoon in Alameda Central Park, 1947, fresco, 1,560 × 470 cm (614 ⅛ × 185 in.), Museo Mural Diego Rivera, Mexico City

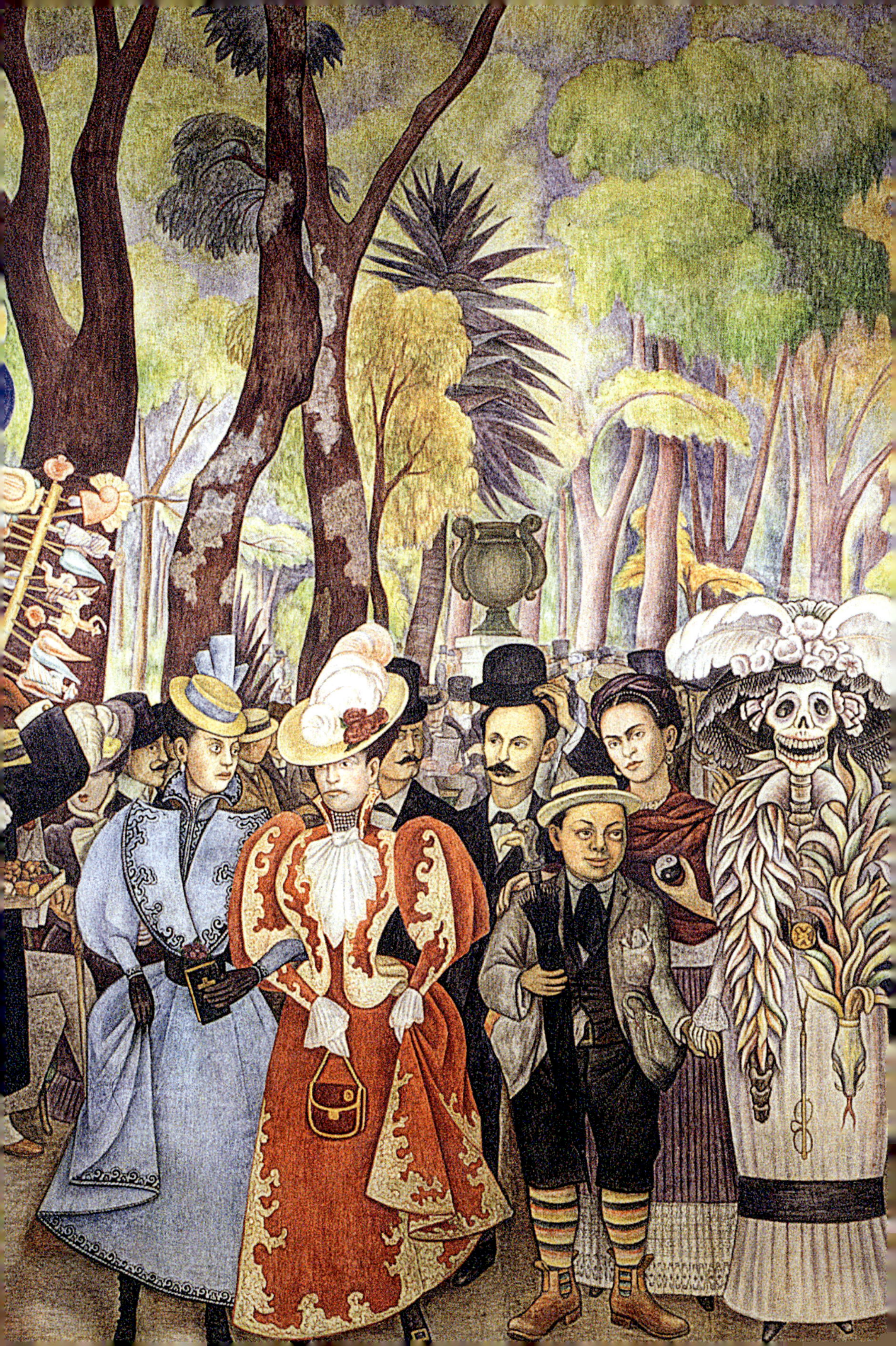

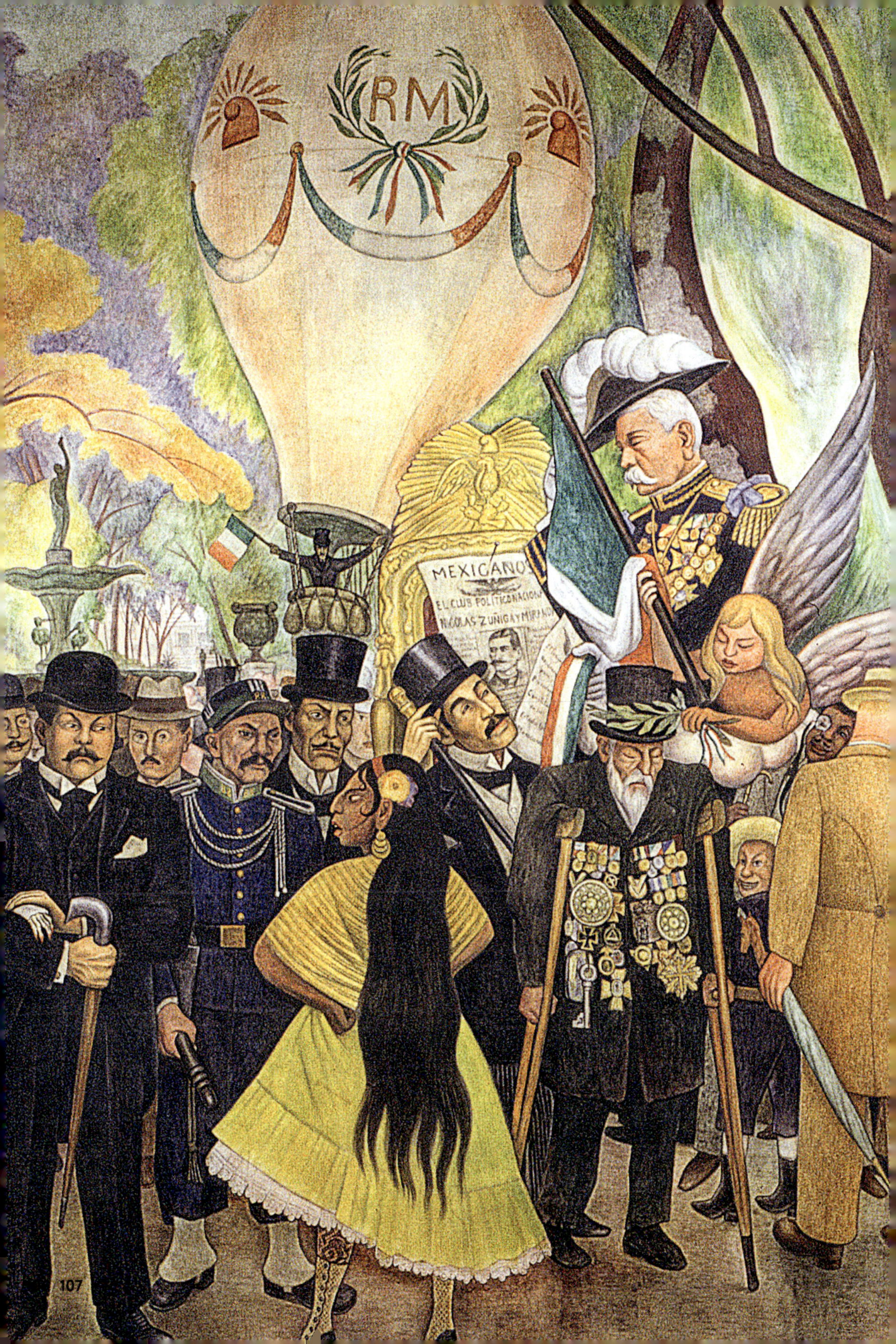
RM
MEXICANOS

GRETE STERN
1904–1999

Now then, what is a photomontage? An approximate definition: the joining of different photographs, preexisting or taken for this purpose, in order to create a new photographic composition. In this way numerous possibilities for the composition arise, among them the juxtaposition of implausible elements.

GRETE STERN, 'NOTES ON PHOTOMONTAGE' (1967)

The graphic artist, photographer and Bauhaus student Grete Stern emigrated from Germany following the Nazi seizure of power in 1933 – first to London and later to Buenos Aires together with her Argentinian husband Horacio Coppola, whom she met at the Bauhaus. The couple's studio in Argentina soon became a gathering place for progressive artists and intellectuals. Stern's avant-garde pictorial language, shaped by her experimentation with unconventional perspectives, photograms and collage, was something new in Argentina. Her photomontages for the column *El psicoanálisis te ayudará* (Psychoanalyst Will Help You) in the newly founded magazine *Idilio* (Idyll), produced between 1948 and 1951, were particularly celebrated. Female readers were invited to submit accounts of their dreams along with a completed questionnaire on childhood memories and personal circumstances. Under the pseudonym Richard Rest, the sociologist Gino Germani, who had emigrated from Fascist Italy, and the psychologist Enrique Butelman provided weekly psychoanalytically inspired interpretations, with Stern supplying the accompanying illustrations.

Of the 140 collages, forty-six have survived as negatives, while all of the originals have been lost. The images were printed prominently on the first page of the periodical, which was intended for middle-class women and had a weekly circulation of 350,000 copies. They include not only striking montages with a distinctly Surrealist inflection that give the dreams themselves a vivid and immediate visual form, but also radical interrogations of traditional gender roles, sometimes subtle, sometimes more forceful. This sustained critique of the reactionary ideal of womanhood of the time, promoted by the dominant Peronist ideology and centred on motherhood and domestic roles, was a remarkable act of emancipatory intervention.

In the photomontages, the dreaming woman is always the central figure. As a rule, the model was someone from Stern's circle of friends or family, in particular her daughter Silva. Many of the images depict oppressive situations in which women are threatened, overwhelmed, powerless, confined or under strain. Again and again, women are reduced to little more than ornaments or accessories to men. In this example, which shows a woman confined in a cage, the message is so unambiguous that it requires no further explanation.

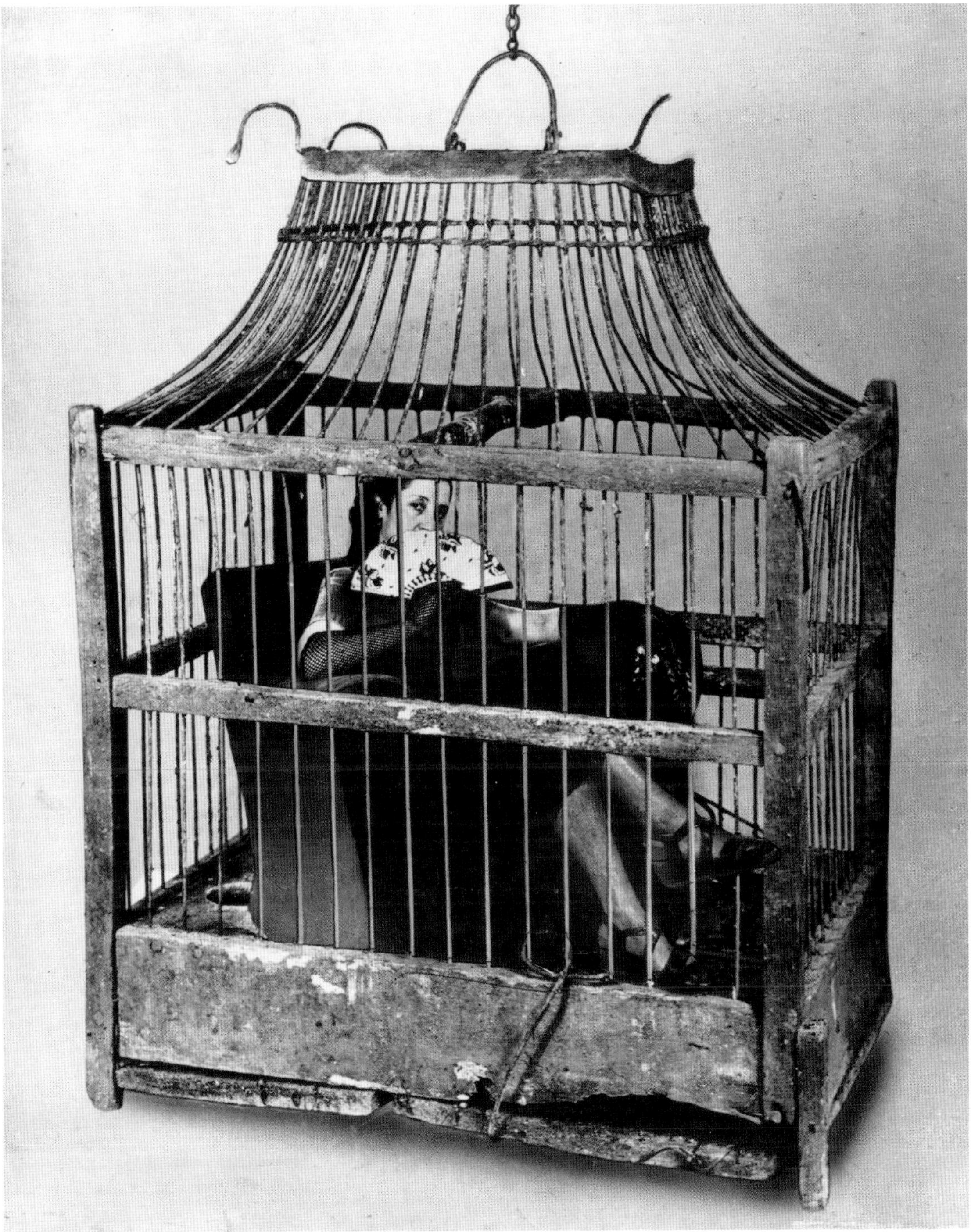

Dream of Imprisonment, no. 45 from the series *Los Sueños*, 1949 (print 1996), gelatin silver print on paper, 30.4 × 23.8 cm (12 × 9 ⅜ in.), Institut Valencià d'Art Modern (IVAM), Valencia

CLIFFORD POSSUM TJAPALTJARRI

1932–2002

A central meaning of The Dreaming is that of a sacred, heroic time long ago when man and nature came to be as they are; but neither 'time' nor 'history' as we understand them is involved in this meaning. […] Although, as I have said, The Dreaming conjures up the notion of a sacred, heroic time of the indefinitely remote past, such a time is also, in a sense, still part of the present. One cannot 'fix' The Dreaming in *time: it was, and is, everywhen.*

WILLIAM EDWARD HANLEY STANNER, 'THE DREAMING' (1953)

The term 'Dreamtime', or 'The Dreaming' – which describes the mythic core of Australia's Indigenous cultures – is as popular as it is suggestive, yet the translation is misleading, since it does not refer to dreams in any conventional sense. Dreamtime denotes a spiritual realm inhabited by heroic ancestral figures. But this sacred time does not simply exist in the past; the everyday physical world of the present emerges from it continuously, while also feeding back into the Dreamtime and filling it with new happenings. Within this spiritual network of relationships, Dreamtime and the events occurring in it retain a presence in the mundane world, shaping the everyday lives of its inhabitants. The events taking place in Dreamtime, known as Dreamings, are reflected in the landscape, in springs, cliffs, caves, plant life and other natural phenomena, and are readable by the initiated and the knowledgeable. These Dreamtime stories, transmitted orally and in some cases thousands of years old, together with the landscape intimately bound up with them and imbued with sacred meaning, form the dominant themes of contemporary Indigenous Australian art, whose practitioners began painting on canvas with acrylic in the 1970s.

Among the most important of these artists is Clifford Possum Tjapaltjarri, whose best-known work is *Warlugulong*. The title refers to a specific sacred site, located roughly three hundred kilometres (185 miles) northwest of Alice Springs, which is associated with numerous Dreamtime stories. Central to it is the story of the ancestral being Lungkata. When his two sons refused to share a kangaroo they caught with him, he ignited a bushfire in which they perished.

The picture, painted not on an easel but with the canvas laid out on the floor, shows the landscape from above, rendered in paint as a multiplicity of juxtaposed points. At the centre is the bushfire, recognizable as a red, radiating star-shaped form. Along the right edge lie the skeletons of the two sons, surrounded by smoke and ash. Eight further stories bound up with the site are grouped around this narrative, indicated, for example, by the footprints of various humans and animals. White, meandering lines trace dream paths across the landscape, along which ancestral beings travel. The image is more than a work of art; it is part of a living spiritual practice, one that is continually evolving.

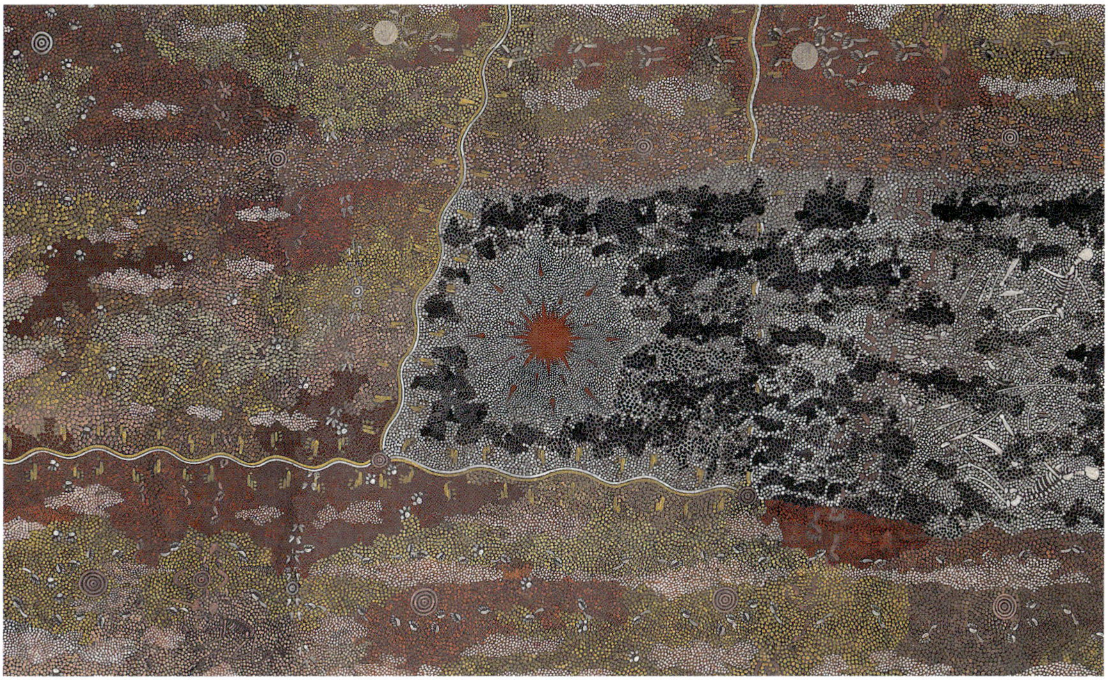

Warlugulong, 1977, synthetic polymer paint, oil, natural earth pigments and binder on canvas, 202 × 337.5 cm (79 ½ × 132 ⅞ in.), National Gallery of Australia, Canberra

MARINA ABRAMOVIĆ

born 1946

The purpose is to concentrate on your bloody dream and dream.

MARINA ABRAMOVIĆ, IN CONVERSATION WITH KATYA TYLEVICH (2015)

The tiny, remote village of Uwayu is nestled in the mountains of Japan's Niigata Prefecture. In winter, the region receives the heaviest snowfall in Japan; in summer, green rice terraces dominate the landscape – a place of extraordinary calm and striking natural beauty. In 2000, for the first Echigo-Tsumari Art Triennale (ETAT), Marina Abramović, possibly the most influential performance and conceptual artist of our time, conceived and realized her *Dream House* here, for which she selected and redesigned a traditional farmhouse built more than a century ago. The only stipulation of the commission was that the work respect the surrounding nature and hamlet, and that it create a connection between people – ideally between the locals and the wider world.

The exterior was simply repaired, but not otherwise altered, so that it would not stand out from the neighbouring structures after its conversion into the *Dream House*. In the interior, however, Abramović installed a sequence of rooms whose design and assigned functions were intended to provide visitors with a highly memorable experience, one that revolves around time, ritual, discipline and personal transformation, and whose core is the experience of dreaming at night. The project marks an important juncture in Abramović's artistic development, which has evolved from individual performance towards the inclusion and active participation of the public, resulting in a more intense experience.

For a small fee, guests can spend the night in the *Dream House*. If they choose, they may perform a simple ritual of purification, of changing their clothes and of allowing themselves to dream, although this is not obligatory. There are four bedrooms on the upper floor, each dominated by a different colour – red, purple, blue and green – and containing a single narrow 'bed' reminiscent of a coffin. The tinted light streaming through the windows bathes the bedrooms in an unreal, mystical glow. The lower level contains two bathrooms, a kitchen, a reception room where visitors are introduced to the house, a changing room with its own specially designed 'dream pyjamas' in the colours of the individual bedrooms and a dream library. This last room, with its walls covered in sayings written in red, houses the dream books in which visitors record the dreams they recall from the previous night. One hundred of these dreams have been and continue to be printed in the artist's *Dream Book*.

Conceived as a temporary installation, the project has been maintained at the initiative of local residents. They even restored the house when it sustained heavy damage in an earthquake in 2010. When Abramović visited the *Dream House* again for the first time in twenty-five years in October 2025, around 3,700 people had spent the night there and 82,000 had visited the site.

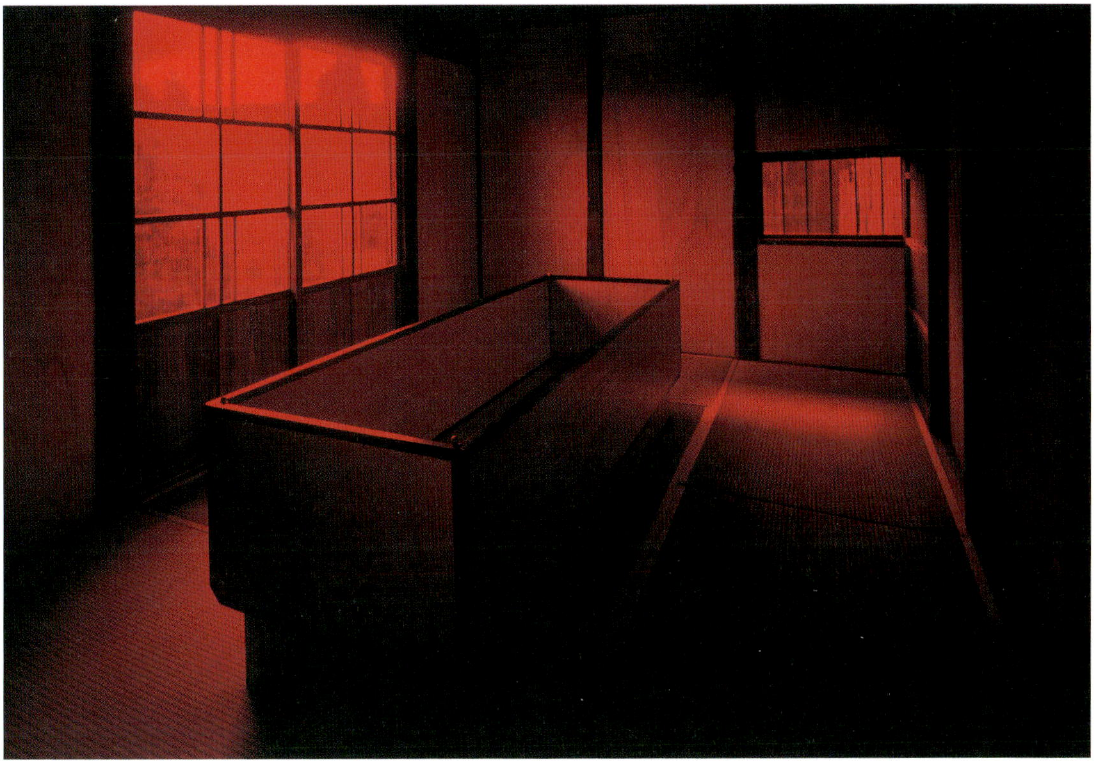

Dream Bedroom (I), from *Dream House*, 2000, site-specific project, snowflake obsidian, wood, paint and Dream Book, Echigo-Tsumari Art Triennale, Echigo-Tsumari, Japan

EL ANATSUI
born 1944

Art is a product of the imagination, and that's always been universal.

EL ANATSUI, IN CONVERSATION WITH WILLIAM KHERBEK (2024)

El Anatsui is one of the best-known and influential artists of the twenty-first century. His monumental objects in particular, assembled from the caps of liquor bottles, were internationally celebrated following his resounding success at the Venice Biennale in 2007, and have since been exhibited in museums worldwide. Anatsui's compositions draw on both classical and traditional African modes of design, fusing them into a fascinating, visually overwhelming aesthetic experience.

According to his own account, El Anatsui first came across the material that would eventually define his work in 1998, when he found a bag of metal bottle caps from Nigerian distilleries by the roadside, while passing through the eastern Nigerian city of Nsukka. Cut, compressed, flattened and joined together with copper wire in a time-intensive process involving numerous assistants, the caps – now supplied in large quantities by regional firms – are transformed from insignificant everyday objects into dazzling works of art. At the same time, multiple levels of meaning closely associated with the recycled material are revealed. The elaborate processing of thousands of individual elements renders the enormous investment of physical labour immediately tangible, creating a connection between the viewer and those involved in its production. Through its brand labels, the caps tell their own regional stories, but also comment on colonial oppression: the alcohol brought by Europeans to Africa had enormous significance as a valuable currency and was exchanged for human cargo during the transatlantic slave trade. The shiny metal alludes to the term 'Gold Coast', in use in West Africa from the seventeenth century onwards, a region from which the modern nation of Ghana emerged in 1957, and from which Anatsui himself originates. This economical material, available in large quantities, naturally lends itself to large, monumental forms.

Recycled Dreams (Uniting the World with a Stitch) is a striking early example of El Anatsui's large-scale hanging wall sculptures. The precise shape is never fixed, as intended by the artist, since the network formed by the rounded tops and flattened foil seals creates different folds with each new installation. From a distance, the interplay of light, transparency, physicality and colour, gives these metallic tapestries a dreamy, unreal shimmer, while close inspection reveal the ordinary found objects, the craftsmanship that joins them together and the brand logos of the individual distilleries.

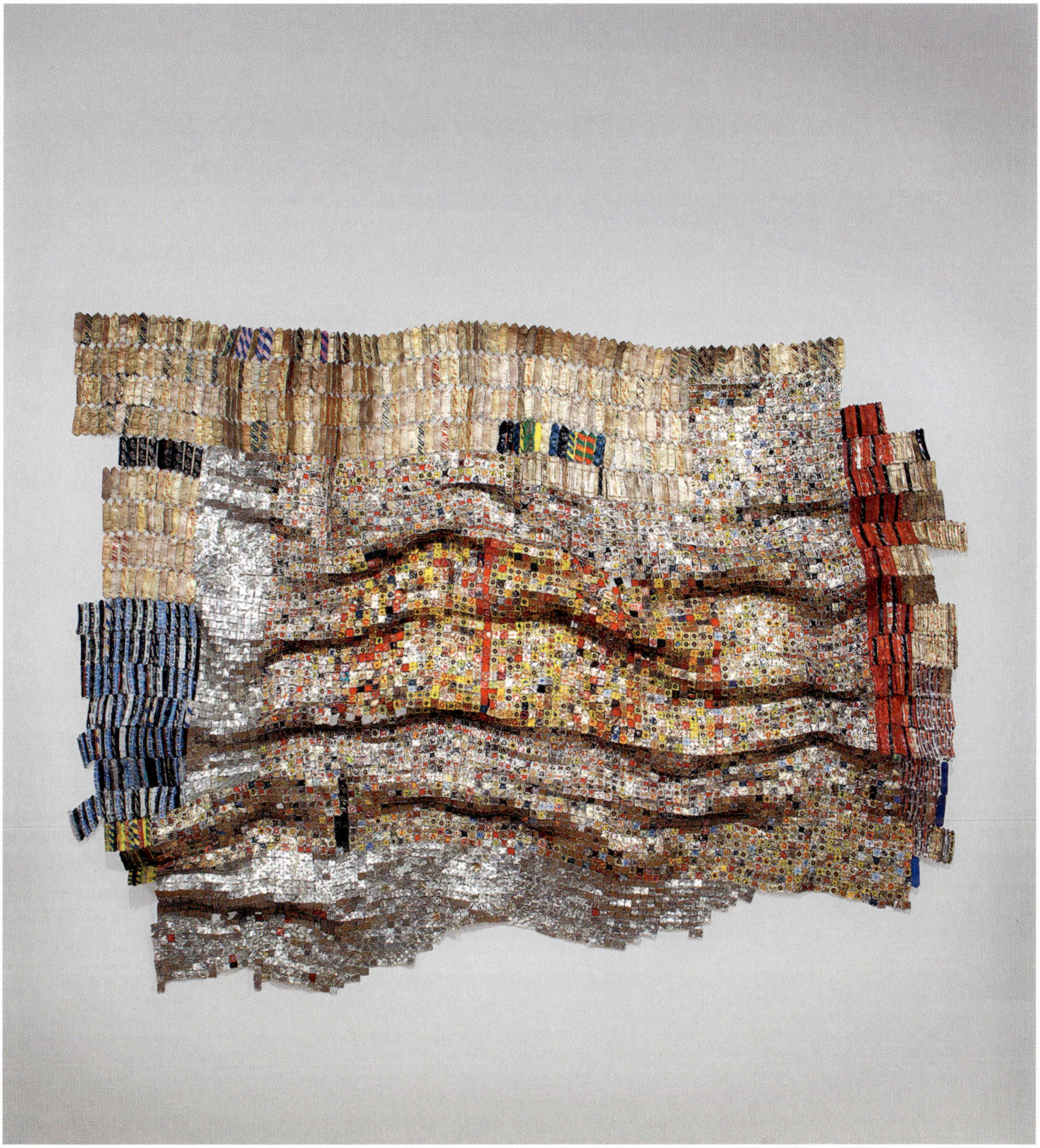

Recycled Dreams (Uniting the World with a Stitch), c. 2005, aluminium bottle caps and copper wire,
186.7 × 251.5 × 10.2 cm (73 ½ × 99 × 4 in.), Private Collection

DAMIEN HIRST

born 1965

The truth seems to be a kind of impossible search really.

DAMIEN HIRST, IN CONVERSATION WITH MIRTA D'ARGENZIO (2004)

Damien Hirst's best-known work is probably the 1991 installation *The Physical Impossibility of Death in the Mind of Someone Living*, featuring a tiger shark, its mouth gaping, preserved in a formaldehyde solution. Like *The Dream*, it is part of the series *Natural History*, begun in the early 1990s and now comprising dozens of works. All display dead animals preserved in formalin in large glass cases. They explore the boundaries of art and examine the relationship between nature, technology, myth, commerce, art, life and death.

The Dream presents a white foal that has been transformed into a unicorn through the addition of a horn on its forehead. At its core, this object is less a representation created by an artist than the creature itself, which the viewer can approach closely and observe from all sides. The eyes are wide open, and the dead animal is so well preserved that at first glance, it almost seems alive. The work gives rise to a fascinating interplay between the beast of myth and fable, which seems to have emerged from a world of dreams, and a seemingly scientific presentation in a hard, cold container of steel and glass, its artifice underscored by the chemical bath in whose absence the specimen's organic body would immediately begin to decay. Here, the world of Romanticism, of mythology and dreams, emblematized by the unicorn since time immemorial, together with all of its evocative facets, is enclosed in a vitrine and exposed to the inquisitive gaze of a modern public. There is, however, no scientific benefit to the contemplation of this object, as the technically complex method of conservation might suggest, familiar from natural history museums; instead, a decidedly commercial aspect emerges alongside its artistic claims. *The Dream* highlights the instrumentalization of fantasy and dreaming – and therefore its decline – in the postmodern world of consumerism.

In September 2008, over a period of two days, more than two hundred works by Hirst were auctioned off by Sotheby's directly from the artist's studio, among them *The Dream*. With a total of £111 million, the sale far surpassed expectations and was, at the time, the most successful auction ever devoted to the work of a living artist.

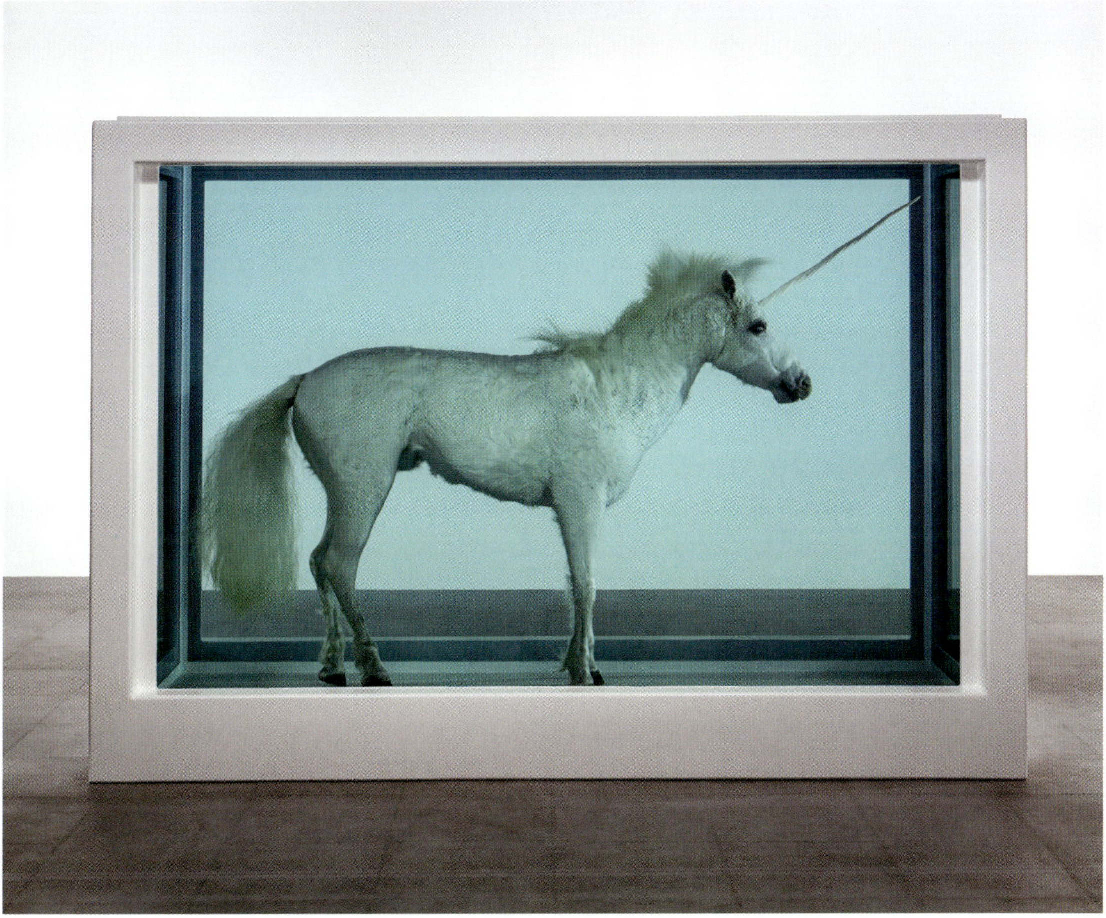

The Dream, 2008, foal, glass, steel, resin, silicone and formaldehyde solution,
231 × 332.6 × 138.1 cm (91 × 131 × 54 ⅜ in.), Private Collection

BANKSY
date of birth unknown

There's nothing more dangerous than someone who wants to make the world a better place.

BANKSY, *EXISTENCILISM* (2002)

Although the British street artist Banksy, a native of Bristol, has been active since the 1990s, with his works visible in cities around the world and some fetching prices in the millions, his identity remains shrouded in uncertainty. Through his imagery, some of which has become iconic, he has succeeded as virtually no other living artist in shaping the visual culture of the contemporary world. One of his most recognizable images, *Follow Your Dreams, Cancelled*, was executed in May 2010 in Boston's Chinatown.

Standing against a white background, wearing a disillusioned, resigned expression, is a man who holds a paintbrush in his right hand and a bucket in his left, with rolls of paper under his arm. Alongside him, in large, bluish-grey lettering, appears the phrase 'Follow Your Dreams', a motto that is central to America's cultural self-image – while stamped diagonally in red paint across it is the word 'Cancelled'. As is typical of Banksy, this composition was executed quickly on the wall using stencils, but also with nuance and a distinct graphic intensity. While the paint drips beneath the optimistic slogan suggest it was applied by hand, the precision of the stamped word conveys bureaucratic regularity; the figure's pose and facial expression, meanwhile, subtly convey his dejection.

In its reduced, compact form, the work becomes a kind of pictogram, as emblematic as it is powerful, with pointed political and activist force. Here, the American Dream – according to which anything is attainable by anyone, provided they are capable of seizing the opportunities available to them and orienting their lives towards a consistent goal – is exposed as a mere platitude. For most working and middle-class Americans (and Banksy's figure is clearly identifiable as one of them by his dress), the pursuit of personal dreams is obstructed by structural disadvantages such as unemployment and financial insecurity. The stamped word 'Cancelled' gives this reality the force of an official decree, dismissing the individual dreams of the majority in order to maintain the privileges of a small economic elite. Banksy's Boston mural therefore fits seamlessly into his larger oeuvre: visually appealing and innocuous at first glance, it relentlessly exposes social injustices, subjecting them to radical critique.

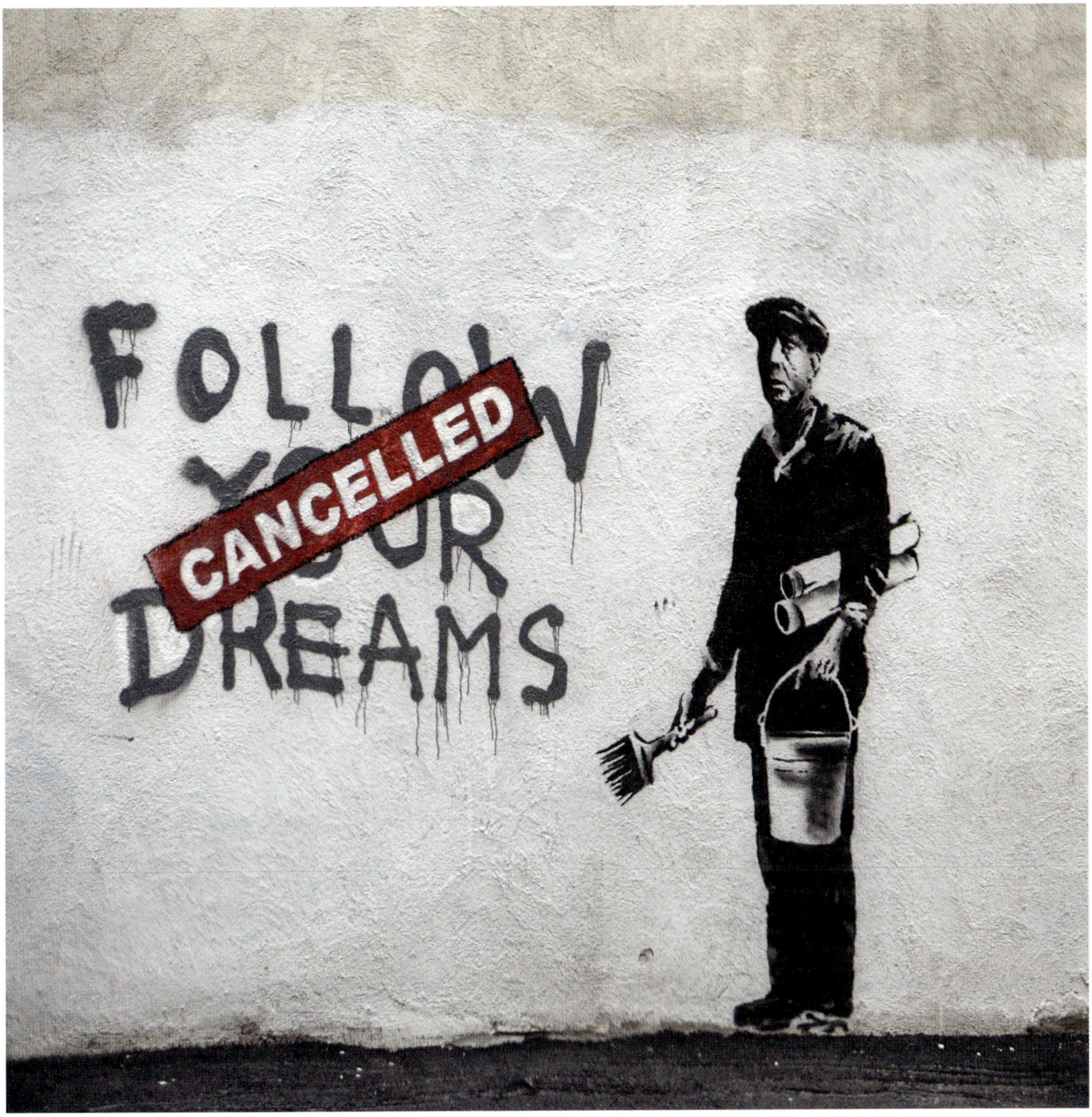

Follow Your Dreams, Cancelled, 2010, spray paint, 134 Essex Street, Chinatown, Boston

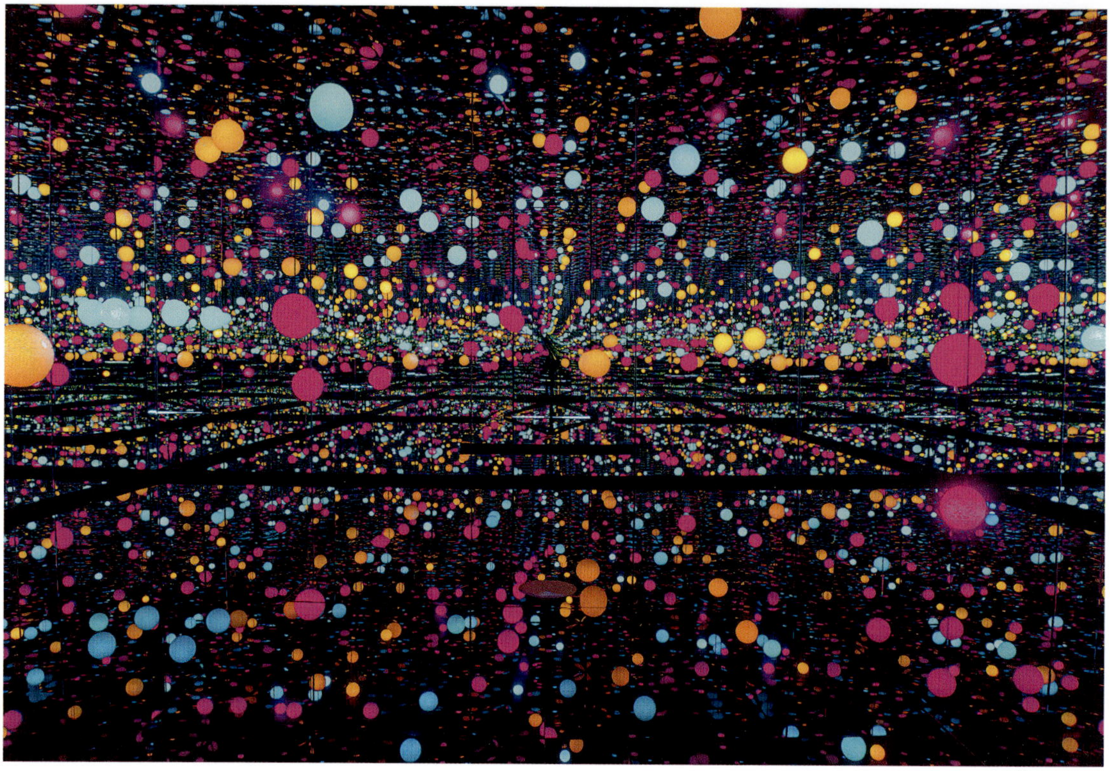

Infinity Mirrored Room – Brilliance of the Souls, 2014, mirror, wooden panel, LED, metal, and acrylic panel,
287.4 × 415 × 415 cm (113 ⅛ × 163 ⅜ × 163 ⅜ in.),
The Museum of Modern and Contemporary Art in Nusantara, Jakarta

YAYOI KUSAMA

born 1929

One day, after gazing at a pattern of red flowers on the tablecloth,
I looked up to see that the ceiling, the windows,
and the columns seemed to be plastered with the same red floral pattern.
I saw the entire room, my entire body,
and the entire universe covered with red flowers, and in that instant,
my soul was obliterated and I was restored,
returned to infinity, to eternal time and absolute space.

YAYOI KUSAMA, *INFINITY NET* (2011)

In the twenty-first century, with her singular and unmistakable mode of expression, Yayoi Kusama has become a globally recognized icon of contemporary art. Beginning as a child, she was plagued by hallucinations, during which patterns of dots, nets and blossoms spread across her entire visual field, covering everything around her. In this context, she tells of her terror of disintegrating as an individual. A major portion of her oeuvre, including above all the so-called *Infinity Mirror Rooms*, seeks to transform these perceptions into works of art. In these installations, a sophisticated arrangement of mirrors and objects generates a seemingly endless repetition of forms within a visually infinite space, producing an effect akin to mystical visions or dreams. In these works, beginning in 1965 with *Infinity Mirror Room – Phalli's Field*, the work of art is no longer an individual object, but a situation created by the artist, one that surrounds viewers and in which they are fully immersed. Here, infinite space is not simply depicted; it is experienced in the moment. The boundaries between reality and illusion, dreaming and wakefulness blur, and the endless juxtaposition and repetition of identical forms results in an intense, overwhelming experience.

Infinity Mirrored Room – Brilliance of the Souls is a relatively small room and can be entered by only a few people at a time. A narrow platform is surrounded by water. Circular lights slowly change colour, seeming to hover in an infinite space – an effect created by the water's surface as well as by mirrors covering the walls and reflective material on the ceiling. The result is psychedelic and, surprisingly, simultaneously alarming and soothing. This unfamiliar sense of limitless expanse is designed to evoke the feeling of sinking into boundlessness, thus enabling a radical experience of the dissolution of individuality, a dreamlike state and a lingering echo of the hallucinations that haunted Kusama.

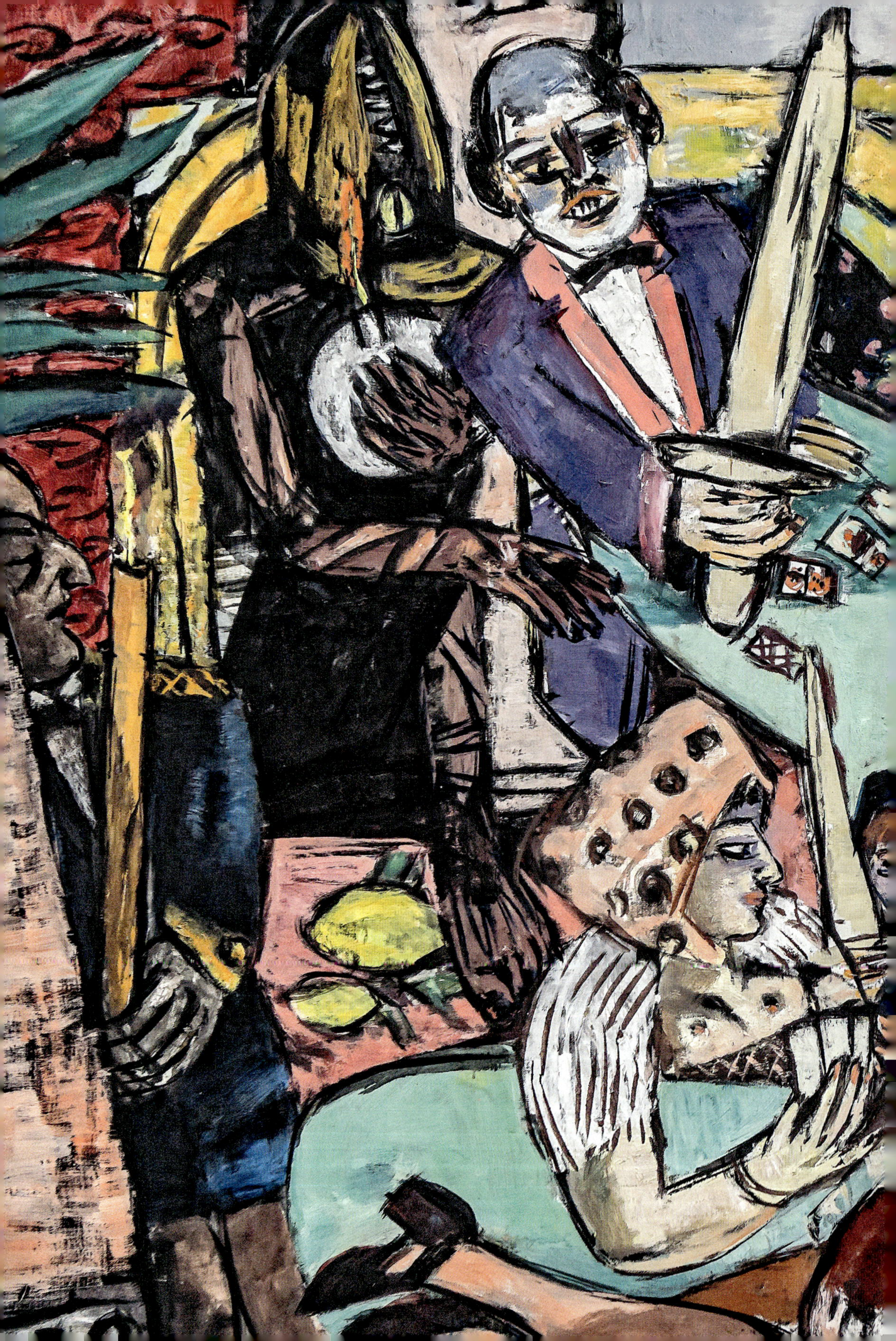

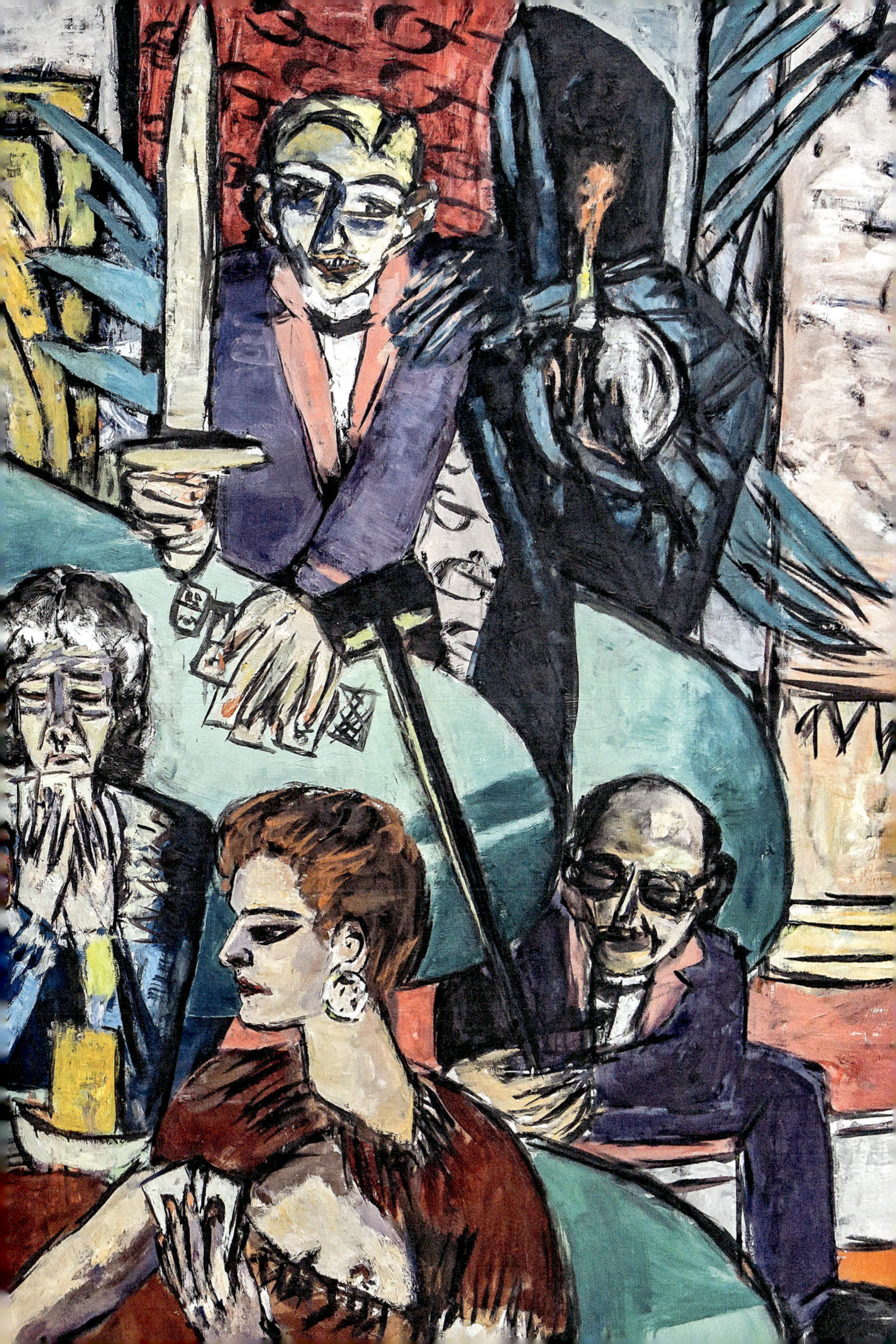

SOURCES OF QUOTATIONS

p. 9 Rainer Maria Rilke, '...Und sagen sie das Leben sei ein Traum', in *Gedichte 1906 bis 1926, Sammlung der verstreuten und nachgelassenen Gedichte aus den mittleren und späteren Jahren*, ed. Rilke-Archiv with Ruth Sieber-Rilke (Wiesbaden: Insel-Verlag 1953), p. 303.

p. 14 Inscription, *Dream Stele of Thutmose IV*, trans. in Selim Hassan, *The Great Sphinx and Its Secrets: Historical Studies in the Light of Recent Excavations* (Cairo: Government Press, 1953), p. 95.

p. 16 Pausanias, *Description of Greece*, vol. 1, *Books 1 and 2*, trans. W. H. S. Jones, Loeb Classical Library 93 (London: William Heinemann, 1918), p. 187.

p. 18 *The Play in Full: Lalitavistara*, trans. Dharmachakra Translation Committee, 84000: Translating the Words of the Buddha, p. 46, https://84000.co/translation/toh95.

p. 20 Dante Alighieri, *The Divine Comedy: Purgatorio*, trans. Henry Wadsworth Longfellow (Boston: Houghton, Mifflin and Company, 1899), p. 60.

p. 22 Genesis 28:11–12 (New International Version, NIV).

p. 25 Jacobus de Voragine, *The Golden Legend: or, Lives of the Saints*, trans. William Caxton, vol. 4 (London: J. M. Dent & Co., 1900), p. 177.

p. 28 Canon Nicolas of Liège, *Passiones Vitaeque Sanctorum Aevi Merovingici*, ed. B. Krvsch and W. Levison (Hanover and Leipzig: Impensis Bibliopolii Hahniani, 1913), MGH SS rer. Merov., vol. 6, ch. 16, p. 425.

p. 30 Lactantius, *De mortibus persecutorum*, ed. and trans. J. L. Creed (Oxford: Clarendon, 1984), p. 63.

p. 32 Proverb, trans. in Elizabeth Scurfield, *Complete Mandarin Chinese* (1999; Blacklick: McGraw-Hill, 2010), p. 290.

p. 34 Genesis 41: 25–28 (NIV).

p. 36 Job 33:15–16 (NIV). Also, *The Writings of Albrecht Dürer*, ed. and trans. William Martin Conway (New York: Philosophical Library, 1958), p. 145.

p. 38 Michelangelo, 'XLIV: The Defence of Nicht', in *The Sonnets of Michael Angelo Buonarroti and Tommaso Campanella*, trans. John Addington Symonds (London: Smith, Elder, & Co., 1878), p. 77.

p. 40 Virgil, *The Aeneid*, trans. Robert Fagles (New York: Penguin, 2006), book 6, lines 1029–1033, p. 212.

p. 42 Matthew 2:13–14 (NIV).

p. 44 Gérard de Lairesse, *Groot schilderboek*, qtd. in Julius S. Held, 'Jordaens' "Night Vision": A Rejoinder', in *Journal of the Warburg and Courtauld Institutes* 25, nos. 1–2 (January–June 1962), p. 131.

p. 46 Inscription, Nicolas-François Regnault's engraving (1791) of Fragonard's *The Warrior's Dream of Love*.

p. 49 Henry Fuseli's 'Aphorism 231' in John Knowles, *The Life and Writings of Henry* Fuseli, vol. 3 (London: Henry Colburn and Richard Bentley, 1831), p. 145.

p. 52 Charles Baudelaire, 'Quelques caricaturistes étrangers', translated as 'Some Foreign Caricatures: Hogarth – Cruikshank – Goya – Pinelli – Bruegel', trans. P. E. Charvet, in *Baudelaire: Selected Writings on Art and Artists* (1972; Cambridge: Cambridge University Press, 1981), pp. 236–237.

p. 54 From Jean-Auguste-Dominique Ingres's notebooks, 1812, qtd. in Daniel Ternois, 'Ingres et le "Songe d'Ossian"', in *Walter Friedländer zum 90. Geburtstag: Eine Festgabe seiner europäischen Schüler, Freunde und Verehrer*, ed. Georg Kauffmann and Willibald Sauerländer (Berlin: Walter de Gruyter, 1965), p. 186.

p. 56 Inscription, Hokusai's *The Dream of the Fisherman's Wife*, trans. in James Heaton and Toyoshima Mizuho, 'Erotic Expression in Shunga', in 'Eros', ed. Ueno Chizuko, Murakami Ryu and Araki Nobuyoshi, special issue, *Kyoto Journal* 18 (1991).

p. 58 Novalis, *Heinrich von Ofterdingen*, part 2, 'Die Erfüllung' (Berlin, 1802), p. 7.

p. 60 Sigmund Freud, *Introductory Lectures on Psycho-Analysis*, in *The Standard Edition of the Complete Psychological Works of Sigmund Freud*, vol. 15, *1915–1916, Introductory Lectures on Psycho-Analysis, Parts I and II*, trans. James Strachey (1963; London: Hogarth, 1991), p. 135.

p. 63 Thomas Cole, letter to Robert Gilmore, 25 December 1825, in Louis L. Noble, *The Life and Works of Thomas Cole, N. A.*, 3rd ed. (New York: Sheldon, Blakean and Company, 1856), p. 93.

p. 66 Odilon Redon, *À soi-même: Journal, 1867–1915; Notes sur la vie, l'art et lest artistes*, qtd. in Klaus Berger, *Odilon Redon: Fantasy and Colour*, trans. Michael Bullock (London: Weidenfeld and Nicolson, 1964), p. 116.

p. 68 Marius Vachon, *Puvis de Chavannes: Un maître de ce temps* (Paris: Société d'Édition Artistique, 1900), pp. 214–215. Also, Pierre Puvis de Chavannes, *Le Rêve*, Musée d'Orsay, https://www.musee-orsay.fr/fr/oeuvres/le-reve-9484.

p. 70 Inscription, the original frame of Hodler's *The Night*, qtd. in Hans Christoph von Tavel, *Ferdinand Hodler: Die Nacht* (Stuttgart: Reclam, 1969), p. 11.

p. 72 Edvard Munch, MM N 59, fol. 3, 1890–1892, eMunch: Edvard Munch's Writing, https://www.emunch.no/HYBRIDNo-MM_N0059.xhtml, qtd. in Jay A. Clarke, 'Munch's Living Nature', in *Edvard Munch: Trembling Earth*, ed. Ortrud Westheider, Michael Philipp and Daniel Zamani, exh. cat. (New Haven: Yale University Press, 2023), p. 12.

p. 74 Edward Burne-Jones, qtd. in Laurence Binyon, 'Burne-Jones, Sir Edward Burne', in *The Encyclopædia Britannica*, 11th ed., vol. 4 (Cambridge: Cambridge University Press, 1910), p. 850.

p. 76 Henri Rousseau, poem accompany *The Dream*, qtd. in *Henri Rousseau*, exh. cat., trans. Richard Miller (New York: Museum of Modern Art, 1985), p. 252.

p. 78 Franz Marc, letter to Maria Franck, 10 May 1907, qtd. in Klaus Lankheit, *Franz Marc: Sein Leben und seine Kunst* (Cologne: DuMont, 1976, p. 37); translation from Wolf-Dieter Dube, *Expressionism*, trans. Mary Whittallm (New York: Praeger, 1973), p. 126.

p. 80 Ardengo Soffici, 'Soffici a Milano', *Lacerba* (Florence) 2, no. 13, 1 July 1914, p. 207, qtd. in James Thrall Soby, *Giorgio de Chirico*, exh. cat. (New York: Museum of Modern Art, 1955), pp. 47–48.

p. 82 Theodor Däubler, 'Über Klee', *Das Kunstlatt* 2 (1918), p. 25.

p. 84 Max Ernst, 'Biographische Notizen: Wahrheitgewebe und Lügengewebe', in *Max Ernst: Retrospektive zum 100. Geburtstag*, ed. Werner Spies and Karin v. Maur, exh. cat. (Munich: Prestel, 1991), p. 291.

p. 86 Wassily Kandinsky, *Point and Line to Plane* (1926), trans. Howard Dearstyne and Hilla Rebay (New York: Solomon R. Guggenheim Foundation, 1947), p. 68.

p. 88 Joan Miró, 'Comment and Interview', by James Johnson Sweeney, *Partisan Review* (New York) 15, no. 2 (February 1948), p. 209.

p. 90 René Magritte, 'Les mots et les images', *La révolution surréaliste* 5, no. 12, 15 December 1929, translated as 'Word vs. Image', in *Magritte: Word vs. Image*, trans. E. L. T. Mesens (New York: Sidney Janis Gallery, 1954), n.p.

p. 92 E[fstratios] Tériade, 'En causant avec Picasso', *L'Intransigeant*, 15 June 1932, qtd. in *Picasso on Art: A Selection of Views*, ed. Dore Ashton (New York: Viking, 1972), p. 78.

p. 94 Henri Matisse, 'Notes of a Painter' (1908) in *Matisse on Art*, ed. Jack D. Flam (London: Phaidon, 1973), p. 38.

p. 96 Marc Chagall, *My Life* (1923), trans. Elisabeth Abbott (New York: Orion, 1960), p. 65.

p. 98 Frida Kahlo, letter to Carlos Chávez, in *The Letters of Frida Kahlo: Cartas Apasionadas*, ed. Martha Zamora, trans. Jorge Gonzalez Casanova with Daniela Garaiz (San Francisco: Chronicle Books, 1995), pp. 104–105.

p. 100 Max Beckmann, letter to Mathilde 'Quappi' Beckmann, 3 July 1925, in *Max Beckmann: Briefe*, vol. I, *1899–1925*, ed. Uwe M. Schneede (Munich: Piper, 1993), no. 309, citation 322.

p. 102 *The Unspeakable Confessions of Salvador Dalí: As Told to André Parinaud* (1973), trans. Harold J. Salemson (London: Quartet Books, 1980), p. 143.

p. 104 Diego Rivera, interviewed by Alardo Prats, 'Sueños de un domingo en la Alameda', *Hoy* (Mexico), 6 March 1948, qtd. in Raquel Tibol, *Diego Rivera, luces y sombras: Narración documental* (Mexico City: Lumen, 2007), p. 233.

p. 108 Grete Stern, 'Apuntes sobre fotomontaje' (1967), in *Grete Stern: sueños*, exh. cat. (Valencia: IVAM Centre Julio González, 1995), p. 195, translated as 'Notes on Photomontage', trans. Rachel Kaplan, in *From Bauhaus to Buenos Aires: Grete Stern and Horacio Coppola*, ed. Roxana Marcoci and Sarah Hermanson Meister, exh. cat. (New York: Museum of Modern Art, 2015), p. 241.

p. 110 William Edward Hanley Stanner, 'The Dreaming' (1953), in *White Man Got No Dreaming: Essays, 1938–1973* (Canberra: Australian National University Press, 1979), pp. 23–24.

p. 112 Marina Abramović, qtd. in Katya Tylevich, 'Casket Case: An Artwork Best Seen with Closed Eyes', in *My Life as a Work of Art: The Art World from Start to Finish* (London: Laurence King, 2016), p. 143.

p. 114 El Anatsui, interviewed by William Kherbek, *Burlington Contemporary*, 21 August 2024, https://contemporary.burlington.org.uk/articles/articles/el-anatsui.

p. 116 Damien Hirst, interviewed by Mirta D'Argenzio, in *Damien Hirst: The Agony and the Ecstasy: Selected Works from 1989–2004*, by Eduardo Cicelyn, Mario Codognato and Mirta D'Argenzio, exh. cat. (Naples: Electa Napoli, 2004), p. 145.

p. 118 Banksy, *Existencilism* (Weapons of Mass: 2002), n.p.

p. 122 Yayoi Kusama, *Infinity Net: The Autobiography of Yayoi Kusama*, trans. Ralph McCarthy (London: Tate Publishing, 2011), p. 69.

For this publication, the translations of Beckmann, Däubler, Ernst, Ingres and Canon Nicolas of Liège are by Ian Pepper. The translations of Hodler, Novalis, Rilke, Rivera, Regnault and Vachon are by José Enrique Macián y Fijałkowski.

IMAGE CREDITS

p. 15: Mohamadkassem (https://commons.wikimedia.org/wiki/File:Giza_Plateau_-_Sphinx.jpg), detail, https://creativecommons.org/licenses/by-sa/4.0/legalcode; p. 17: George E. Koronaios (https://commons.wikimedia.org/wiki/File:Votive_relief_depicting_Amphiaraus_and_a_patient_(4th_cent._B.C.)_at_the_National_Archaeological_Museum_of_Athens_on_22_July_2018.jpg), detail, https://creativecommons.org/licenses/by-sa/4.0/legalcode; p. 19: Biswarup Ganguly (https://commons.wikimedia.org/wiki/File:Dream_of_Queen_Maya_-_Medallion_-_2nd_Century_BCE_-_Red_Sandstone_-_Bharhut_Stupa_Railing_Pillar_-_Madhya_Pradesh_-_Indian_Museum_-_Kolkata_2012-11-16_1834.JPG), 'Dream of Queen Maya - Medallion - 2nd Century BCE - Red Sandstone - Bharhut Stupa Railing Pillar - Madhya Pradesh - Indian Museum - Kolkata 2012-11-16 1834', https://creativecommons.org/licenses/by/3.0/legalcode; p. 21: ALINARI / ARTOTHEK; p. 23: From the British Library archive / Bridgeman Images; p. 24: Stefano Bianchetti / Bridgeman Images; p. 29: CC0; p. 31: Piero della Francesca creator QS:P170,Q5822 Sailko (https://commons.wikimedia.org/wiki/File:Piero_della_francesca,_cappella_bacci,_1452-69_circa,_sogno_di_costantino_01.jpg), 'Piero della francesca, cappella bacci, 1452-69 circa, sogno di costantino 01', https://creativecommons.org/licenses/by/3.0/legalcode; p. 33: © Freer Sackler Gallery / Freer Gallery of Art, Smithsonian Institution / Bridgeman Images; p. 35: CC0; p. 37: CC0; p. 39: Photo © The Courtauld / Bridgeman Images; p. 41: Photo © Luisa Ricciarini / Bridgeman Images; p. 43: ARTOTHEK; p. 45: Christoph Sandig / ARTOTHEK; p. 47: Heritage Images / Fine Art Images / akg-images; p. 48: Detroit Institute of Arts, Founders Society Purchase with funds from Mr and Mrs Bert L. Smokler and Mr and Mrs Lawrence A. Fleischman, 55.5.A.; p. 53: *The New York Public Library Digital Collections*. 1799. https://digitalcollections.nypl.org/items/311c84f0-c610-012f-fc9e-58d385a7bc34; p. 55: © Erich Lessing / Bridgeman Images; p. 57: CC0; p. 59: CC0; p. 61: CC0; p. 62: CC0; p: 67: CC0; p. 69: Pierre Puvis de Chavannes artist QS:P170,Q216873 (https://commons.wikimedia.org/wiki/File:Le_Reve-Pierre_Puvis_de_Chavannes-IMG_8260.JPG), 'Le Reve-Pierre Puvis de Chavannes-IMG 8260', https://creativecommons.org/licenses/by-sa/2.0/fr/deed.en; pp. 70/71: CC0; p. 73: Photograph © 2026 Museum of Fine Arts, Boston. All rights reserved / Ernest Wadsworth Longfellow Fund / Bridgeman Images; p. 75: Bridgeman Images; p. 77: CC0; p. 79: ARTOTHEK; p. 81: digital image, The Museum of Modern Art, New York/Scala, Florence; p. 83: bpk / Nationalgalerie, SMB, Museum Berggruen / Jens Ziehe; p. 85: Artepics / Alamy Stock Photo; p. 87: public domain sourced / access rights from Artium / Alamy Stock Vector; p. 89: public domain sourced / access rights from Peter Barritt / Alamy Stock Photo; p. 91: Bayer&Mitko /ARTOTHEK; p. 93: Christie's Images Ltd / ARTOTHEK; p. 95: Centre Pompidou, MNAM-CCI / Bertrand Prévost; p. 97: The Phillips Collection, Washington, DC, Acquired 1942; p. 99: © Jorge Contreras Chacel. All rights reserved 2026 / Bridgeman Images; p. 101: CC0; p. 103: ARTOTHEK; pp. 104/105: Bridgeman Images; p. 109: © Institut Valencià d'Art Modern, IVAM (Photo: Juan García Rosell, IVAM); p. 111: Vivien Johnson, The Art of Clifford Possum Tjapaltjarri (Basel: Gordon and Breach Arts International, 1994), pp. 56–57; p. 113: © Marina Abramović, Courtesy of the Marina Abramović Archives; p. 115: © El Anatsui; p. 117: © 2026 Damien Hirst and Science Ltd. All rights reserved, DACS Images. Photographer: Prudence Cuming Associates Ltd.; p. 119: Boston Globe / Kontributor via Getty Images; p. 120: arthipo.

https://creativecommons.org/licenses/by-sa/2.0/fr/deed.en
https://creativecommons.org/licenses/by-sa/3.0/legalcode
https://creativecommons.org/licenses/by-sa/4.0/legalcode

A member of Penguin Random House Verlagsgruppe GmbH
Neumarkter Strasse 28 · 81673 Munich

1st edition 2026

produktsicherheit@penguinrandomhouse.de

Details: pp. 6/7: p. 77; pp. 12/13: p. 43; pp. 26/27: p. 24; pp. 50/51: p. 48; pp. 64/65: p. 62; pp. 106/107: pp. 104/105; pp. 122/123: p. 101.

A CIP catalogue record for this book is available from the British Library.
Library of Congress Control Number is available.

Editorial Direction Prestel: Markus Eisen
Translation: Ian Pepper
Copy-Editing: José Enrique Macián y Fijałkowski

Design and Layout: April, Joana Niemeyer
Production Management: Martina Effaga
Separations: Reproline Mediateam GmbH, Unterföhring
Printing: TBB, Banská Bystrica
Typeface: Certeau Pro, Canela, Figue
Paper: 170 g/m², Magno Volume

Printed in the Slovak Republic

ISBN 978-3-7913-9469-5 (English Edition)
ISBN 978-3-7913-9468-8 (German Edition)

www.prestel.com